ANALYSTS AT WORK

Practice, Principles, and Techniques

Edited by
Joseph Reppen, Ph.D.

JASON ARONSON INC.
Northvale, New Jersey
London

THE MASTER WORK SERIES

First softcover edition 1994

Library of Congress Cataloging-in-Publication Data

Analysts at work: practice, principles, and techniques / edited by
   Joseph Reppen.
      p. cm.
   Originally published: Hillsdale, NJ : Analytic Press, 1985.
   Includes bibliographical references and index.
   ISBN 1-56821-423-5
   1. Psychoanalysis. I. Reppen, Joseph.
RC509.A53 1995
616.89′17 – dc20   94-36490

Manufactured in the United States of America. Jason Aronson Inc. offers books and cassettes. For information and catalog write to Jason Aronson Inc., 230 Livingston Street, Northvale, New Jersey 07647.

Contents

Preface

The idea for this work grew out of long-standing curiosity to know how other analysts conduct an analysis, what informs their thinking and methods and what motivates their work. This volume contains twelve original papers by ten American and two European psychoanalysts, all of considerable renown and all of whom accepted my invitation to speak to others. In words that are deeply personal, incisive, and stimulating, these twelve individuals describe the nature of their methods and techniques, and their personal commitment to analysis – an unusually fresh view of seasoned analysts analyzing.

Analysts at Work contains samplings of specific treatment situations, the nature of the patient–therapist interaction, and useful clinical vignettes. Above all, it allows the reader to see how broad the Freudian perspective can be, and how deeply personal is the work of a psychoanalyst. I am very grateful indeed to these twelve analysts who were able to speak to others with openness and candor about their own work. The presentation of papers is alphabetical by author; the presentation of the inner world of the analyst is, I believe, unique.

Joseph Reppen, Ph.D.

1 An Analyst at Work: Reflections

Peter L. Giovacchini, M.D.

When I finished reading Dr. Reppen's letter asking me to write a chapter for this book describing how I work, my first instinctive impulse was to hurl it in the wastepaper basket. Without any deliberation, the idea seemed absurd. I even felt that I was being imposed upon and, perhaps, slightly exploited. After this short flush of emotion, I began to allow some secondary process to prevail, and I had to wonder about the strength of my reaction.

I have always felt that psychoanalysis is a unique science, unique in many ways but still a science. Therefore, it should not be at all inappropriate to let observers, in this instance readers, enter the consultation room and view the analytic interaction. This has been done often enough by prominent psychoanalytic investigators such as Merton Gill. However, the practitioner describing what he believes he is doing is quite different than allowing interested professionals make impartial observations.

Obviously, in describing what we are doing, we are introducing a personal bias. I do not consider bias in this context as necessarily being a negative quality. It may be an advantageous outlook that can help cement the analytic bond and facilitate the analysis of the transference. Still, analysts show great reluctance (even though much less today than in the past) to reveal how what in many circles continues to be viewed as extraneous factors become involved in the treatment process. For analysts of my generation (the post-World War II group), analysis had a purity of its own (Freud's "pure gold of psychoanalysis," which should not, if possible, be alloyed with any other element). We were supposed to maintain analytic neutrality and not contaminate the relationship with personal reactions to the extent that what we did determined how critical colleagues and teachers would be of our analytic competence.

I can now better understand my exaggerated reaction to the invitation to write this chapter. To a large measure, it was determined by a need to be honest, because otherwise there would be no point in agreeing to make a contribution to this book. I am not required to make public what I do with my patients as I had to as a candidate when I presented patients at clinical seminars. If I am to reveal what happens in the consultation room, it is something I have chosen to do, so I cannot withhold what I today believe to be one of the most important factors in the treatment relationship, the analyst's personal responses and countertransference. Feeling this need to be frank, however, is not altogether comfortable. It generates conflict, which leads to reluctance.

Besides stimulating conflicts about exhibitionism, it stimulates superego conflicts that received sizable accretions during my training at the Chicago Institute for Psychoanalysis. Although many years have passed since then, old thinking habits are hard to break, and if these habits become imbricated with our moral values, they become even harder to relinquish. Analysis then was a religion for most candidates, and our mentors were the priests who allowed us privileged few to learn about the esoteric mysteries of the therapeutic ritual. Even though we were required to present our control cases to an audience, it was a closed audience, and our attitude generally was one of secrecy.

In part, not discussing patients was the outcome of the clinical necessity for confidentiality. But much more was involved inasmuch as we placed classical psychoanalysis on hallowed ground, and we had to conduct ourselves in a manner befitting such sacred surroundings. The blasphemy of personal emotions, anxiety, or needs was strictly out of place. I realize that I am stating attitudes of several decades ago in a melodramatic and histrionic fashion, but basically, I do not believe I am indulging in hyperbole. These attitudes still persist, and I believe that my resistance to reveal my modus operandi derives from vestiges of these early orientations.

This resistance is compounded by the fact that many of my patients are also therapists who practice analysis or psychoanalytically oriented psychotherapy. To reveal how I think or to emphasize my personal quirks might be harmful to their treatment because most of them would make it a point to read this chapter. I know if my analyst had written such a chapter, I would have been eager to get my hands on it. Again on reflecting further, I know that such glimpses as my patients may have from my "confessions" are simply grist for the transference mill and, at most, would become a subject for analysis. Regarding patients learning about our technical maneuvers and countertransference, our sensitivities are also determined by the aura of secrecy that was dominant during our training. However, the introduction of reality once again is reassuring. What we do and think during analytic sessions is neither startling nor scandalous. It is rather ordinary, and as Freud taught us not to be prudish about sexual matters, we should feel similarly free to discuss candidly attitudes that define our analytic identity.

Before discussing how I work, I believe it is important first to supply some background that focuses on the question of what motivates a person to become an analyst. There are many reasons for such a choice as there are for the choice of any profession. However, when it comes to selecting psychoanalysis as one's life work, the circumstances leading to such a decision have some unique features. Apart from mundane factors such as financial reward and prestige, there are special reasons for wanting to be an analyst that do not apply significantly to other vocations and professions.

To begin, let me put to one side accidental factors such as being the son or daughter of an analyst or having encountered a charismatic teacher who has a profound influence upon the construction of a professional identity. These are variables that have no special connection to analysis; they would be equally significant for the selection of any career.

The choice of analysis as a career is, in a sense, puzzling. Because of the many negative attributes associated with analysis, it may seem to be a masochistic decision. During my undergraduate years, psychoanalysis and Freud's theories were constantly maligned and misrepresented. This happened during the era of Hutchins and Adler at the University of Chicago, probably as liberal-minded an atmosphere as could be found anywhere and whose faculty and students filled my practice when I started my private clinical work. Even there, psychoanalysis was called a Jewish profession, a cult whose members were intellectually limited misfits. This was not a propitious introduction for a young Gentile student who considered himself dedicated to science. To have voiced an intention to become a psychoanalyst would have immediately labeled one "peculiar."

Many analysts frankly admit that they pursued analysis because they were aware of their own emotional problems and saw it as a way of working them out in an accepting atmosphere. Although considered a good enough reason by analysts, nonanalysts naively view this as a negative approach, making the practitioner suspect. This pejorative assessment ignores the contribution of psychic determinism in the making of any decision.

Psychoanalysis is a subspecialty of the specialty of psychiatry. At least that is how it was presented to me, though this classification in recent years has been seriously challenged and there has been intense controversy about separating psychoanalysis both from psychiatry and medicine. Nevertheless, everyone agrees that psychoanalysis is a highly specialized area, and the course of training that is currently required to obtain certification is as long, if not longer, than many other highly specialized areas in medicine and surgery.

Consequently, students decide to seek analytic training when they are far advanced in their studies, and in many instances, they may already be established clinicians or academicians. It is not a particular youthful decision that is made impetuously or prematurely. I was quite surprised when a well-known colleague told me that he wanted to dedicate his life to psychoanalysis since he was in high school, after he read Brill's translation of the basic works of Sigmund Freud. This struck me as odd and still does. It is interesting that my colleague has become an ardent foe of psychoanalysis.

I and many colleagues decided to obtain psychoanalytic training relatively late in our careers as the outgrowth of a progressively deepening interest in how the mind works. As an undergraduate, I majored in the physical sciences, chemistry as a major, with more than the required courses in physics and mathematics needed for medical school. My fellow premedical students had the same number of courses in the biological sciences, but because they did not have to spend as much time in the laboratory as a chemistry major, they left college after 3 years and started medical school without a Bachelor's degree. I mention this to indicate that my primary interest was in science and not in medicine. Only during my senior year did I realize that life in the laboratory could be lonely, as I felt the need, intensified undoubtedly by the adolescent process, to relate to people and share feelings. I surmised that a physician could maintain a scientific orientation, but it would not cause him to withdraw from human interactions.

During the latter half of my freshman year, I was formally introduced to the unconscious. The awareness of the existence of the unconscious mind had a tremendous impact on me and completely upset what had already been a weakly held mechanistic outlook. One of my fraternity brothers performed hypnosis. When he began, I had thought of hypnosis as something done by charlatans, an act designed to dupe the audience. But after his first demonstration, I became completely converted, and I viewed the unconscious as something powerful and mysterious. I felt in awe of it, and I started hypnotizing anyone who was foolish enough to let me.

I became an experienced, if not an ignorant, hypnotist and boldly and recklessly experimented with techniques of induction as well as probing into the past lives of many hapless students. I still find it interesting as to how many fellow students, both male and female, were willing and even eager to be hypnotized. Perhaps the students of that generation were more hysterical or naive than today's.

Besides gratifying my narcissistic and exhibitionistic needs, my excursions into hypnosis influenced me profoundly. I was constantly amazed by how past experiences are retained and stored in the mind and how they are not accessible in the conscious state. I was demonstrating the existence of the dynamic unconscious as I was experimenting with posthypnotic suggestion. I had not, at that time, read Freud's description of posthypnotic suggestion when he observed Bernheim's demonstrations in Nancy, France. I was deeply impressed by how powerfully the mind could influence the body. In some instances, I had been able to make headaches disappear and could cause vasomotor changes simply by suggestion. Experienced hypnotists are familiar with such reactions, but to me, a young, impressionable student, these phenomena were astonishing.

Since I have become a psychiatrist and am in a more appropriate position to hypnotize patients, I have seldom done so. Since I completed my analysis, I have never used it, feeling it has no place in my therapeutic armamentarium. However, I should acknowledge the place hypnosis had in shaping my career plans.

As the outcome of my sophomoric explorations in hypnotic phenomena, I decided I wanted to pursue the influence of the mind on the body further. I had become especially interested in the nervous system. I knew nothing formally about psychosomatic medicine, but it seemed as if my interests were somewhere in that area. Consequently, I decided to go to medical school with the intention of fulfilling my ego-ideal of being a research scientist, but in the context of a healing relationship rather than remaining isolated in a laboratory.

I was fortunate in that my clinical mentors were both skillful and humane. They were dedicated persons, a full-time faculty devoted to teaching, research, and their patients. They felt psychiatry was nonsense, but they nevertheless had tremendous respect for their patients. I was especially moved when our group of junior medical students was making rounds with the venerable head of the department of pediatrics. This veteran clinician asked one of my fellow students a question about the management of a patient. The student's reply began in the following fashion: "Well, I would start by giving the kid a shot of . . .," whereupon he was interrupted with the angry and loud rebuke: "Doctor, here we do not shoot goats." There was nothing callous or cynical about the pediatrician's attitude, even though he had been working with children for over 40 years. He insisted that patients be treated with respect.

As would be expected, I found a similar probity in the members of the department of psychiatry, especially in the chairman, a charismatic character who gave brilliant lectures at the medical student level. It was not so much the content that was impressive, but his attitude and enthusiasm were stimulating and inspiring.

I was fortunate in that he liked me, and as my student years went by, we formed an affectionate bond. My interest in psychosomatic medicine had now become generalized to the whole field of psychiatry and included neurology. As was to be expected, I was offered a residency, and my choice of psychiatry as a specialty was established. Inasmuch as all the faculty members were either certified psychoanalysts or candidates in training, it was also predetermined that I would pursue analytic training. This was the thing to do then, and a residency's prestige was determined by how easily their residents gained admittance to the Chicago Institute for Psychoanalysis.

The Chicago Institute was an ideal place for a person who wanted to probe the depths of the human mind from a psychoanalytic perspective and still remain a doctor immersed in the study of biological processes. Franz Alexander was in charge, and for a while, I considered him a deity. In my enthusiasm, I believed that he had traversed the "leap" between the mind and body, and many of us concurred with the opinion that he was truly the father of psychosomatic medicine. His specificity theory permitted us to maintain both our medical and psychoanalytic identities, and that is why it had so much appeal for so many young psychoanalysts and psychoanalytic candidates.

Furthermore, the practice of psychoanalysis, as we learned when we began treating our control patients, provided me with that combination I had been seeking: research, learning, and treatment. As Freud had described in his papers on technique, each patient represented an enigma that had to be solved. Psychoanalysis furnished a conceptual background that supplied us with an organization that made understanding possible. Still, at the beginning, each patient had to be approached with an open mind and without any preconceived formulations, in other words, as a mystery that would unfold as the patient gradually revealed himself through free associations and transference projections. As we understood the patient further, we also learned about mental processes, psychic structure, and developmental forces.

During the early post-World War II years, Alexander had a profound influence upon his students, not only because of his appealing specificity theory but also because of the innovations of psychoanalytic technique that he and French wrote about. His modifications and the corrective emotional experience that had become the essence of his therapeutic approach satisfied our needs to break away from traditional restrictions as well as to embark upon something that was exciting and innovative.

Therefore, I was surprised when colleagues from other cities were not quite as enthusiastic as our group of candidates. We also became aware of the fact that there were some senior analysts in Chicago who were violently opposed to Alexander's ideas and advocated a strictly traditional psychoanalytic treatment. It was over this issue that I first became aware of how bitter and factional psychoanalysts could be, as I heard them shout at each other at the monthly scientific meetings of the Chicago Psychoanalytic Society. I was especially confused because I had embraced Alexander's position, which he would eloquently present at a meeting, but I could be just as dazzled by Gitelson's acerbic critique or Blitzten's erudite and witty dogmatic pronouncements. I would leave these meetings feeling that everyone had convincingly established their position, but of course, that could not be true. I also felt sad about the vituperation of men I admired and idealized.

From this turbulent background, and Chicago is far from unique in having a stormy psychoanalytic history, I had to find myself as a professional and determine the direction I would follow both conceptually and technically.

In view of what I have described, it may seem odd that my first analyses were conducted according to classical guidelines and did not follow Alexander's principles. In retrospect, I am aware of two reasons that determined my technical stance.

First, in spite of the attraction of changing technique to conform to psychopathology, what Alexander and French were advocating seemed inordinately difficult to carry out. The therapist would have to understand fully the characteristic trauma of the infantile past and then behave in a fashion contrary to the patient's expectations. As many analysts have objected, this would involve role-playing because it would be a contrived response based on conscious insight, which differs from a spontaneous response as a reaction to intuitive understanding.

Classical psychoanalysis, by contrast, has definite guidelines and rules that are often seized by the neophyte to make his level of anxiety manageable. There is security in the ritual, and the withholding of personal feelings, although at times difficult, is a safe position. I note that beginning analysts are often more catholic than the Pope, more traditional than the senior classical analyst. However, it is a rigid stance and in actuality represents a caricature of analysis.

The second reason I did not practice according to Alexander's dictates relates to my personal analysis. I suppose the only justification for calling analyses conducted during training "didactic analyses" is because candidates tend to identify themselves with their analysts and emulate their techniques. My analyst was the silent type and went months on end without saying a word to me, let alone make an interpretation. I consoled myself by believing that this technique was designed to let the transference spontaneously unfold. In any case, other than feeling occasionally annoyed, it did not seem to do me any harm.

At the beginning of my psychoanalytic practice, I also said little to my patients, though it was considerably more than my analyst. I had more frequent interpretations because, frankly, I feared losing my patients if I had remained as silent as my analyst. When I had felt my greatest irritation at him, I had strong urges to quit, but I knew I would not because I was afraid I would be expelled from the Institute and I very much wanted to be certified. I had no such hold on my patients, and I felt it was important for both patients and myself not to have patients leave treatment because they could not stand my silence.

However, I was constantly amazed by the continuity of the analytic process. In my analysis, in spite of my discontent with a passive analyst, I was able to see various patterns emerging that gave the transference a characteristic shape. I became increasingly aware of character defenses, and an occasional interpretation helped accelerate this awareness. Something similar was happening with my patients.

The clinical seminars at the Institute also illustrated the power of the psychoanalytic process if it is not impeded by an intrusive analyst whose interpretations are inaccurate but close to the mark. Students often revealed a plethora of mistakes when treating their first control patients. According to the classroom and the senior analyst instructor, their formulations were all wrong, and their interpretations simply did not apply. I wondered why the supervising analysts did not realize how their supervisees were damaging their patients. But, in fact, they were not harming them. In spite of the therapist's ignorance and mishandling, the treatment was progressing as it should, perhaps in spite of, rather than because of, the candidate's interventions. But nevertheless, it was progressing.

Now I have to reveal another reason—the most obvious reason—for why I gave only sparse interpretations. I often said nothing because I had nothing to say. I often did not understand what was happening, and rather than force an interpretation, I chose to remain silent. Sometimes patients felt that my silence meant wisdom and profundity and that I was withholding my insights. I believed that this was the situation with my analyst, but then I did not think it was the case for me and my patients.

However, I believe there was some truth in patients' assertions that underneath my silence I knew a good deal, that I was not totally ignorant. This occurred to me as a retrospective insight after I had been in practice for at least 5 years. On occasion a patient would reminisce about an earlier period of treatment, recall an exchange between the two of us, and then tell me of the effective interpretation I had made at that time. I do not remember having made such an interpretation, which seemed to be eminently correct. But in some way, certainly not directly verbal, I must have conveyed such an insight, and consequently, I must have had more understanding about the patient's psychopathology than I was consciously aware of.

The question of how much of our knowledge about patients during a session is either unconscious or preconscious is important because it is very much related to how analysts work and how they think when they are seeing patients. Do analysts constantly make formulations as they listen to free associations? I doubt that many do. As stated, I was aware of the feeling that I knew nothing when I was with a patient. This bothered me at first, but I felt considerably reassured that when asked about a patient – as might occur with a supervisor, in the classroom or even by a colleague – I could give a fairly comprehensive formulation. Later, I wrote papers to pull together my thoughts about clinical situations. To some degree I suspend my secondary process when I listen to patients. Freud apparently advocated a special type of listening to analytic patients when he wrote about evenly hovering attention.

Still, the free-floating nonintellectual attention that is optimal for the analytic relationship can be phenomenologically similar to the silence of the analyst who, both consciously and unconsciously, does not have a grasp of what is happening in the patient's mind. This was my situation with my first long-term, extremely difficult patient who turned out well, as was the case with the candidates at the Institute I have mentioned. I believe that I did some things that were correct, namely, not to be too overwhelmed or too frightened, and to survive.

The patient was the middle-aged wife of a prominent professor on the faculty of the university where I was serving as a resident. She was brought into the emergency room in a state of disruptive agitation. She was moaning, screaming, and incoherently cursing. Because I was the only psychiatric resident at the time, I was called upon to make a diagnosis and recommendations for treatment. Although there were some features about her confusion that suggested an acute schizophrenic episode, I was more inclined to view her as an agitated depression. She had bruises all over her body, which were the result of numerous and daily physical beatings from her husband. I recommended hospitalization, but the patient vehemently objected, shouting that she was not crazy.

Sensing that this was a delicate matter, especially in view of her husband's academic status, I decided to consult with the head of the department about how to proceed, believing that in view of her position it might be discreet for a experienced senior faculty member, perhaps the head of the department himself, to take over her treatment. When I made that suggestion, his objections were almost as strong as the patient's feelings about hospitalization. He instructed me to ask all of the members of the senior staff (there were only two) and to report back in 10 minutes. I was able to find them easily, and after hearing who the patient was, they did not hesitate to refuse. All of them, including the head of the department when I reported back, suggested that I treat the patient, emphasizing that I needed the experience. They also strongly suggested that I give her daily appointments. I knew that this decision was more political than clinical, but I decided it was prudent for me to go along with my mentors, even though I was frightened of the consequences of my attempts at treatment, not a propitious attitude regarding the beginning of treatment. Nevertheless, when I proposed to the patient that we set up a schedule of sessions, she accepted the prospect of therapy with me, and we began the next day.

For the remaining 2 years of my residency, this patient never missed a session, but she ranted and raved throughout most of her interviews and would frequently throw plastic ashtrays at me. At this moment, I do not recall anything I said to her during her agitated period other than perhaps rephrasing something she had said or attempting to clarify her feelings. In the meantime, her life at home steadily deteriorated, with her husband continuing his brutality and constantly depreciating her treatment. However, he never attacked me personally and never mentioned that I was just a resident, something he knew because he was very much aware of academic status.

During the second year of treatment, I began my first control case at the Chicago Institute for Psychoanalysis, and almost on signal, the patient insisted on lying down on the couch. The patient continued feeling agitated and depressed, but now she expressed her feelings in a much more subdued fashion, and her violent behavior ceased. In fact, she began expressing positive feelings about the treatment, which she referred to as "analysis." She remained with me for 6 years as a private patient after completing my residency. She had divorced her husband, remarried, and had two children. Her parting words when we terminated treatment were: "When my children grow up and find themselves on an analyst's doorstep, they will be good candidates for treatment."

I have given this patient much thought throughout the years and wonder as to what actually happened during 8 years of treatment. When she first came to the emergency room, she was as close to commitment as any patient I have ever seen. She was totally unable to function, and her masochism had reached life-threatening proportions. My initial trepidation about treating the wife of an important person soon vanished as I learned that I could survive all of her anger and destructiveness, that it was not as bad as it seemed. The fact that I had little to say apparently was beneficial rather than detrimental inasmuch as my silence indicated an acceptance of her rage, whereas interpretations might have been experienced as attempts to explain away her feelings so that she would behave calmly and rationally. I was and still am impressed with the importance of creating a setting in which the patient can get in touch with the primitive parts of the self and express regressed feelings and adaptations.

My formal training and supervisors, however, stressed the importance of insight gained by interpreting the transference. From a conceptual viewpoint, this seemed eminently logical and reinforced my belief that the psychoanalytic process is part of a scientific framework. The question that concerned my colleagues and myself was the content of insights and interpretations. With my early patients and control cases, I followed the formulations that were discussed at the Institute, as well as the sparse interpretations my analyst made, and passed them on to my patients.

I was facing a dilemma. The idea of using transference interpretations made sense. But the content of these interpretations seemed to be limited to what, in my mind, sounded like a few standard clichés. From the defensive layer, the patient supposedly formed an oral dependent transference that could manifest itself in various ways, such as indulging in regressive immature behavior or jealous competitive actions founded on sibling rivalry. After these infantile orientations were worked through, the patient would bring in oedipal material and become immersed in a father or mother transference based on incestuous fantasies or death wishes. I recall how intensely I focused on the patient's dependency as I was beginning to consolidate a working style.

I was a relatively silent analyst, maintaining neutrality and confining the majority of my comments to transference interpretations. The latter concentrated mainly on what I was formulating as regressed oral dependent defenses, although on occasion anal-sadistic and controlling configurations entered the patient's free associations and had their influence on behavior. I had also been taught that the patient's silence was a resistance that had to be overcome as quickly as possible. Silence by patients was not to be tolerated.

I was comfortable enough in my professional stance, but not altogether comfortable. First, I became increasingly aware of the stereotypic nature of the content of interpretations and the regularity of the sequence from specific pregenital defenses to the Oedipus complex. In view of the variability of human character, it was difficult to believe that all analytic patients could fit into a relatively simple formulation. I had the feeling that we had built a Procrustean bed. Nevertheless, it was interesting that my patients seemed to accept my interpretations and produced free associations and dreams that apparently confirmed them.

Next, I detected moral overtones in the formulations we discussed in the classroom. They were never overtly expressed, but the note of disapproval was unmistakable. Certain types of behavior were simply unacceptable. For example, the patient was often labeled as immature, and this had a definite pejorative connotation. When we pointed out to patients that they had infantile expectations or were behaving childishly, we were expecting them to change their behavior and attitudes. Nothing was ever said about the adaptive value of symptoms.

In essence, our attitudes were critical about regressed and infantile behavior. This extended even to the length of analysis. I recall a prominent senior analyst telling me that he would not let his patients remain in treatment after 5 years of analysis. "The lion jumps only once," said Freud when he told the Wolf Man about a termination date. The patient had to get well in a prescribed length of time. I started wondering what happens if he does not, as in the case of the Wolf Man. The patient is still emotionally disturbed and consequently needs treatment. I reasoned that if we are going to deny treatment because we do not want to make the setting of a termination date into a meaningless gesture, then all we are doing is forcing the patient into changing therapists. Hence, I was ambivalent about the length of treatment.

A colleague's experience proved very valuable in helping me resolve the problem of how long treatment should last. His patient, a very intelligent and talented woman, was dying of tuberculosis when he first saw her. She had a pneumothorax and extended care in a sanitorium, but her course was steadily downhill. This occurred before there was effective chemotherapy for tuberculosis. The patient and her family sought psychoanalysis as a last lifesaving resort. Her response to treatment was miraculous. At least it appeared to be so from a medical viewpoint inasmuch as she totally recovered from what had been a moribund state. She also made considerable progress in her analysis, which had no end in sight.

After 7 years of treatment, her analyst, who had also been taught that there should be limits to the length of treatment, suggested that they should start to think about termination. The patient arrived at the next session holding a handkerchief to her mouth. As she sat on the couch, she held the handkerchief so her therapist could see that it was soaked with blood. She said that she would decide how long she needed to be in analysis, that her needs were involved, and that if she had to stay in treatment for the rest of her life, why should anyone object. Analysis had kept her alive, functional, and reasonably happy, and if she wanted to carry treatment to its ultimate, that is, to help her die, there was no reason why she should be deprived. If her analyst had problems with accepting her interminable need for treatment, then he should work them out, perhaps get further analysis for himself, which, incidentally, he did. Several of my contemporaries and I profited from this exchange. Analysis for this lady was life sustaining. Though it may not be so vital for most patients, it is still a very important relationship that has deep significance for them. The holding environment and the understanding that treatment provides may both sustain and promote integration. Why is it necessary to impose a time limit upon a process? We are aware of the timelessness of the unconscious; yet we were taught that we had to keep an eye on the calendar because otherwise the patient will develop an unhealthy dependency and stagnate. My colleague's patient helped me deal with some of my patients who had similar needs.

As I viewed my analytic orientation while gaining more clinical experience, I was becoming uncomfortable with certain implicit attitudes that my mentors had passed on to me. I can sum them up by using the word "judgmental," and although Freud had admonished us against taking such a stance, he and many others nevertheless did. Freud believed that analysis had to be carried out in a state of abstinence, and he was very critical of his patients' behavior. In one instance, he made a patient break up an engagement, and in another, he forbade a patient from masturbating. Resistance was also handled in a peremptory fashion and had to be abolished as quickly as possible. As I have discussed, I was struck by the setting of time limits on treatment and the disapproving reactions to pregenital orientations and defensive behavior. Regarding the latter, I recall a friend asking me to define psychoanalysis. I replied that that was easy: Discover the symptoms and then forbid them.

This may sound like a sarcastic oversimplification, but many of my peers found this formulation to be compatible with their beliefs. They may have rejected it if stated in those terms, but clothe it with clinical material and various syndromes and it becomes believable and respectable. For example, I was frustrated in my treatment of severely acting-out masochistic patients. At a postgraduate seminar, I conjectured that such patients were impossible to treat unless they gave up their masochistic escapades before they started treatment. I was suggesting that these patients had to stop allowing their partners to beat them up or otherwise inflict pain. This condition for treatment was accepted by most of the members of the seminar without hesitation. Needless to say, not many of us were able to keep masochistic patients in treatment, but we consoled ourselves by concluding that they were unanalyzable.

In fact, I wondered if analyzable patients existed. I was well aware of Freud's criteria of analyzability, of how he excluded all patients except those that he could classify as transference neuroses. With Freud's restrictions in mind, I recall asking a colleague after we had both been practicing for 2 years whether he had as yet seen an analyzable patient, and he replied that he had not. I remember my four control cases that purportedly had been carefully selected by a committee of senior analysts so that they would be suitable for a neophyte psychoanalyst. My first patient was an adolescent male who later revealed that he was an active homosexual and also had paranoid delusions. My second patient was a grandiose character who claimed he had actually had sexual intercourse with his mother between the age of 15 and 18. My third patient seemed to be a hysterical character neurosis and my fourth was a drug addict and alcoholic who frequently acted out violently. Three of these carefully selected patients did not, in any way, meet the standards for analyzability that are supposedly found in the transference neuroses. Rather, they would have been diagnosed as psychotic or borderline.

Regardless of how our present-day DSM-III would classify these patients, my supervisors paid no attention to the primitive aspects of their psychic makeup, and I must confess that I did not concentrate on the psychotic core, so there were no objections to continuing their analyses, something I was eager to do because I wanted to graduate. In summary, my first experiences in treating severely disturbed patients were matters of expediency and not the outcome of any carefully thought out therapeutic strategy.

The question of selection of patients was extremely important from several viewpoints. As stated, it was at first a matter of expediency. But then it became a practical issue that concerned the preservation of an analytic identity. It would also involve my modus operandi and whether I would, to some extent, have to abandon some elements of my professional ego-ideal if I needed to modify my technique in order to be able to treat these so-called difficult patients.

The practical issue centered around the fact that we seldom encountered patients who could be diagnosed as classical neuroses. All of my peers lamented this, and it seemed that we were all trying hard to find the analyzable patient. I recall a workshop held at the meetings of the Western Psychoanalytic Societies that I cochaired where I asked the question of how many classical neuroses the members of the workshop had seen or treated. There were 18 experienced analysts in this group, but none could honestly say that they had ever seen any. One analyst jokingly stated that he had been referred a patient who had been labeled as an oedipal neurosis. When he arrived at the therapist's office, he was hallucinating.

My generation of analysts was faced with a dilemma that threatened to undermine our existence as analysts. This involved our conceptual system both as a frame of reference to help us understand our patients as well as to construct a technique of treatment compatible with the psychoanalytic doxology. I felt that it would be awkward, if not therapeutically defeating, to treat the patients that were being referred to me in the classical neutral tradition. Furthermore, if I tried to explain their problems on the basis of psychodynamic factors, that is, conflicting intrapsychic forces, I found myself on a dead-end street. At this stage in my career, about 2 years after I had graduated from the Chicago Institute for Psychoanalysis, I began thinking in terms of structural problems, defects in and lack of psychic structure rather than exclusively on the basis of unconscious conflict.

I as yet had no idea how these new ways of formulating would affect my technique. The only point I was trying to convince myself of was that patients suffering from characterological defects were treatable, and in part, this was motivated by my wanting to do analysis with the patients who came to see me. But as I reflected back on the cases I was currently treating analytically, very few if any could be considered examples of the transference neuroses. As mentioned, even my control cases were best understood as character disorders. Throughout the years, analysts discussing my work have frequently stated that I see more borderline and psychotic patients than most analysts because of my interest in this group, and therefore, my position about the number of psychoneurotic patients seeking treatment is unrealistic. However, the workshop on the west coast indicated that my experience is in no way atypical.

I differed from my colleagues in that I began paying little attention to diagnosis and simply started analysis and followed how it developed. I used Winnicott's concept of a therapeutic diagnosis, which concentrated on the unfolding of the transference and whether it is manageable and capable of being resolved. I was also concerned with the acquisition of new psychic structure as the consequence of regression, the giving up of infantile adaptations, and the decathexis of constricting introjects permitting what I believed to be an arrested developmental drive or impetus to once again be set in motion. Granted, this is an oversimplification, but my widening clinical horizon forced me to look at patients from a structural context. I suppose this represented my moving in the direction of ego psychology.

This viewpoint did not seem to change my therapeutic stance or technique. I was in some respects less rigid than my colleagues but in others perhaps more so. I charged, and still charge, for missed appointments unless I am given 48-hours notice. I have some flexibility about this now, and in an emergency or following some unforeseen event, I may waive the time limit, recognizing that there is an unconscious determinant in every event but that in some instances to charge the patient may cause an unproductive disturbance in the patient and may severely damage the treatment relationship. In other situations, I may charge no matter how far ahead of time the patient may have informed me. These are patients who may habitually and cavalierly cancel appointments, disdainful in a way that provokes untoward countertransference reactions. In these instances, I maintain a comfortable equilibrium through the fee.

I bring up this very specific technical detail because it is illustrative of my developing therapeutic philosophy. Rather than relying on the formal elements of the patient's psychopathology, I was more concerned about the interaction between myself and the patient. This shifts the focus of the indications and contraindications for analysis. Treatability depends on the "fit" between analyst and patient. Some analysts can treat patients that others cannot. I felt much more comfortable when I stopped thinking in terms of rules and tried to adapt myself to what I felt was best for the analytic process. Often this meant what I could do to preserve the relationship. For example, if insisting on a fee for a missed appointment would cause the patient to leave treatment, then it would be wise not to charge if I wanted the analysis to continue.

There are, of course, limits as to how far an analyst will go to preserve treatment. In my writings, I have given examples of analysts accommodating themselves to patients in ways I could not. In one instance, an analyst could tolerate his patient defecating on the couch, and in another, the therapist had to hold sessions for a while outside the consultation room because the patient refused to leave at the end of the session. I do not like my furniture to be smeared, and I am not adaptable to changing my work setting. So for me, these patients are not analyzable, though they were with other analysts.

The analyst's idiosyncrasies are variables involved in the determination of treatability. They work either way, making the patient more or less treatable. One of my negative idiosyncrasies is that I do not want to treat patients who do not have a telephone. I feel a need to have an open avenue of communication, especially because, on occasion, I have to change appointments.

There are limits to analytic tolerance. Some patients are so destructive or vulnerable that they are totally disruptive to the analytic setting. However, these may be transient psychic states, which may require hospitalization and can often be followed by analysis.

I have frequently wondered about how willing analysts are to analyze. Most of my current patients have seen at least one and more often two to three analysts before me. Their descriptions of previous therapies may have undergone considerable distortion, but there are enough similarities in various histories from which some general conclusions can be drawn. Basically, their former therapists abandoned analysis and sought to be helpful by giving the patient support in handling difficult reality problems.

One of my patients had seen three analysts before me. In each instance, she specifically requested analysis. Her first therapist treated her for a year and was constantly giving her advice. He wanted to be her friend. She liked him and did not want to offend him, but she felt she did not need a friend. She needed an analyst. She terminated treatment, convincing her therapist that she had had a good treatment experience, and went immediately to another analyst. For some reason, this second therapist could not take her seriously and, according to the patient, told her Jewish jokes. This was entertaining, but not exactly what she wanted, so she went to see a third analyst. The patient was an excellent mimic, and various regressed ego states would be reflected in the tone of her voice. During an early session with this last analyst, she changed her tone of voice from that of an adult to a baby. Her analyst angrily retorted, "Is that the way a grown-up woman should talk?" whereupon the patient got up from the couch and never returned. She next came to see me, and I admired and wondered about her stamina in pursuing analysis. With all these experiences, I would have expected her to have become discouraged, but she did not. Her analysis was difficult and long, but it was rewarding for both of us.

Concentrating on the feasibility of the relationship between patient and analyst made formal history taking less important. Strictly following the medical model, evaluation and diagnosis are important. As a beginning clinician, I took extensive histories, sometimes extending over two to three sessions, and then asked the patient to lie down on the couch. I was shocked when a classmate told me that his analyst greeted him at the door on his first interview, asked him his name, and then told him to get on the couch. On further reflection, I started questioning what use I made of all the material I acquired by taking histories. Knowing details about parents and siblings did not help me understand what was going on in the therapeutic relationship. I have sat through many lengthy case presentations where all sorts of data were presented— social worker's reports, psychometric testing, psychiatric histories— and yet the data I had did not give any real feeling for the patient's problems. I learned much more from hearing how the patient interacted with the therapist than from the voluminous amount of data that did not emphasize any particular aspect of the patient's character structure and defensive adaptations.

Today, I do not interview a patient with the view of reconstructing the past as it contributes to the present illness. This is information that I wish to acquire eventually, but I find it best for the patient to reveal himself at his own pace. I may from time to time interject a question, but I try to keep it in context with what the patient is discussing. If I were to ask questions either to complete a history or to satisfy my curiosity, I would not be focusing on what is really significant. Active history taking reflects the interviewer's bias or gives everything equal weight. Though Freud apparently practiced differently than he wrote, I became increasingly impressed with his advice that the therapist let the material spontaneously unfold and be surprised at every turn.

My modus operandi is based on having as few rules as possible. This means I do not have many expectations of patients. They are not, for example, required to give me a history or to "tell me everything that comes to mind." I have modified the fundamental rule and ask patients to tell me what they choose to tell me. They can feel free to reveal themselves or to hide things from me if they have such a need. One of the aims of analysis is to achieve maximum autonomy, and I believe this goal is best served by introducing autonomous choice into its methodology.

I have been asked about silent patients. Do I let them remain silent? Silence could be resistance, and by being accepting of it, the therapist is encouraging the obstacles the patient is setting up against treatment. The analyst, by accepting silence, is reinforcing the patient's resistance. This is what my supervisors taught me. I recall Dr. Thomas French telling me how Freud reminded an anally fixated, silent patient how his silence was a waste of money, whereupon the patient began talking.

How do I reconcile the fostering of autonomy with the elimination of resistance? Actually, I cannot, but I return to this question shortly. First, I want to expand further upon the problem of the silent patient, a patient most beginning analysts either dread or find tedious.

There have been a fair number of articles written about silence in recent years, and most analysts are recognizing its adaptive nature. Depending on its specific meaning, our reactions may differ. Countertransference continues to be significant.

I have found that as the years go by I become increasingly comfortable with most patients' silence and realize that it is important for me to respect it. An adolescent patient who had been diagnosed as having had an acute schizophrenic breakdown but who had reconstituted fairly quickly spent his first session giving me monosyllabic answers or saying nothing at all. He was a shy, frightened, withhdrawn young man, and I quickly felt that my questions were bothersome, intrusive, and designed to fill silent gaps. I felt too uncomfortable to continue trying to extract information, so I told the patient that he must find my questions burdensome and that it might be best if he lie down on the couch where he could relax and keep his thoughts to himself if that is what he wanted.

Or if he wished, he could communicate his thoughts to me, and I would be nearby. The patient was visibly relieved, lay down on the couch, and remained silent. This continued for several weeks, but then he began gradually to speak.

Silence represented a protective withdrawal for this patient. He was too frightened to relate directly to me, and he had to pull away. My function was to provide a setting in which he could comfortably withdraw so that the analytic process could be set in motion, but first he had to feel safe. To my mind, urging him to talk would have been a technical error and disruptive to treatment.

Circumstances vary, however, and silence has different meanings depending on the patient's character structure and the range of adaptive modalities. For example, a married woman in her 30s, after 2 years of producing fairly spontaneous free associations, became increasingly silent to the degree that she said nothing at all during some sessions. For some reason that I was unaware of, I found this intolerable and would make the usual grunts that are supposed to encourage patients to talk or badger her by asking what was on her mind. My reactions puzzled me because it was contrary to my usual response.

The conclusions I finally reached were derived from both what I knew about her after 2 years of analysis and from examining my own feelings, what constituted my countertransference reactions. I saw the patient as running away from me; sometimes, in my mind, I had very distinct images of her running out of the office. I could also see myself chasing her. I then knew I had assumed the role of her parents as they related to her in the infantile past. Her method of controlling her environment was to withdraw and then get others to pursue her. This mode of relating had also become significant in determining how she conducted heterosexual relationships.

Once I understood what was going on, I relaxed, and it did not matter whether she talked or did not talk. The patient was able to sense the change in my mood and actually asked me about it, not making it necessary to give her what might have seemed to have been a gratuitous interpretation. We discussed what I believed to be the transference–countertransference interaction, and she brought up considerable material, including dreams, as confirmation. Of course, now she was no longer silent, and her analysis continued to a successful termination.

The fundamental principle that determines my therapeutic philosophy is to respect the patient's adaptations and not to interfere with the manifestations of psychopathology. As I have already discussed, there are limits to what an analyst can tolerate depending on how disruptive the manifestations of psychopathology may be. I believe it is possible to let patients reveal themselves in a characteristic fashion based on their emotional problems. This raises the question of the desirability of eliminating resistance.

Freud defined resistance as the patient's attempts to resist treatment. At first, in the *Studies on Hysteria*, he described it as a conscious phenomenon, but later he attributed to it unconscious motivation. It would be absurd to put resistance outside the psyche, as if it had an existence apart from the rest of the personality, sui generis, especially if Freud recognized its unconscious derivation. Still, in prohibiting its expression as Freud described and as many of us were taught, we are treating it as if it were simply a malevolent manipulation purposely designed by patients for the sole purpose of defeating us in our therapeutic endeavors. Analysis would then become a battleground and a power struggle, and it often has.

I remember discussing these attitudes about treating resistance as if it were just another defensive adaptation with Winnicott. He stated that the word was no longer in his vocabulary. He believed it had developed such a pejorative connotation that it was incompatible with the supportive nonjudgmental attitude that is so necessary in constructing the holding environment, which is an indispensable part of the psychoanalytic process. Winnicott reinforced my belief that resistance is another defensive modality specifically detected against the therapy, but which has to be analyzed in the same way as any material that the patient presents.

There are special situations, usually with severely disturbed patients but also with the better integrated patient. There are some patients who have a need to get the analyst to function as a nonanalyst. They may want him to intrude into their lives, help them manage, and give them advice. Some patients cannot or refuse to free associate and ask the therapist incessant questions. Often these patients are so concretely oriented, that is, they do not seem to have any capacity for psychological mindedness, that they make a mockery of the analytic relationship. Frequently, these patients tell the analyst how he should be helping and reassuring them without having any substance to their demands. The latter seem insatiable. There are many varieties of such interactions that can be very frustrating for therapists who want to analyze these patients, patients who create innumerable obstacles to setting up an analytic relationship.

We have to admit that not everyone is analyzable, and some of these patients, even with the most tolerant and patient therapists, prove to be unanalyzable. Still, if I do my best to preserve the analytic setting, some of these seemingly impossible patients eventually become involved in an analytic relationship. In some instances, patients may seek another type of treatment, but if we have maintained our analytic orientation, they may return. This has happened to me in about half a dozen cases.

As an example of the vicissitudes of engaging such patients in an analytic relationship, I briefly present the case of a middle-aged lawyer who was very anxious to start analysis with me. He waited, against my advice, 8 months for his first appointment. With such motivation, it was surprising that halfway through his first hour on the couch he demanded that I give him a summary of what we had done and the amount of progress we had made. He asked other similar, concrete questions such as our goals and how we planned to reach them. I had no inclination whatsoever to respond to what I experienced as an assault. Consequently, I said nothing.

The patient was furious and continued his barrage for the next two sessions. I finally realized that my "analytic silence" represented an oppositional stance. We were involved in a power struggle. I began to wonder whether analysis was suitable for this patient, but I was further perplexed by his patience and tenacity regarding seeing me, who was clearly identified as a psychoanalyst. Furthermore, he was not unsophisticated about analysis, having read a good deal and having many friends in analysis who freely discussed their treatment with him. Yet, he acted as if he knew nothing about the analytic method.

I decided that I would have to declare my position and told him that what I wanted to do was analyze him and that I did not consider it part of my analytic function to give summaries, make evaluations, or answer questions on demand. I found the need to reply to him intrusive, and as we wanted to foster his autonomy, I also had to feel free to reply to him or treat his demands as declarative statements. This was the only way I could work, and he had to choose whether he would accept my approach or wished to be referred to someone who would answer questions and give summaries. He chose to stay and had a good analysis. He did not stop making demands, but having established my position, I was able to be relaxed in spite of his attempts to get me to relinquish my analytic attitude.

As we understand more about psychopathology, we can see more clearly how patients may need to disrupt the analytic relationship. This may require specific maneuvers to preserve the treatment. The question of whether analysis is either feasible or desirable for these patients is still an open one. There is much that we do not know, and many of our attempts at treatment can still be considered experimental. How effective can interpretation of the transference be for patients suffering from severe ego defects or whose adjustment to the external world is based on delusions?

Interpretation is an analytic tool designed to give the patient integrative insights. Previously, the analyst interpreted unconscious sexual feelings that are related to Oedipal issues or defenses against Oedipus. In some institutes, this is about all that is said about interpretation. In terms of the types of psychopathology I have been discussing, this is a narrow and unproductive viewpoint.

I believe that in general there are two types of psychoanalytically relevant interpretations which are very much related. First, the conventional type of transference interpretation consists of identifying various aspects of the transference such as infantile feelings displaced onto the analyst, projections of parts of the self, and the reenactment through the repetition compulsion of infantile traumatic constellations. Next, I sometimes feel the need to define the analytic setting, which I consider to be a second type of transference interpretation. Especially with severely disturbed patients, it may be necessary to clarify the limits of the analyst's participation in the treatment process and just what the analytic orientation for the particular patient will consist of. Winnicott gives an example of a patient who felt elated over some success he had achieved in his daily life as a consequence of the progress he had made in analysis. Noting that Winnicott was not as excited as he was, he complained about what he felt to be his analyst's indifferent attitude, whereupon Winnicott replied that he did not get as excited or as elated as the patient, but neither did he get as depressed or as hopeless as he did. Winnicott had defined the spectrum of his reactions. Any other expectations the patient might have would stand out as transference expectations.

I do not limit all my comments to these two types of transference interpretations, but I believe they are the most important interactions in terms of patients assimilating experiences, which help lead to endopsychic structuring of potentially helpful experiences. In turn, the latter lead to an expansion of the ego accompanied by the acquisition of more efficient autonomous adaptive techniques and a strengthening of the self-representation. This type of interaction, to my mind, is the foreground of the treatment process and represents the nurturing-growth potential that is found in ordinary development.

With certain patients, I allow myself to have interchanges that are not transference interpretations. This can be risky because there are patients who will feel threatened by the introduction of anything that goes beyond strictly adhering to the investigation of how their minds work, and these are usually the more vulnerable and severely disturbed patients. With many patients, however, it is desirable, even necessary, to respond and at times initiate communications that, on the surface, appear to be extraanalytic. These may also be very sick patients whose needs are different from the group that would experience such overtures as intrusive. The former usually feel more or less assaulted by extraanalytic exchanges, whereas the latter require them to construct a comfortable background, to produce a setting that will support the nurturing foreground of interpretation.

Infants are nurtured when they are held and soothed, that is, the nurturing process consists of the foreground of feeding and other caregiving activities and the background of soothing. There is a similar duality in analysis. Winnicott divides mothers into nurturing and environmental mothers, as they represent nurturing and soothing elements.

If such extraanalytic maneuvers are designed to preserve or make analysis possible, I wonder if I am justified in calling them extraanalytic. In any case, I can give a brief example of such an interchange. The patient I discuss is the some schizoid young man I previously described as being shy and withdrawn and who felt somewhat relieved when I suggested he lie down on the couch so he could be alone with his thoughts. I would be nearby, and he could determine whether he wanted to tell me about them.

He eventually did talk to me, and this took the form of asking innumerable questions. He asked me how to do things, that, for most persons, would be pedestrian. For example, he wanted to know how to dress for certain occasions, including what clothes are proper to wear in the downtown section of the city. He even asked how to make a phone call and what to say when asking a young lady out for a date. In contrast to the lawyer, I felt it was absolutely necessary to answer his questions as completely as I could. I also believe, now in retrospect because nothing was consciously thought out at the time, that if I had handled his questions in a more conventional analytic fashion by reflecting the question back to him and inquiring about his motives for his questions, treatment would have quickly ended. Furthermore, in this situation, unlike that with other patients, it would have been unnatural for me not to respond. I enjoyed replying, partly I suppose, because the patient had said very little or nothing at all. So anything from him, even a barrage of questions, was welcome.

More important, this withdrawn patient was able, for the first time in his life, to make an emotionally meaningful contact with another person that was directed to his needs. In the treatment, this created a mutually exciting atmosphere insofar as we both experienced our dialogues as stimulating but relaxing. This led to the establishment of a background soothing environment that later enabled us to examine transference projections.

The purpose of this book is to describe how various analysts work. As clinicians are well aware, modes of treatment are strongly influenced by the therapist's personal style. I have described my attitudes about indications for treatment and attitudes about various types of psychopathology, resistance, interpretations, and so-called extraanalytic interchanges. Undoubtedly, many of my technical maneuvers are determined by some idiosyncratic factors, but these refer mainly to surface phenomena. The source of my modus operandi is based on my conceptual orientation. Throughout the years, my concepts about patients have been gradually modified, and this has determined how I relate to them. In describing my technical orientation, I was also implicitly indicating its theoretical substrata, but now I discuss, explicitly and briefly (as this book concentrates on techniques), how my conceptual frame has developed.

In spite of being considered an ego psychologist and an object relationship theorist, I want to emphasize that the foundations of my conceptual system are rooted in freudian principles. Freud furnished us with a unique viewpoint based on the existence of a dynamic, unconscious, and psychic determinism. He also furnished monumental insights about various forms of psychopathology, and his recommendations about treatment are, for the most part, valuable for a large range of emotional disturbances. Freud's ideas are still the essence of psychoanalysis.

As discussed in the introduction of this paper, Freud limited psychoanalysis to a select group of patients. At least, this was his theoretical position because, if we examine the cases he presented as paradigms of classical neuroses, they do not appear, from a characterological viewpoint, to be that different from the patients we see today. As our range of experience widened, the id-ego conflict hydrodynamic model was not too helpful in achieving the understanding that would permit us to maintain a psychoanalytic perspective with the vast majority of patients seeking treatment. However, Freud provided us with the foundation of a model that would contribute to our construction of appropriate psychoanalytic techniques by furnishing us with the structural hypothesis, the beginning of ego psychology.

Putting the ego in the center of the psychic apparatus, a mediating energy between the inner and outer world, stresses adaptation or the lack of adaptation in psychopathology. Symptoms and aberrant character traits are the manifestations of defective techniques to cope with the exigencies of the outer world. Keeping this in mind causes analysts to modify their ideas about directing patients to change their behavior so that it conforms to the norm the therapist has in mind. This is an oversimplification. However, moving away from the id-ego conflict model has an effect on our scale of values, causing us to modify our expectations about changing patients' adaptive modes as long as they need them to preserve psychic equilibrium.

Loewald and Winnicott have had a strong influence in helping me construct my theoretical orientation. I first heard Loewald in 1957, at the meetings of the American Psychoanalytic Association in Chicago, presenting parts of his paper "On the Therapeutic Action of Psychoanalysis," which was later published (1960) in the *International Journal of Psycho-Analysis*. Although throughout the years this article has appeared in many bibliographies, its content has for the most part, been ignored. I recently assigned this paper to fairly sophisticated and clinically experienced members of a seminar, and they were amazed by its wealth of ideas, which are just being discussed today by mainstream psychoanalysts.

In 1957, I found these ideas useful in helping me understand psychopathology and the therapeutic interaction. A colleague then introduced me to Winnicott's works, which broadened my perspective. Because of Winnicott, I began reading Melanie Klein, and after discarding her developmental timetable and separating elements that she felt to be crucial to psychic differentiation as manifestations of psychopathology, her ideas also contributed to my comprehension of primitive forms of psychopathology and revised the then current attitude about treatability. Loewald and Winnicott emphasized the interaction of the environment with the developing psyche; Klein outlined in detail primitive psychic mechanisms.

Throughout the years, I have paid increasing attention to primitive mental states, and my technical orientation has been influenced pari passu. Fortunately, I have received considerable support from colleagues whose clinical attitudes have been proceeding in a similar direction; the two that have been most supportive and have contributed extensively to our clinical knowledge are L. Bryce Boyer and Harold F. Searles.

To write a chapter about an analyst at work requires that technical maneuvers be placed in their proper context. This involves an appraisal of a person's motivation to become an analyst as well as an assessment of the influence of training and the special impact of various teachers, especially charismatic ones.

There are usually some fortunate, fortuitous experiences that help shape the pursuit of a professional career. The student can become attached to a renowned mentor, and the idealization of a teacher is generalized to the area that the mentor represents. This may serve as an impetus to learning and dedication. From such encounters, motivation gains momentum, which is translated into action and study.

In my case and that of some colleagues with whom I have exchanged confidences, this early idealistic attachment has to be loosened, but not necessarily broken. We need to discover our true professional selves and make them compatible with our emerging beliefs as we integrate them into our ego-ideal and self-representation. Our analytic styles are the outcome of such an integration. As we seek professional autonomy, we are enabled to help our patients seek a similar autonomy to help liberate them from the crippling and constricting effects of psychopathology.

REFERENCE

Loewald, H. (1960). On the therapeutic action of psychoanalysis. *International Journal of Psychoanalysis, 41,* 16–33.

Random Notes on the Art and Science of Psychoanalysis from an Analyst at Work

2

James S. Grotstein, M.D.

As I cast a searchlight into the corridors of memory to summon my past experiences in psychoanalytic practice, I find that it first illuminates an intense, guileless, innocent young man who romantacized the Gothic mystery of the unconscious, who believed in the universality of the application of psychoanalysis for all problems of the world, and who worshipped the pantheon of the famous ones who ruled this field. I became aware that my having become interested in being a practitioner of psychoanalysis was most extraordinary insofar as I came from a very small suburb of a modest sized city in the midwest, which to this very day has no analyst but yet does have psychiatrists, psychologists, and social workers. In my childhood, those who knew of the profession linked it indissolubly with psychotic patients and shunned both.

I realized that in my interbellum childhood, I had witnessed the ocean crossing of many Europeans fleeing Nazi persecution who had brought this new German science of the mysterious unconscious with them. To this very day, parenthetically, I find psychoanalysis had, in retrospect, been very German in its ambiance, in its traditions, and in its institute rituals. With this massive change, there had been a sudden translocation of the center of psychoanalysis to London and ultimately to the United States, maybe even before either country and culture was ready for this responsibility. For me, at any rate, psychoanalysis was European, mainly German, was Gothically mechanistic, and the unconscious held untold dark, unruly secrets. The unraveling of evil had become a medical specialty. I recall two "psychoanalytic movies" current when I was a child–*King's Row* and *Spellbound*–both of which portrayed the then new practice of psychoanalysis in glowing colors. The unconscious had entered the Zeitgeist of the American way of life, where it remains to this very day, but the long dark shadow of the silent movie, *The Cabinet of Dr. Caligari*, was to hover over the newfound importance our culture was to place on mental health, especially insofar as the latter movie dealt with the theme of psychiatric sadism, a belief that is yet to be dispelled.

I also believed as a young man that the very existence of psychoanalysis was connected with a certain Medieval search for the Holy Grail. It somehow represented a heroic pursuit of Truth through the Forest of (contaminating) Experience. I recall having been in awe of those august few who had actually been through psychoanalysis (let alone who *were* analysts) and was secretely feeling pity toward those who could only afford the experience of "psychotherapy."

The naivete of a would-be knight errant has departed, but what has remained undiluted to this very day is my respect for the capacity psychoanalysis has to generate powerful, awesome experiences, especially transference. To this very day, I cannot quite get over what can happen when "two strangers" get together to listen to the experiences of one of them. By this time, the whole world knows about the phenomenon of transference, and it is so taken for granted inside and outside of psychoanalysis that the term loses its magic and mystery. We now realize that transference is more plural than not insofar as it has many usages, the original being the well-known phenomenon of the repetition of past significant relationships with the analyst as if the latter were the same figure as the ones in the past. It also came to mean that the patient's experience of him- or herself could be "transferred" to the analyst. Finally, a newer meaning has been added—that of events which should have but did not take place sufficiently, either of a mirroring of one's infantile grandiosity by the parent or of the development of an unblemished idealization by the infant of a parent, and a twinship concordantly and/or complementarily with the parent-analyst. In this latter case, self psychologists advise us that the empathic validation by the analyst of the patient's experiences of this loss constitutes a new form of transference and may even help to evoke the experience of making up for it through the retrospective validation.

I should like to add yet one more meaning of transference. The original putative meaning of transference conveys the actual "transfer" of mental pain from the infant to its mother, from the parishioner to his or her confessor, from the patient to the analyst. The latter meaning borrows so heavily from the religious tradition that it is rarely discussed in serious works on technique, yet it seems to be one of the principal reasons for the evocation of a phenomenon that is now being widely discussed, namely, *countertransference.* Between the poles of transference and countertransference there occurs the whole panoply of emotions that two people are capable of engendering in each other in this rich energy chamber of interaction. Having come from the medical tradition and having been imbued with the safety of being the doctor who offered detached "prescriptions" to his patients, it took me a long time to realize that my self, body and soul, were to be the very sense organs that were to experience the pain of the other person *and* were to be "invited" by command performance to experience my resonance with them.

The advent of the importance of countertransference has represented a very big change in the analyst's attitude toward the practice of his or her profession. It represented the beginning decline of the old medical model of scientific observation and the emergence of a newer conception of intersubjectivity, that of two human beings in an ongoing experience with each other. In order to be intersubjective, analysts must submit to more assault on themselves than ever before, not only from patients, but now from themselves in the form of self-questioning. Although countertransference is technically considered to be unconscious, we nevertheless do have indicators of our emotions and distress when we are with patients. I have often had profound feelings about patients, sometimes extrasensorily perceptive and at other times deeply negative and disturbing. I have also had the experience of being the object of what would appear to have been extrasensory perception by patients. I recall an event of many years ago when I scheduled a week vacation in February. One of my borderline patient's felt constrained to ask me if I were getting married and going off to San Francisco for a honeymoon. Of course, she was right, but how did she know?

This episode is but one of a countless number of extrasensory "knowing," which seemed to have crossed the gap of apparent separation between the patient and me. We analysts have progressed far enough to recognize that the patients themselves may be more keenly aware of our countertransferences and inner emotional states than we are; patients can help us with them. This has certainly been true for me. What has been especially disturbing were those occasions in which feelings were being "transferred" by the patient to me, and at the same time, feelings within me were being evoked—all beyond or underneath my awareness or the patient's awareness. It is almost as if the patient has been broadcasting in a certain frequency band to which my receiver was sensitive, and the analysis we know of takes place within that frequency band; yet at the same time, the patient may be "sending" on an ultrasensory band to which I was unconsciously, but not consciously, sensitive. Often, I would go home in the evening after what I believed were interesting, revelatory hours with patients and have to plead with my family to allow me to "debrief" for a half an hour or so, during which time I would be aloof from them, mysteriously perturbed, and highly irritable in general. After a while, the feelings would pass (God knows where they went), and I would recover my normal personality once more. It was, and often still is, as if I am occupied by nameless demons of unrest, ghosts of a story that has yet to be told more fully, disturbing previews of coming unattractions.

When I carefully examined these feelings and tried to associate them to particular patients, I retrospectively discovered that they had often developed during sessions with patients whom I was later destined to be surprised. These were the patients who may have been undergoing what I had believed at the time was a good analytic relationship with me in which a good to and fro dialogue existed. Then there would be a turn in the bend, a sudden interruption of unexpected negative feeling by the patient toward me and, in a few instances, a sudden abruption of the analysis. In other cases, where there were no sudden surprises, I had experienced the aforementioned feelings in long analyses that were characterized by the virtual absence of any positive feelings. In these cases, I felt closest to being like Job and had the feeling that I was to pay the price of ostracism and bewilderment (in its most literal sense) in a way not too dissimilar to the patients' experiences in their own childhoods.

Whatever the reason, I gradually came to realize that the analyst is more like an exorcist than not and suffers the transference of bad demons from the patient to him- or herself. The analyst, in other words, must subjectively "know" the torment of the patient by experiencing it. I had never been taught this but came to realize that it was part of the healing function. It was only a step to the realization that the analyst's mental health is under more jeopardy than has been believed, whether this jeopardy is by transference influence or by transference-countertransference stress. Later, I discuss analysis as play. For now, let me merely allude to the "role" function that analysts inadvertently find themselves in. Included in the umbrella conception of countertransference is our tendency to behave at times in subtly altered ways so as to appear, in retrospect, as if we have been ensorcelled by the requirements of the patient's drama to portray aspects of him or her without actively knowing it. With nearly every case I presently see, I ask myself: "I wonder who I'm going to be now!" (with apologies to Kurt Vonnegut).

Perhaps the most formidable experiences I have had with patients, however, are those where I have to share silently their failures, their lonelinesses, and their losses. I seldom escape intact from the occasions of their tragedies. I believe the term "countertransference" is not suitable for these occasions; I should rather use the term "bonding" – oftentimes despite myself until I understood that that was what it was. Psychoanalysis, I came gradually and inescapably to realize, is not just a profession that is "practiced" in the office during office hours. The phenomenon of the special transference that accrues to us has been surprising to me. Transference expectations of a patient within the confines of the analytic procedure are easy enough to comprehend. What I was not prepared for were the "transference" expectations imposed upon me outside the office, not only by patients, but by patients' relatives and friends and by the culture – even to the point of "transference" expectations imposed upon my wife and children by teachers at school and people at large. I then began to realize that the life of an analyst (and that of his family) is not unlike that of a movie actor, of a person high in government, or even of a monarch – where one is on public display and is expected to conform to a mythical protocol which designs to fashion us in roles of heroes, of ideal personages who are powerful, all-knowing, and mysterious, detached and secretely caring, but also gently and poisefully uninvolved. Practicing in a large city dilutes only slightly the difficulty of leading a normal life with relative impunity. Yet how understandable it is that hero-starved, ideal-starved people will experience disappointment when someone whom they hold in such august, mysterious, and complex esteem would betray their hopes by appearing "too human" publicly.

When I was still a first-year psychiatric resident at the Pennsylvania Hospital, I consulted Dr. Robert Waelder to become my analyst. He accepted, but reminded me of his long waiting list. My subsequent plans led me away from Philadelphia to Los Angeles, so I was denied the privilege of being his analysand, but as fate would have it, I wound up in analysis with *his* analyst, Dr. Robert Jokl. A statement Waelder made to me during that interview, however, has rung down through the years. He stated: "Dr. Grotstein, are you sure you wish to spend the rest of your life seeing a very few patients, when all is told whose importance to you will be out of proportion by virtue of their long stay with you?" In the early days of my practice, when patients were hard to come by, I gave little thought to his statement, but later, after my reputation had been established, I began to ponder this question more seriously. It was Bion who pithily repeated this same injunction as follows: "We really don't know who it is who is coming to consult us for analysis. By the time we become properly introduced, it's too late to do anything about it. We just have to make the best of a bad job." Bion's statement did not reflect cynicism but rather resignation to the inescapable fact that we allow strangers into our intimate lives to affect us, to impact upon us in ways that can be beautiful or horrendous.

We may believe that we have a choice and that we can act on what appears to be a choice, but more often than not, we select whomever comes along at a time when we have an opening and we try hard, if at all possible, not to have a waiting list, although I must confess that I do have one, but am apologetic for it. Having a waiting list presupposes one's agreement with patients that one is indeed the only analyst who can analyze them. On the other hand, when we turn a patient down, and I rarely have, we are put to the question of what it was that got to our inner core, that so disturbed us that it vibrated with the fundamental. An analyst does not like to be caught with the proof that his personal feelings have been evoked to the point that he cannot bear a certain patient, but alas, this happens all too often. One dislikes disliking because it interferes too dreadfully with one's self-image as a healer.

On the opposite side of the scale, however, are those choices of patients we make which promise to anoint and to appoint us to fame and fortune. I have often caught myself wanting to analyze this or that prospective patient and realized later that I had confused patientdom with friendship. We spend so much time with these few people, following Waelder's all too cogent warning, that they inescapably become our friends and companions through the long, dark winter of the analytic odyssey. The general medical practitioner is spared this problem because of the dilution of intensity by his or her patient load. A general practitioner or internist may have several hundred people on his or her panel and see each of them very occasionally, whereas we see each of our patients frequently and intensively. The grounds for friendship and its corollary, hostility, are rife. It begins to matter far too much, despite the fact that it should not count at all, what our patients think of us, what they report about us to their friends, how they represent us in public, and so forth. There have been too many times when I have felt too helpless to present my side of the issue after hearing indirectly what patients were saying about me. Yet there were times when the patient's view was dangerously close to the truth and my view was less so. Those were the times that I would momentarily regret not having chosen internal medicine or surgery so as to realign myself with the authority of medicine's grandeur and be more immune to the vicissitudes and vulnerability of reputation.

I have found that people who practice psychoanalytic psychotherapy are generally torn between a tendency to adhere strictly to the so-called rules of abstinence and those who desire to be more natural in their dialogues with patients. The former group can be characterized as those who were thought to be purists and who believed largely in the power of the "word" that their interpretations delivered to the patient. The latter seemed to be more humanistic and empathic (in the older meaning of the term) and were more interactional in their attitudes. In my practice, I have vacillated between these two polarities and have never felt too comfortable with either. To this very day, I have been unable to make up my mind about the preferential value of the highly disciplined approach as opposed to the interactional one. More recently, I came to realize that the history of the more rigorous approach was based on Freud's concept that the instinctual drives release through instant gratification. An ego and a superego were needed, therefore, to withstand their pressure, to postpone their discharge, and to transform their more meaningful aspects into action while curtailing the others. The id and its drives had apparently acquired very bad "press" in psychoanalysis, had become associated with a "seething cauldron" of infamy within us, and had required a philosophy of life in general and an analytic technique in particular that would change these instinctual drives into properly dressed ego attitudes. I no longer believe this paradigm and have criticized it in some of my publications as being the inescapable result of using a one-track theory that highlights one aspect (the ego) but must of necessity demonize the other (the id). I came to the next realization that the id is also an "I" and therefore is as much an ego as the one that seeks to discredit it.

I was thus able to envision a cooperative partnership between the two, but I could also envision the need for the two agencies to be kept separate with a repressive barrier between them which protected one from the other so that they could continue to function separately without interference. From here it was only a very short step to another idea that analytic technique is optimally experienced in a field of abstinence, not in order to convert the instinctual drives into substitute verbal associations (the classical theory), but in order for the unconscious to reveal itself in the form of narrative plays which require their actors, the patient, and the analyst, to remain in their roles.

I have always been struck by how rigorously children assign roles to themselves and their playmates in their games and how they adhere in such a disciplined manner to the roles in which they have cast themselves. Further, I was interested in the fact that children generally do not need referees or umpires in their games. Each child seems to understand the nature of the role and plays it to the hilt. Might this not be true for analysis as well, I reasoned. Is not the practice of analysis by an analyst an artificial role to enact, and conversely, is not the role of a patient absurd by the standards of everyday life? In short, the analyst and his or her patient are experiencing a play—and a series of plays within the larger play—which can only be played out when the analyst and patient undergo the disciplined performance of their respective roles. The play being played is a most arcane one, however, insofar as the analyst and the patient do not know the nature of the play except in ever-continuing retrospect. With this in mind, it helped me to justify being more disciplined in my approach to patients but never fully dispelled the desire to be an actual "player" within the play the patient was writing—a "playmate," as it were. I believe this is a desire on the part of many therapists and causes them to yield to the temptation to be supportive psychotherapists, another term that has generally been vilified in our field. It may very well be that there are a variety of roles for the analyst to play in addition to the transference roles, and I believe this is a fruitful area for future research.

Of all the patients I can think of in this regard, the one that comes most easily to mind is actually a screen writer who was able to make successful professional use of some of these "plays" that took place in the analysis. I often had the feeling during his analysis that I was not merely his analyst, but was actually an active guide to his internal world of undiscovered plays. When one of the "plays" was over and had actually been successfully launched, I felt like Ulysses who was no sooner home from his Odyssey from Troy than he wanted to go on his second voyage. With this and other patients, I also learned that being a psychoanalyst is not unlike being a method actor insofar as the analyst must be able to evoke within him- or herself those experiences that most closely approximate those of the patient.

How does analysis work? I have often asked myself this question and have answered varyingly and in general without the conviction of certainty. Do people get better because of catharsis or because they are now able, perhaps for the first time, to communicate meaningfully with another person? Is the interpretive word the mysterious element that resonates with the secret, repressed truth and unlocks it via this resonance? Psychoanalysis is an agency of transformation, and the nature of this transformation, I more and more believe, is mysterious. I recall having been puzzled when a patient reported to me that he had given up smoking and credited the analysis for this. Naturally, I was pleased, but I was bewildered because I had not even known that he smoked. He had never brought it up in his analysis. Events such as this convince me that analysis is more mysterious than it would seem and that our understanding of the phenomenon of "understanding" is in need of revision.

I was greatly helped in this regard by my analysis with Wilfred Bion, who eschewed "understanding" altogether. Unlike my experiences in my first two analyses, I found many of his interpretations incomprehensible mentally, but nonetheless effective emotionally. I recall commenting once, when I thought I did understand him, "I follow you." His reply I shall never forget: "Yes, I was afraid of that." Another interaction between us may make the point a bit more clear: After a particularly beautiful interpretation of his, which I had been able to "understand," I stated, "You're absolutely right! That was a magnificent interpretation!" His rejoinder jarred me. He stated: "Yes, you would have me be right and would credit me with having given you a magnificent interpretation but seem to forget that my interpretation is only a second opinion on my part based upon your associations. I could just as easily say that your associations were absolutely right." What I learned from this and other such interactions has had a profound effect on my development. It helped me to get underneath and, therefore, beyond the barrier of "understanding." It is one thing to understand or comprehend a text that a lecturer is propounding; it is quite another thing to realize one's experience as the result of the impact of one's echo through the experience of one's self by another. Thus, Bion's "second opinion" was his echoing of my initial announcement of my inner experience via free association. I realized then that it was my duty to heed, not so much his interpretation, but its impact on me as a transformation of what I had initiated and which had coursed through him on its way back to me. My attention shifted from him to myself and to my capacity to "realize" my "experience." I therefore realized that "understanding" is misleading if one "stands under" the word of the other and neglects one's *self* in the transaction.

This clarification profoundly affected my attitude toward analytic technique. I became aware that there was no such thing as a correct interpretation, but rather that there were only my second opinions of what the patient was sending to me to echo, and that my interpretations were the best approximations at the moment but could never be accurate in the true sense of the word, insofar as truth is unknowable. Analytic growth, therefore, occurred in the absence of "understanding" and comprehension, but it *did* occur in the presence of experiencing (realizing) the experience, a phenomenon which "understanding" seems to arrest, forestall, or at worst, pervert by attempting to convert moving, unknowable experiences into tangible icons of seeming knowability. Ultimate growth seems to have taken place in the act of the sharing of feelings. Perhaps analysis works when two people are able to live one life for a moment in time.

Earlier in this presentation I mentioned the phenomenon of the development of the power of feelings in analysis. It must be acknowledged that analysis borrows from mind-control techniques insofar as the patient is invited to come to speak only of distress and, upon failing to do so, is often subjected to interpretations about resistance. The passport to the analytic relationship, therefore, is based on one's continuing to betray one's weaknesses and to reveal one's suffering to a stranger. This exclusive concentration of emphasis on suffering certainly mobilizes the shadow side of the individual and is often in danger of eclipsing the positive side, a phenomenon many analysts have recently addressed. The dangers of analysis, therefore, are not so much the revelation of the id, as had previously been thought, but rather the exclusive mobilization to the surface of the dark side of the individual at the expense of the positive aspects. Sometimes I have thought of it as being very much like a deep "abscess" migrating to the surface on its journey to "expressing" itself. At the same time one is concentrating on the patient's abscess, however, one also becomes gradually aware of the human being who has the abscess. This latter phenomenon may seem so obvious that the reader might wonder why I bring it up. It is my experience, both with myself and with my colleagues and supervisees, that their references to their experiences with patients are heavily loaded in terms of the patient's illnesses and seem not to contact the patient as a human entity in his or her own right. I believe every therapist does wonder about a patient's life aside from the illness, but it takes a very long time to get to know the person and to have a mental representation of that person which is independent of his or her illness. Their suffering is what bonds us and, therefore, what may "bind" us. Similarily, I have often caught glimpses of patients that cause me all the more to realize how trapped their free souls felt in the prison of their personalities or temperaments.

As I think about the various patients I have treated in the past, several come to mind as deserving awards for poignancy. One of the most poignant involved a Mexican laborer, born in a small Indian village in Mexico, who was, strangely, tall, blond, and blue-eyed. He was a construction worker and prior to seeing me had frequently consulted the company doctor because of stomach pains. He told me that the doctor was unable to help him because the pains were "not in the stomach, but in the soul." As he continued to suffer, he tried to think of other ways of getting help. He went to church and confessed to his priest, but to little avail. His wife would read the newspaper to him and one day read to him about psychiatry and how it dealt with bodily pains. He then found his way to the Biomedical Library at the UCLA School of Medicine and had the reference librarian give him some literature about "psychoanalysis for bodily pains." He then somehow got to the Neuro-Psychiatric Institute and obtained my name for referral.

What I saw before me was a tall, handsome, blond enigma who had been the last of 15 children and the only blue-eyed blond among them. Allegedly because of poverty, he was sent away from his family and grew up with his father's compadre, but he always had a feeling of being the bad one, the evil one, the one who should not have been born. Hour after hour we dealt with his feelings about the guilt of being born and about the shame he brought onto his family, and I had unveiled before me a Mexican version of Hans Christian Andersen's *The Ugly Duckling*. Of all the things that struck me about this patient, the most forceful was how long a journey he had to make in order to get analytically "exorcised" from his feelings of "original sin," how he had an idea about analysis even before he knew analysis existed, and how he knew he had a pain that could only be relieved through the "therapy of the word."

Another patient narrative that still clings to me is that of a furniture salesman, my second control case. I remember his analysis as being a gratifying one for me insofar as transferences and resistances developed in such a way that I was relatively able to interpret to him successfully and thereby please my supervisor as well as myself. In the third year of the analysis, however, there occurred a sudden change in his demeanor. He became very depressed and silent for quite some time and then revealed to me something he had never wished to discuss: He had killed his brother in childhood. Apparently, when the patient was 4 years old and his younger brother was 2, he had pushed his brother out the window of their second-story New York apartment, and the latter fell to the ground dead. His mother and father never talked about the matter with him, and the event constituted the family ghost.

Much of the rest of the analysis was spent on feelings of atonement and reparations for this ancient act. One day, when the patient's father had come from New York to visit him and his family, the patient felt bold enough to ask his father about the details of the tragedy. The father stated: "You didn't push Sidney out of the window. You were at the other end of the room at the time. He fell out onto the awning of the downstairs apartment. He wasn't hurt by that. He died of polio 2 months later." What followed in the analysis was deeply moving. The patient was relieved to some extent by the realization of his factual innocence, but he was somehow outraged by having his tragic guilt robbed from him. The "fact" of the accident had constituted the central core of his identity, the North Star of his tragic selfhood, and was now summarily discredited by a resurrection of facts from the past. It was now as if his entire life had been that of a liar, of a false self, rather than that of a depressed man whose depression had been authenticated by an ancient guilt. I learned an important lesson from him about the organizational power of depression to be a pathological container for the development of a personality's raison d'etre.

It sometimes happens that the analyst gets caught in the experience of extraordinary coincidence and in the position of frustration because of the vows of discretion. I recall a patient of many years ago who was tall, lanky, and Gary Cooperesque with his Oklahoma accent. He was married, had two children, and worked as a television writer. He often related stories of his moody father, an Oklahoma rancher, who was distant from his child and prejudiced in his views about people, especially in his anti-Semitism. When the patient would refer to his father's attitude about Jews, he would pronounce the word "Jew-ish" with a hyphen between the two syllables in imitation of his father.

The patient who saw me in the following appointment was a doctor's wife from a nearby suburb, Jewish by upbringing, who had come from a large industrial center in the midwest. Her married name was obviously Jewish, but one day she parenthetically mentioned her maiden name, which happened to be identical to the name of the patient preceding her. Upon discussing her family history following the revelation of her maiden name, she mentioned the family "ghost," an eccentric uncle who had come from the same city and who had forsworn his family of origin to resettle in Oklahoma and became a rancher. The coincidence was extraordinary. There I was with the dilemma of not being able to tell my Southern writer patient that, without his realizing it, he was indeed "Jew-ish"! My second patient confirmed this relationship by relating she had heard that she had a cousin in Hollywood who was a TV writer. Would it have done any good to break silence and introduce the two of them? Naturally, I preserved analytic discretion, and to the best of my knowledge, the two do not know each other to this very day. I later came to understand that my desire to break analytic vows and to introduce the two had been due to an impulse on my part to heal an ancient breach in a tormented family, which each patient had somehow or other intuited to be present. I had to settle for healing whatever breaches I could fix within the individuals themselves.

One of the most surprising discoveries to penetrate the immunity blanket of my naivete was the phenomenon of extraordinary hatred for each other amongst analysts. When I was a young man and had entered the analytic "priesthood," I was aware of deviant schools populated by poor fools who listened to inferior gods. Yet even in Philadelphia, where my psychiatric career began, I had to contend with the fact that there were two psychoanalytic institutes, an "orthodox" and a "reformed" one. Naturally, I chose the orthodox with which to affiliate, and when I came to Los Angeles, I continued my orthodox affiliation. Only very gradually did I discover the human condition and the presence of politics and group phenomena generally. Our profession may very well be handicapped by the absence of concrete, mechanistic procedures, which the specialities of our medical brethren have at their disposal. We have, after all, only the therapy of the word; therefore, we can deliberate only on how to and how not to use this word. This is certainly a stricture that lends itself to the arbitrary as much as it does to the considerate. Alongside these disquieting ruminations, I also came to the realization that there seemed to be a conflict in psychoanalysis as to who or what was more important: psychoanalysis or the patient. Disturbing statements arose such as: "This patient was not analyzable." "I only did psychotherapy with him because he couldn't come often enough."

I then became entreated to the great ecclesiastical wars of psychoanalysis: those in Europe between Anna Freud and Melanie Klein and those in this country between Franz Alexander and "classical" analysis, Klein and classical analysis, object relations and classical analysis, and so on. When actual warfare finally broke out in Los Angeles because a site visit committee of the American Psychoanalytic Association had decreed that the Los Angeles Psychoanalytic Institute must either rid itself if its Kleinians or be decertified, I was in moral anguish. It had not really dawned on me until that moment that I could lose my status as a training analyst because I used such words as "splitting" and "projective" identification rather than "repression" and the "Oedipus complex." It took the threat of a lawsuit to dispel the threat provoked by the site visit recommendation, but the problem lingered on. I could not grasp for the life of me why Melanie Klein and Anna Freud had been such enemies and why their ancient hatred should cast such a dark shadow so many miles away from their strife. I do not believe that people in the profession know what a holocaust had developed in Los Angeles. Friendships and collegial relationships were forever strained by this "McCarthyism." It brought to an end my naive notion that the healing profession of psychoanalysis was pure. It was, and is, like all organizations subject to the deterioration of group process, of decay, of personal motives, of political expediency. Sacrifices were continuously necessary in order to maintain the purity of the original beliefs, which founded the group in the first place, and the group would choose which revolutionary ideas were the proper ones to be accepted, the latter being regulated by the choice of speakers at semiannual conventions and by the papers selected for publication in its official journals. It was a long journey from Camelot.

Although I never used to think of it when I was young in the profession, the advent of the women's consciousness movement made an enormous impact on me, and I am amazed in retrospect at how I had been ensnared by a philosophy that placed women in a second-class position. Psychoanalytic theory and practice resounded with this prejudice and would not take corrections gladly. At the same time, I became aware that psychoanalytic institutions, particularly in the United States, had been so dominated by medical authority and orthodoxy that nonmedical people were not allowed equal opportunities to become analysts. I found myself developing feelings that surprised me when I analyzed clinical psychologists, social workers, and educators who thought and felt analytically and yet whose ambitions to become analysts were too easily thwarted. When I was very young and had just entered analytic practice, analysis itself had been under so much attack that it was seen as the medical underdog. Today, not unlike the United States, which despite its pretentions to being an "ingenue," is politically one of the oldest countries in the world, psychoanalysis constitutes a respectable establishment and authorizes from the power of this establishment position statutes and regulations that continue to be unfair to a large number of individuals seeking training under its auspices.

Earlier in this essay, I alluded to the high, romantic idealism with which I and so many others had invested in psychoanalysis. It came as a shock, therefore, when I realized it was the very "holiness" of psychoanalysis that was to become the instrument of persecution of so many people in the mental health field, even of psychoanalysts themselves. An "appointed" establishment has felt continuously constrained to preserve the sanctity of psychoanalysis and to become an eternal protective body by being able to choose its own successors (training analysts) and to choose which theories and morals of practice outside psychoanalysis should be condemned or which theories and morals within psychoanalysis should be ostracized and expelled. The engima arose in psychoanalysis, therefore, as it had in religion and in other cultural institutions before it: the rise of group politics and the need for someone to be sacrificed in order to preserve the "system's purity." Freud and Bion, particularly the latter, have helped reconcile us to the inevitable problem, which all groups are subject to. It is an area that the psychoanalytic organization understands the least and ignores at its peril.

Psychotherapy is an ancient profession. Savage tribes and ancient Greeks knew well about the therapy of the word. Many primitive tribes have had forms of psychotherapy in which an afflicted member of the tribe would be heard by all the other members who would attempt to give interpretations to his distraught feelings. Other primitive, savage tribes placed a high degree of importance upon dreams and would subject them to the group process for interpretation. The ancient Greeks, even before the rise of Hippocratic medicine, knew of the therapy of the word and used rhetoric, dialectic, and catharsis as the techniques of cure, while they bade their patients to the couch to examine their dreams. Psychoanalysis is therefore an ancient practice, one that has been admired in ancient and savage times and has only recently become resurrected.

The question is: Will psychoanalysis survive into the next century? Those who believe in it often seem to believe in it absolutely and, at times, to the exclusion of its natural interfaces with other disciplines, particularly psychosociology, psychobiology, and anthropology. The question always arises: What must practitioners of psychoanalysis have in mind when they listen to patients? Do their minds shift for a moment to the possibility of the patient being endogenously depressed or hypomanic, or do they wonder for a moment how traumatically influential the patient's upbringing and cultural background were in reference to the presenting symptoms? The bewilderment of today's analyst, especially myself, is to determine what had really constituted the important influences in the development of the patient's pathological belief systems while at the same time trying to keep an open mind, one which is purposely lacking in the *memory* of the patient's past and in the desire to cure, so as to achieve a more effective analysis. If psychoanalysis survives into the next century, it will be because people at long last have come to value the imperishable truth that there is something to be said for being heard by an objectively neutral but empathically interested person who can withstand the rigors and bear the joys of an inner journey with a stranger.

3 The Use of the Self: The Analyst and the Analytic Instrument in the Clinical Situation

Theodore J. Jacobs, M.D.

In this paper, I focus on the analyst's use of himself in the analytic situation. In it I will try to show how one analyst utilizes himself, describe the influences that have led to his particular approach, and comment on how the analyst's perception of his own mental and bodily responses may aid in deciphering the unconscious communications of his patients.

Central to my view of the analyst's role in the clinical situation and to many of the ideas contained in this paper is the concept of the analyzing instrument. Associated most closely with the name of Otto Isakower, who elaborated on Freud's original metaphor, this conceptualization of the relationship between the minds of the two participants in the analytic situation is one of the more creative ideas that has been developed in psychoanalysis.

Freud's notion of the analyzing instrument was that of a telephone, with the patient's unconscious tramsitting a message and the analyst's receiving it. Recommending in one of his technical papers that the analyst listen in an open-ended way, Freud (1912) observed the "he must turn his own unconscious like a receptive organ to the transmitting unconscious of the patient. He must adjust himself to the patient as a telephone receiver is adjusted to the transmitting microphone" (p. 115).

Taking as his starting point Freud's notion of a transmitting and receiving device, Isakower developed it into a way of viewing not only the analyst's role in the treatment situation but the analytic process itself. In recent years, his ideas have been explicated by Malcove (1975) and by Balter, Lothane, and Spencer (1980). For Isakower, the analyzing instrument is, in essence, a set of mind existing in analyst and patient that facilitates the grasping of the latter's unconscious communications.

Isakower presented his ideas at two faculty meetings of the New York Psychoanalytic Institute in October and November of 1963. Minutes of those meetings record that he described the analytic instrument as "a constellation of the psychic apparatus in which its constituent structures are tuned in a way that makes the apparatus optimally suited for functioning in a very specific manner." In its activated state, it is "in rapport with its counterpart in the patient." He added, "One might see it as a composite consisting of two complementary halves." An essential feature, however, "is the unique and specific setting-in-relation to a near identical or analogous constellation in a second person. It represents an *ad hoc* assembly for a special task and it is of a transitory nature."

Isakower made clear that when functioning optimally the analyzing instrument is inaccessible to conscious observation. Its characteristics can best be distinguished in retrospect when its work is temporarily ended, "most opportunely, perhaps, when that short phase of its intense functioning has occurred just before the end of an analytic session."

At the second of the two faculty meetings, Isakower described the kind of subjective experience that, not uncommonly, an analyst may have at the end of an hour when the analytic instrument is in the process of being dismantled:

> The session is broken off. The patient is leaving the room. You, the analyst, are in the process of emerging out of the analytic situation, that near dream-like state of hovering attention. The patient is being separated from you and you are left alone. In this short moment of the severance of the "team" you are left in mid-air and you become aware of the denuded raw surface of your half of the analyzing instrument, the surface which is opposite the patient's half. This surface now becomes accessible to observation because its cathexis is not bound to the surface of the patient's half of the apparatus. Now you, in a slow motion replica, can make observations. The slow motion comes from the induced process of re-integration of that part of you within yourself, a re-integration required by the withdrawal of the patient's half. There is a re-distribution of cathexis and while this is going on you can, in fortunate instances, observe it. It can be observed because your observing function is no longer glued to its former object—the patient's half.

What Isakower himself observed in such circumstances was a variety of visual and auditory phenomena related to the material of the previous hour. Included were representations of the manifest content of the patient's verbalizations as well as representations of visual and auditory responses that occurred in the analyst.

It is clear that for Isakower the essence of the analyzing instrument is a particular state of mind experienced by both analyst and analysand. Central to this mental set is a variable degree of regression in both participants. This state of regression, which is a necessary condition in patient and analyst alike for understanding the unconscious communications of the other, is closely allied to the kind of ego regression that occurs in the artist during moments of creative activity. For Isakower, analysis was an art, and his mode of perception in the analytic hours was that of an artist.

The factors that foster regression in both members of the analyzing team and that allow for the development in them of the requisite mental states have been elucidated by Balter et al. (1980) in their article on the analyzing instrument. In analysand and analyst alike, they have identified three preconditions necessary for the effective functioning of the analyzing instrument. For the analysand, these include: (a) an increase in the attention he pays to his own psychical perceptions; (b) suspension of his normally critical attitude toward the thoughts and perceptions that arise from within; and (c) the capacity and willingness to report verbally all that he is experiencing. For the analyst, these prerequisites involve: (a) the concentration of attention on the analysand's communications; (b) the concentration of attention on the analyst's own internal perceptions; and (3) the suspension of critical activity regarding these two objects of the analyst's attention.

When the requisite conditions are met in the analysand, the result is a state of ego regression that allows for the process of free association to develop. When they are fulfilled in the analyst, the complementary regression that takes place fosters the receptive state of mind that Freud (1912) termed "listening with evenly suspended attention" (p. 239). In both participants, the capacity to give oneself over to regression is an essential element that allows analogous mental processes to take place in each. When the unconscious of patient and analyst are "set in relation" to each other, the analyzing instrument may be said to be operative.

For the contemporary psychoanalyst, Isakower's notion of the analyzing instrument is as evocative and useful a concept as it was when articulated in the 1960s, but it is even more valuable when reformulated in light of new knowledge gained since that time. For Isakower, as for Freud before him, the analyzing instrument was closely associated with verbal communication and with the auditory sphere. Although both were aware of the fact that communication in the analytic situation occurs through a number of modalities and both were sensitive to the nonverbal dimension, the notion of the analyzing instrument was conceived of as an apparatus constructed for the sending and receiving of verbal messages. For Isakower, these referred primarily to words, but they also included the sounds of an hour – the pitch, tone, and rhythms of speech – as well as its silences. Advances over the past decade in our understanding of the important role of nonverbal behavior in human communication and of the place of such communication in the transmittal and reception of unconscious messages in the analytic situation have allowed us to revise and expand Isakower's original model of the analytic instrument. Whereas initially it was conceived of as a system operating primarily through the verbal-auditory spheres, we may now regard it as a multichannel system containing components that register not only verbal and acoustic signals but also movement patterns, autonomic responses, and visual stimuli.

Every analyst is aware that important communication takes place on a nonverbal level during each analytic hour. Understanding the meaning of such communications, however, has been relatively slow to develop in analysis, and their role in the expression of conflict and resistance, as an aspect of empathy and as a conduit for memory, is only now becoming more widely appreciated.

In my own analytic work, I pay particular attention to the kinds of postures, gestures, and movements that accompany the verbalizations of patient and analyst alike. In a previous publication (Jacobs, 1973), I have tried to demonstrate the way in which certain aspects of the analyst's nonverbal behavior may occur in response to the patient's communications. When he is listening well, the analyst automatically and unconsciously uses his body as a kind of seismograph that registers and reverberates with the steady stream of kinesic stimuli emanating from the patient. Awareness of his own bodily responses, as well as of the thoughts and images that accompany them, often provides the analyst with useful cues both to the nonverbal communications coming from the patient and to countertransference reactions of which he has been previously unaware. I would like, through a few brief clinical examples, to illustrate the way in which the analyst's use of himself as an instrument that registers not only the sounds of an hour, but also its sights and movement, may enhance his capacity to grasp the unconscious communications of his patients.

For me, the analytic hour begins before I rise to greet the patient. With the previous patient gone and the temporarily assembled analytic instrument now in the process of being dismantled, I turn my thoughts to the patient now waiting. Spontaneously, with as little restriction as possible, I allow an image of that patient to arise in my mind. At the same time, I try to become aware of my own inner experiences in doing so. Sometimes I find myself picturing the patient as I last saw him, and material from his previous hour may arise in my mind. Sometimes I picture him in a scene from his childhood or in a fictional scene that I have invented. I pay particular attention to the emotions I am experiencing as I conjure up images of the waiting patient. Often, these images and the feelings that accompany them tell me a great deal about the particular state of my countertransference feelings at the moment and the way in which those feelings resonate with the transference that has been developing. Sometimes the emotions that I am aware of in myself are consonant with the image I have of the patient. Thus, in the case of a woman whose recent hours have been filled with childhood memories of long hours spent alone and with a sense of despair in an empty apartment, I may find myself feeling sad and even protective as I imagine her in that situation.

Sometimes, though, the feelings that I am aware of seem to run counter to the image I have conjured up. In the case of a young man who has been complaining bitterly of indifference and mistreatment by his girlfriend and members of his family and who, in my imagination, I have pictured being so treated, I have at times found that the predominant emotion that I have felt was one of irritation. The disparity between what I fantasize and what I experience emotionally is, to me, a useful clue to countertransference responses that, while active, have been kept out of awareness. I believe this to be an important matter because I have found that, when present, such countertransference reactions are inevitably communicated to the patient through posture, gesture, tone, or phrasing. The material of an hour or even entire segments of an analysis may be decisively influenced by them. Because they are often effectively defended against, however, such responses may, without self-scrutiny, go undetected.

As I approach the waiting room, I try to become aware of my posture, of my facial expression, and of the affect that I communicate in my greeting. Although I try to be reasonably consistent in the way I greet patients, end sessions, and bid them goodbye, subtle variations do occur in the course of any analysis. Such changes often reflect shifting countertransference responses and may exert a significant influence on the analytic work. Even slight alterations in the analyst's usual nonverbal communications can be detected with regularity in the material of the accompanying hours. Although awareness of such reactions in himself may require consistent and repeated self-scrutiny on the part of the analyst, such awareness is a necessary condition for understanding the myriad nonverbal communications between himself and the patient that accompany their verbalizations.

I make efforts to be aware of my inner experiences as I enter the waiting room, and I make an equal effort to observe the patient. Child analysts, and particularly those colleagues whose interests lie in infant research, have taught us the unique value of close and careful observations of children. The advances in both theory and practice derived from such observational studies have been widely recognized, but the value in adult analysis of comparably careful observation has not been fully appreciated. It is rare for case reports of analytic work to contain information on the patient's nonverbal behavior, its shifts and transformations in the course of analysis, and its relation to transference and countertransference phenomena.

Observation of a patient as one approaches him in the waiting room can yield a good deal of useful data. His posture, facial expression, and movements often reveal affects of which he himself is not aware. It is not unusual for the analyst to encounter a patient who, revealing through body language clear signs of depression, seeks to conceal his feelings upon seeing the analyst and who, in the ensuing hour, displays strong resistance to the conscious recognition of his depressed affect. Also commonly encountered is the patient who reveals through a shift in his facial expression that one aspect or another of the analyst's appearance has registered strongly on him, but who avoids reference to this in his session. In these and similar circumstances, the analyst's observation of the patient as they encounter one another and his judicious use of those observations is an important, if sometimes neglected, aspect of analytic technique.

Of equal importance is observation of the patient on the couch. Although as early as 1893 Freud pointed out the importance of posture, facial expression, and bodily movement as a vehicle for the transmission of messages in the therapeutic situation, these early observations were not further developed, and the phenomena of nonverbal communication remained, for many years, unintegrated into psychoanalytic theory or technique. Understanding this aspect of the patient's communications has continued to be a relatively neglected area. Despite evidence from a number of studies that have emphasized the consistent, and often predictable, relationship between a patient's verbalizations and his nonverbal behavior on the couch, it is not unusual in analytic work for such nonverbal behavior to be overlooked or to remain as isolated and dynamically nonintegrated observations on the part of the analyst.

Of particular interest is the fact that few analysts observe a patient's face while he is on the couch. With his chair positioned behind the patient, the analyst of 1984, like his counterpart of 60 years ago, is in no position to do so. Because facial expressions are so rich a source of communication in the analytic situation, the analyst may thus rob himself of a significant, even vital, source of data.

Dr. Annie Reich, an early supervisor of mine, pointed out to me the unique value of viewing, as well as listening to, the patient. Borrowing from some of the work of Wilhelm Reich as well as her own observations, she made consistent efforts to integrate the patient's movements, gestures, and facial expressions with his verbalizations. To do this, she pointed out, one had to place his chair in a position so that he could see the patient in his entirety and not simply catch a glimpse of his head, as often occurred in the usual analytic setup. Dr. Reich's chair was placed essentially at a right angle to the couch at approximately the level of the patient's head. This allowed for a full view of the patient. After experimenting with various positionings of the chair, I have found that placing it at slightly less than a right angle to the couch allows me to remain out of view and yet be in a position to observe the patient's bodily movements and most, if not all, of his facial expressions.

In Isakower's model, visualization of the patient is not mentioned as a source of data. Rather, visual experience in both patient and analyst is regarded as aspects of the ego regression taking place in each. As he associates freely, the analysand may convey certain inner experiences relating both to past and present through visual imagery. The analyst, listening to this material as he listens to dreams, may visualize the images being described. In this way, many analysts not only dream along with the patient, but continually engage in a process of "seeing" along with him. Even when listening to nonvisual material, such analysts may find arising in themselves fantasies and memories that have a strong visual element. As Isakower suggests, when properly attuned, the analytic instrument often decodes messages by means of the visual as well as the auditory apparatus.

Omitted from Isakower's formulation is a consideration of how the process of visualization itself both contributes to and is an integral part of the analyzing instrument. Visualization in the analytic situation is analogous to the phenomenon in the auditory sphere that has been variously termed "evenly suspended" or "freely hovering attention." Just as the analyst listens with equal attention to all of the patient's verbalizations and tries not to fix any particular aspect of the material in mind or make a conscious effort to concentrate on it, so he observers all of the patient's nonverbal behavior. Looking as he listens, he takes in and registers what he sees, but does not focus on any particular bodily movement or facial expression. The visual imagery that he registers makes contact via associative pathways with visual aspects of memory and stimulates the recall of memories that are linked with the patient's nonverbal communications. Often, it stimulates in the analyst kinesic behavior and autonomic responses that are reactions on an unconscious level to nonverbal messages. Thus, the analyst's visual perceptions join with his auditory perceptions to stimulate in him responses that draw on unconscious visual and auditory memory. In practice, both visual and auditory spheres play vital roles in the registration and processing of analytic data. Both are essential parts of the analytic instrument.

Another aspect of the analytic instrument that was underemphasized in Isakower's formulation was the autonomic system and the autonomic responses of both patient and analysand. While Isakower emphasized the analyst's self-observation and his awareness of his inner processes, his focus was on mental phenomena and particularly on the auditory and visual imagery that become available to him during the operation of that instrument. Analytic experience confirms that autonomic responses in both patient and analyst are regular, if often overlooked, accompaniments of the analytic hour. At times, the patient will be aware of and will report such phenomena. Descriptions of sweating, dryness of the mouth, facial flushing, tachycardia, feelings of coldness or warmth, or sexual arousal, although not commonplace, are not rare either. Quite often, however, such phenomena either do not register in the patient's awareness or are not reported. In a similar way, autonomic responses in the analyst, although often providing important clues to the unconscious messages being transmitted by a patient as well as to countertransference reactions, are often overlooked as valuable analytic data.

Material from several analytic hours may be used to illustrate how an analyst's use of himself as an instrument that registers and resonates on multiple channels and through several sensory modalities can enhance his understanding of a patient's communications in the analytic situation.

Mr. A was a short, energetic, affable man whose anxiety over his aggressive and competitive impulses and his consequent fear of the analyst's retaliation led him to smile a good deal and indicate through body language that he was a compliant, nonthreatening individual. Whenever, in the transference, negative feelings toward the analyst were mobilized, the patient would become restless on the couch, begin a tapping motion with a foot, fall silent, and when able to speak, do so in a hesitant and disjointed manner.

Such feelings had been coming up in the analysis against strong resistance, and as I entered the waiting room at the beginning of one hour, I noticed Mr. A sitting upright in his chair, his body taut, and one foot already in motion. As I approached, he looked up, and in the instant before his usual smile covered it over, I noticed an expression on his face that seemed to convey a mixture of surprise and disapproval. In a flash it was gone, and as Mr. A rose and approached me, his smile seemed to broaden. As he passed me he glanced at my face, seeming to seek in it a clue to my feelings about him.

On the couch Mr. A assumed a familiar position, his body held stiffly, legs extended, and hands placed behind his head. In addition, however, I noticed that his elbows were positioned in such a way as to create a protective shield. As I observed him, I felt a tightening of my musculature. I was sitting rather stiffly and experiencing a tension in my body that was not usual for me. I was also aware that my heart beat was rapid. A feeling of tension, in fact, dominated the room. There was an air of expectation as though something dramatic was going to happen. This electric quality was added to by Mr. A's silence. For several minutes he did not speak, but he began to move on the couch as the characteristic restless moments and foot tapping conveyed his irritation.

When he spoke, it was to relate a story of mistreatment at the hands of his girlfriend. The theme was old and repetitive, the content a slight variation of incidents reported hundres of times before. Mr. A's tone was flat, his narration lacking in strongly felt affect. As I listened, I found myself experiencing tedium, compounded by inner feelings of tension and irritation. The atmosphere continued to be charged.

After he had gone on for some time relating his story in a rather bland and controlled way, I took advantage of a moment's pause to direct his attention to the scene in the waiting room. I told him what I had observed in his facial expression and asked if he was aware of his own reaction. Suddenly, as if a reservoir had been tapped, Mr. A gave vent to a flood of feelings about my appearance. How, he wanted to know, did I come to dress the way I did? Who picked out my ties? He was startled by the boldness of the print I wore that day, which went with my sport jacket like oil and vinegar. My shirt did not match either, and my trousers needed a pressing. All in all, I looked like a Samuel Beckett character, fresh out of a dustbin. Mr. A then speculated on the woman who, in his imagination, was responsible for selecting my attire. He considered her inattentive and self-centered. She did not look out for me. She had let me deteriorate, and instead of presenting myself as I should be, a well–turned-out Madison Avenue doctor, I greeted my patients like a schmegge, like an analyst who slept on his own couch.

It was not difficult then for Mr. A to realize that he was experiencing me as the father of his adolescent years, the father whom he wanted so very much to be proud of but whose alcoholism led to a steady deterioration in his dress and behavior. For years, Mr. A had concealed his dismay and anger from his father, and rarely had he allowed himself to come in touch with his own feelings.

The pattern had been reactivated in the transference, and although repeatedly recognized, its understanding had remained intellectualized. Confrontation with a piece of his nonverbal behavior, which conveyed an involuntary reaction of disapproval and disgust, served as a wedge.

It allowed Mr. A to experience more immediately his own spontaneous reactions and his defenses against them. And it was the monitoring of the analyst's own reactions within the analytic hour, as well as his observations of the patient, that aided him in recognizing the field of resistance that had began to cover over Mr. A's spontaneous and important transference response.

A second case, that of Mr. L, bears some similarity to that of Mr. A in that an important reaction to the analyst was concealed in an analytic hour and could be detected through nonverbal clues. Like Mr. A, Mr. L tended to be friendly and outgoing. Unlike the former, however, what Mr. L defended strongly against was not his negative feelings toward the analyst but his love for him. Indirectly but persistently, Mr. L gave hints that he wanted signs of affection from the analyst. Often, this took the form of imagining that the analyst would bring him a gift, and in fact, he often treated the analyst's verbal interventions as though they were gifts.

Unlike Mr. A, Mr. L rarely permitted himself to be silent on the couch. Silence was equated with sadness and depression, affects that very much frightened him and that he vigorously defended himself against.

One day, however, Mr. L seemed more subdued than usual. Although he filled the hour with a stream of talk that related primarily to his weekend plans, there was in his speech a strained and forced quality. It was as though he was trying to be "up." Moreover, his posture on the couch was unusual for him. For most of the hour, he lay on his side with his legs curled under him. As he talked, he fingered the material on the couch, alternately rubbing it and pinching it between thumb and forefinger. He was speaking of the forthcoming weekend. He anticipated a full and pleasurable round of activities capped off by a dance at his country club. But he was sweating, and every now and then he burped, as though he was suffering from a sudden case of indigestion. During the hour, while recounting the fact that one of his cars was in for repair and that he would be forced to take another, he began unconsciously to carry out some driving motions. At the same time a tear came to his eye, and with a quick covering gesture that pretended to flick a piece of dust from a lash, he wiped it away.

As I listened to the material of the hour, I felt a heaviness within myself. An inexplicable feeling of sadness came over me. Memories of a similarly planned weekend in my youth that turned out to be a disappointment filtered into my consciousness. Despite the manifest content of Mr. L's thoughts, the mood in myself and in the room was heavy. Feelings of depression were in the air. When I noticed the tear in Mr. L's eye, I called his attention to the disparity between what he was saying and the feelings that he must have been experiencing. Then he revealed something that had happened just prior to the start of the hour.

I had arrived at my office in the family car, an old and weather-beaten sedan that had seen better days. Being early for his appointment, Mr. L had been waiting on the corner about a hundred yards away and had seen me drive up. As he did so, he was aware of a sudden feeling of disappointment, but quickly he put this reaction out of mind. Now as I pointed out the emotions that seemed to be just beneath the surface, the feeling of disappointment surfaced again with great intensity.

Mr. L could not understand me driving so old and unfashionable a car. He felt very let down, almost tearful. Finally, a memory presented itself that clarified what was happening. Mr. L remembered the night of his high school senior prom and the promise his father had made that a newly purchased sports car would be available to him for the evening. He had conveyed this to his date, and both were looking forward to arriving at the prom in celebrity style. As it turned out, however, the dealer failed to have a new car ready as promised. It was with the keenest sense of betrayal and disappointment that, watching out the window, Mr. L saw his father drive up to their house, not in the Triumph that he had expected, but in the family's aging and battle-scarred station wagon.

This incident, long forgotten, contained within it the essence of Mr. L's relationship with his father, a relationship filled with yearning and disappointment. The memory that was recaptured opened the way to the exploration in analysis of that crucial relationship and its impact on Mr. L's identification symptoms and object relations. And it was primarily by means of his nonverbal behavior on the couch that Mr. L provided the clues to the transference reaction that opened the pathway to memory.

In another case, a critical experience of the past could also be recovered with the help of clues from the patient's body language. In this instance, however, the experience occurred not in adolescence but in the earliest months of life.

Mr. W was a tall, lean, and artistically gifted young man whose artistic career was very much hampered by his fear of failure. So great, in fact, was his anxiety over not succeeding and "falling flat on his face" that he was unable to enter a field for which by virtue of his training and natural abilities he was well suited.

Analysis revealed that one source of his difficulty lay in certain thought patterns laid down in the pre-Oedipal years, particularly during the separation-individuation phase of development. Mr. W's mother was an anxious and fearful woman who had difficulty in allowing her young son to separate from her and to individuate in his own way. Through their close and intimate contact and the strong identification which it fostered, her fears became his own. This factor, as well as his anxiety over revealing his powerful sexual and aggressive impulses toward his mother, made him fearful of leaving her side. He experienced any assertive act as an aggressive one and any move toward independence as a threatened separation. Whenever Mr. W acted in an independent and self-sufficient manner, his behavior stirred up in him profound anxiety that was related to fantasies originating in the separation-individuation period. He imagined that he would be left all alone and in a helpless state. His mother would abandon him, and he would starve or perish. Unable to walk or move, he would be essentially paralyzed.

Although Mr. W's disturbed relationship with his mother played a pivotal role in the development of his neurosis, it was not the only factor of importance. In fact, the degree of his anxiety and the extent to which it incapacitated him suggessted to me that other, perhaps earlier, factors may have exerted important influences on him. Even if they existed, however, I had no idea what they might be.

While observing Mr. W during an analytic hour, I noticed something that I had seen before but which had not registered. While lying on the couch, Mr. W regularly kept his legs in the same position, stretched out perfectly straight with his ankles flexed and his feet always the same distance apart. As I observed this posture, a memory from my internship days arose in mind. I recalled working on the pediatric service and seeing a number of young children with deformities of the legs and hips whose limbs were placed in braces. I called Mr. W's attention to the positioning of his legs on the couch and asked him if anything about his posture came to mind.

Immediately he related a fact that he had long forgotten. Shortly after birth, his feet were noted to turn inwards as the result of a defect in his lower extremities, and for a year thereafter, he was placed in a leg brace nightly. His stance and walking were retarded, and the practicing subphase of the separation-individuation process was substantially delayed. In fact, his mother's anxiety over his well-being, combined with his own weakness of limbs, severely comprised Mr. W's ability to locomote independently. This, in turn, had profound effects on his further development, particularly on his ability to separate from his mother. Again, in this case, Mr. W's kinesic behavior provided an important clue to experiences that had their origin in the preverbal period and that had not surfaced through the channel of verbalization.

In the foregoing, I have cited instances in which the analyst's memories, as well as those of the patient, were valuable in understanding the latter's unconscious communications. Although not specifically identified by Isakower as part of the analytic instrument, the memory system is, in fact, essential to it. The importance of the patient's memories is well known. Perhaps less well recognized is the importance of the analyst's memories. Blum (1980) has pointed out that reconstruction of the patient's childhood is often accompanied by reconstruction of the analyst's childhood and that these are independent, if overlapping, processes. In a similar way, the memories of the patient and those of the analyst arise independently but interweave and overlap. The analyst "knows" his patient not only through the process of being able, for brief periods, to identify with him, but through his own parallel life experiences. It is through his own memories and the affects connected with them that, in large measure, he understands his patient's inner experiences. This way of knowing constitutes an important, if sometimes overlooked, aspect of empathy. For the analyst to be truly empathic, his own memories must be available to him. This is one of the most important effects of the analyst's own analysis. It helps put him in touch with his own memories. When shifted into a mobile state, these memories are then free to rise up to meet those of the patient.

The following may serve as one more example of the analyst's use of his own memories. Mr. Y, a bright, energetic business executive who wished analysis because of persistent difficulties in his interpersonal relationships, was markedly anxious about using the couch. For almost a half hour in his first session he remained seated, feeling confused and embarrassed by his inability to lie down. He made several efforts to do so, only to experience intense anxiety and be forced to resume a sitting position. Finally, on his fourth try, Mr. Y was able to ease himself into a recumbent position, although he maintained his head and shoulders well propped up with pillows. His anxiety had an intensity to it, as well as a childlike quality, that was familiar to me. But, listening to Mr. Y, I could not identify the source of this feeling of familiarity.

Then a memory arose in my mind, a memory of my being driven to the hospital at age 4 to have a tonsillectomy. Although, in all probability, what I remembered was a screen memory, the affect associated with it was undoubtedly related to frightening experiences that were characterized by a threat of bodily injury. The memory and feelings accompanying it were triggered by the material of the hour and particularly by Mr. Y's fear of lying down. This anxiety, which was clearly related to his fear of submitting passively to a doctor, had, through a momentary identification, triggered a memory of my own frightening surgical experience. That this memory from my childhood was meaningfully linked with Mr. Y's behavior became clear when, tentatively, he eased himself into a reclining position. Then I noticed two deep scars behind his ears, the result of a double mastoidectomy performed when he was 6 years old for a life-threatening illness.

As a final topic, I would like to take up another aspect of the analytic instrument: the analyst's communications to the patient. This is, of course, a vast topic to which I cannot at the present time do justice. I comment, therefore, only on a particular facet of it.

In their teaching, Isakower, Arlow, and others have pointed out that when an analyst is listening well and his part of the analytic instrument is tuned in to the transmitting instrument of the patient, an accurate reading of the patient's unconscious communications is very likely to take place with the result that a correct understanding of that message will "arrive" in the analyst's mind. This he communicates to the patient in the form of an interpretation. Thus, in this model, the analyst's interpretations are closely linked with the proper functioning of the analytic instrument.

What was not discussed in Isakower's initial remarks was the way that the analytic instrument operates to promote and regulate the metacommunications between patient and analyst. That this kind of communication exists as an important aspect of every analytic hour is a well-known, if infrequently studied, phenomenon. Close scrutiny of the verbal exchanges that occur within a given analytic hour will reveal not only overt messages conveyed by both participants, but covert messages as well. The manifest content of the communications is accompanied by a latent content that comments on, adds to, or modifies the manifest level. When his part of the analytic instrument is working well, the analyst will register with sensitivity the metacommunicational as well as the denotative aspects of the patient's communications. And his interventions will contain a latent message that reverberates with and responds to the latent messages inherent in the patient's verbalizations.

During one analytic hour, a 55-year-old writer expressed greater distress over a troublesome vaginal condition that was causing her to lose sexual feeling. With anguish, she stated her belief that she was like an 80-year-old woman and was doomed to a life of isolation and celibacy. Listening to her, the analyst found himself picturing the patient's aged aunt. Some years previously, this woman had developed a similar condition.

The patient's identification in fantasy with her aunt was clear, and the analyst was able to interpret it. In doing so, he was able to show the patient that it was, in fact, her fantasy of being like her aunt that contributed to her sense of being old and decrepit. But he contributed something else as well. In response to the patient's fright and anguish, the analyst's voice took on a calm and reassuring tone. Through his manner and phrasing, as well as through the decisive quality of his voice, he was conveying another message. What he was communicating was something like this:

> I hear what you are saying. You are afraid that because of your problem I will find you ugly and unattractive. You are worried that I will see you as an old an shriveled woman. In fact, you are not that way. A large part of your fright stems from the fantasy that you have developed that you are like your aunt and that her fate will be yours. I know this is a fantasy and I do not share it. I see you as you are and do not believe, as you do, that your current problem makes you a less attractive woman.

There is little doubt that this kind of message, the metacommunicational one, plays a significant role in every therapy. As yet its place in theory and technique has not been fully elucidated. But there is little question that every correct interpretation is correct on more than one level. Grasping the essence of what the patient is attempting to convey, the analyst responds with a verbal interpretation indicating that he understands the message. But through his inflection, his tone, his timing, his phrasing, and particularly through the affect that he conveys, the analyst responds to another message, to the covert communication which, often enough, contains within it a comment on the interaction between patient and analyst. When the analytic instrument is operating on only one channel and fails to register the patient's metacommunications, the analyst's "correct" interpretation may elicit little response because it is, in fact, only partially correct. But when the analytic instrument is well tuned and is able to register on several channels at once, the analyst's intervention will reflect his intuitive grasp of the multiple levels of meaning of the patient's communications. It is then that the patient has the experience of feeling truly understood. And it is at such times that his response to the analyst's interpretation will, in all likelihood, contain the confirming affects and associations that have come to be associated with its correctness.

REFERENCES

Arlow, J. A. (1969). Fantasy, memory and reality testing. *Psychoanalytic Quarterly, 38,* 28–51.

Balter, L., Lothane, Z., & Spencer, J. H. (1980). On the analyzing instrument. *Psychoanalytic Quarterly, 49,* 474–502.

Blum, H. (1980). The value of reconstruction in adult psychoanalysis. *International Journal of Psycho-Analysis, 61,* 39–52.

Breuer, J., & Freud, S. (1893–1895). Studies on hysteria. *S.E.*, 2.

Freud, S. (1912). Recommendations to physicians practicing psychoanalysis. *S.E.*, 12, 111–120.

Jacobs, T. (1973). Posture, gesture and movement in the analyst: Cues to interpretation and countertransference. *Journal of the American Psychoanalytic Association, 21,* 77–92.

Kern, J. W. (1978). Countertransference and spontaneous screens: An analyst studies his own visual images. *Journal of the American Psychoanalytic Association, 26,* 21–47.

Malcove, L. (1975). The analytic situation: Toward a view of the supervisory experience. *Journal of the Philadelphia Association for Psychoanalysis, 2,* 1–19.

McLaughlin, J. T. (1975). The sleepy analyst: Some observations on states of consciousness in the analyst at work. *Journal of the American Psychoanalytic Association, 23,* 363–382.

New York Psychoanalytic Institute (1963a). Minutes of faculty meetings, October 14, unpublished.

———— (1963b). Minutes of the faculty meeting, November 20, unpublished.

4 The Communicative Approach of Classical Psychoanalysis

Robert Langs, M.D.

My personal approach to the psychotherapy and psychoanalysis of madness (and I refer to the two treatment modalities interchangeably because I believe that they are on a continuum, whereas I term all forms of emotionally founded disorders "madness") has evolved into an elaborate attitude toward the treatment experience, best identified as the *communicative approach of classical psychoanalysis*. Although there is considerable evidence that many psychoanalytic writers propose one body of clinical precepts, but use rather different techniques in the privacy of their consultation rooms, my own writings on the technique of psychoanalytic therapy rather precisely reflect my own clinical practice. In this paper, I describe the basic philosophy and theoretical foundation of my approach, present in some detail the two main clinical instruments which form the most critical components of the listening and intervening techniques that characterize these efforts, offer a brief illustrative clinical excerpt, and conclude with a brief comparison of my own efforts with those carried out by the hypothetically identified average clinical psychoanalyst and one of the more currently prominent spinoffs from this approach—that of self psychology.

It is my considered opinion, based on an extensive survey of the psychoanalytic literature, that the communicative approach to psychotherapy is the single most comprehensive technique available today. It is a systematic endeavor which nonetheless leaves full room for the therapist's use of empathy, intuition. tact, and other basic means of listening, formulating, and intervening. However, it expands the use of these tools into areas generally overlooked by other approaches. Although the details of the communicative efforts at listening and formulating seem unwieldly to some, it should be understood in advance that the main instruments of communicative listening and intervening can be well mastered and can become a smooth and highly useful technique applied with full sensitivity and yet maximal comprehension. The complexity of the approach is, at bottom, a reflection of the multifaceted dimensions of madness itself, of the therapeutic interaction, and of the communications from both patients and therapists.

Fundamental to the communicative approach is but a single basic tenet: that all human beings are adaptive organisms and that, among the adaptive resources, conscious and unconscious communication are of special significance when it comes to the expressions of patient-madness and their resolution through insight and a sound holding relationship. The therapeutic experience is therefore viewed as a spiraling conscious and especially unconscious communicative interaction between patient and therapist, one that takes place in a particular setting and in terms of a specified set of ground rules and boundaries. Further, the approach relies heavily on the clinical finding that the single most reliable guide to sound techniques in psychotherapy lies in the patient's latent (encoded or derivative) communications to the therapist; indeed, all patients appear to have an *unconscious* sense of the ideal framework for treatment and the qualities of a truly valid (uniquely insightful) interpretation. Thus, the communicative approach is founded on a series of technical precepts that have been consistently validated by patients' indirect and encoded responses through interventions based on the principles so defined (as well as on the elimination of all techniques that do not obtain this particular form of psychoanalytic confirmation).

Empirically, it has been discovered that there is but a single activated truth to the unconscious basis of a particular expression of a patient's madness at a given moment in a therapeutic interaction. Although this truth is overdetermined and multilayered, it is specifically defined in terms of the conscious and especially unconscious implications of the therapist's interventions (verbal and nonverbal, in respect to understanding as well as with regard to the setting) and the patient's highly *selective* reactions to these efforts. The communicative approach claims to offer the most comprehensive means of identifying and interpreting these unconsciously founded truths as a basis of illuminating the underlying factors in a patient's activated expressions of madness. Granted the establishment of a sound holding-containing relationship and setting, it is the specific insights into these unconscious aspects of patient-madness that generate the adaptive resources, conflict resolution, and opportunities for growth that characterize true insight psychotherapy. Such understanding is difficult to achieve, involves the conscious experience of expressions of both patient- and therapist-madness, and is, in all, a highly painful and arduous task for both patients and therapists. Because of the pain involved, there are strong conscious and unconscious motives in both participants to treatment to seek out relief from patient-madness through some means other than a maximal understanding of unconscious factors in emotional dysfunctions. The result has been a proliferation of *lie-barrier psychotherapies* designed unconsciously to collusively bypass the activated truths of expressions pertinent to patient-madness. It is another claim of the communicative approach that it is the epitome of what has been termed *truth therapy* and that it stands for the most viable pursuit of the underlying truths of patient-madness available in today's psychotherapeutic practice.

In practical clinical terms, the basic model of the therapeutic interaction is founded on the paradigm of stimulus and response. For the patient in psychotherapy, when it comes to his or her madness (both its expressions and the patient's communications regarding its underlying nature), the most critical stimuli are virtually always the interventions of the therapist. The patient's responses are best seen as a unified whole with a variety of dimensions, perhaps the simplest touching upon qualities of thought, feelings, and action. However, if we wish to classify the patient's reactions to the therapist's interventions in a manner that is most clinically useful, we would identify two classes of responses: (a) those that are constituted by symptoms and resistances to the treatment process (these are termed *indicators* or *therapeutic contexts* i.e., they are signs of patient-madness and indications for active interventions by the therapist); (b) behavioral and especially verbal-affective communicative material that contains within the patient's associations a series of encoded meanings that illuminate the unconscious factors in the patient-madness expression (these are termed *derivative material* and constitute the derivative complex).

Both indicators and the derivative complex are responses to the conscious and unconscious implications of the therapist's interventions (for the patient, these are termed *adaptive contexts, intervention contexts* and *adaptation-evoking contexts* – the stimuli to which the patient is responding). Because therapeutic contexts are one level of response to an adaptive context and derivative communication another, it follows that the derivative complex immediately illuminates the unconscious meanings of patient-indicators (i.e., because the two are equivalent, the communicative material gives meaning to the symptomatic expression). It therefore follows that the goal of the listening-formulating process is to identify the implications of an intervention by a therapist (an adaptive context), to recognize the patient's symptomatic response to the intervention at hand, and to interpret this response in light of both the stimulus or intervention context and the patient's encoded or derivative communications as the latter illuminate the unconscious meanings of both the stimulus itself and the patient's reactions. Such an approach inherently takes into account the conscious and unconscious implications of the ongoing therapeutic interaction and initiates all understanding of the patient's material in the here-and-now situation of the therapeutic relationship – while tracing out all other components, genetic and otherwise, from this nodal point.

In the actual clinical situation, the most practical approach to the full comprehension of the nature and function of the patient's behaviors and associations begins with the identification of all therapeutic contexts (indicators). These are discovered either through the direct observation of the patient's behaviors or through an examination of his or her manifest associations. In this way, the listening process is geared toward the most active and immediate expressions of the patient's madness in a particular hour. Interpretations and framework-management responses by the therapist (as well as silences) are therefore generated as reactions to immediate and active manifestations of psychopathology rather than touching upon hypothetical or illusory issues.

There are two main classes of patient-indicators: (a) gross behavioral resistances – direct opposition to therapeutic progress (e.g., absences, latenesses, silences, etc.); (b) evident symptoms, self-disorders, and interpersonal disturbances. It is to be recognized that all resistances are interactional products, with inputs from both patient and therapist; furthermore, opposition to treatment is not inherently pathological for the patient, but must be understood in light of prevailing intervention contexts for its unconscious basis and functions.

In general, in a well-run psychotherapeutic experience, most gross behavioral resistances actually do reflect aspects of patient-madness. On the other hand, virtually all symptoms, regardless of their interactional sources, must be understood as psychopathological products to be analyzed in light of the ongoing therapeutic interaction. Ultimately, it is the goal of the psychotherapist to interpret to the patient the unconscious basis of an indicator in light of a conscious or unconscious implication of his or her own intervention and the patient's selected – chosen unconsciously in terms of the patient's own madness – perceptions of this intervention, along with the patient's secondary responses to these perceptions.

In most sessions, patient-indicators appear early in the patient's manifest associations. They are quickly identified and kept in the back of the therapist's mind as the target for his or her own interventional responses. The therapist then moves on to the specific consideration of his or her own prior interventions – the adaptive contexts that are stimulating the patient's material and other reactions in a given hour.

In dealing with an intervention context, the therapist makes three appraisals. He or she will do so from time to time in a given hour, alternating between this type of active and definitive formulation and free, unencumbered, and open listening. Nonetheless, it seems clear that most psychotherapeutic approaches are significantly lacking in systematization. Such careful efforts are essential, lest the therapist overlook very important implications of the patient's behaviors and material.

The first task carried out in regard to the adaptive context is that of simply naming subjectively each known, active adaptive context to which the patient may be reacting. Among the wide range of interventions by a psychotherapist, those that impinge upon the ground rules and boundaries of the treatment relationship and experience are by far the most crucial. Next in importance are all noninterpretive interventions because these violate the therapist's neutrality and tend to have highly disturbing qualities for patients in psychotherapy. Other important interventions include silence (correct silence, which constitutes sound holding, as well as incorrect silence, which constitutes a missed intervention), interpretation–reconstructions (both those that are valid and validated, as well as those that prove to be in error), and all noninterpretive interventions (with utmost consistency, this type of intervention fails to obtain derivative validation from the patient and is in essence erroneous and traumatic). In general, patients react most powerfully to framework deviations, less powerfully to erroneous interventions, and least powerfully to sound and validated interventions.

Once the main adaptive context has been subjectively identified, it is important that the therapist quickly attempt to catalogue the main implications of each critical intervention context that is active in the bipersonal field between him- or herself and the patient. Here, of course, the therapist's capacity for self-knowledge and in-depth insight is of utmost importance. A therapist should be capable of sensing the general power of each major adaptive context to which the patient is responding and of identifying the main conscious and unconscius implications of each of these interventional efforts. Ultimately, the therapist must select one or two intervention contexts as the key organizers of the patient's encoded or derivative material; failure to do so will lead to chaotic listening and an inability by the therapist to organize the patient's material meaningfully. However, the selection is not simply a factor of the therapist's own beliefs; instead, it must also be guided by the patient's derivative material and by a judgment on the part of the therapist as to which particular intervention context best organizes the patient's indirect and encoded communications.

Another important technical measure applied to the adaptive context is the search for all manifest representations (portrayals) of the therapist's interventions. In practical terms, the therapist seeks out all direct allusions to his or her own interventions. This particular effort, although quite straightforward, is crucial to the listening-formulating process in that a manifest representation of an adpative context greatly facilitates the development of an interpretation to the patient. This proves to be the case because it is indeed the interventions of the therapist that are stimulating the patient's unconscious communications as the latter illuminate patient-madness. Thus, in order to provide the patient with a cogent interpretation, the effort is greatly facilitated by a direct and passing reference to the intervention which is actually evoking the patient's main communicative and symptomatic reactions.

In the absence of a manifest allusion to an adaptive context, the therapist searches for a strong encoded representation of a particularly important intervention context. For example, consider a session that has followed upon an hour in which a therapist inadvertently extended a patient's session for 10 minutes. The patient may at some point in the following hour remark directly that he noted the therapist had gone past the end of the session. Or there may be no direct mention of this deviation whatsoever, but the patient may describe a situation in which his boss unfairly kept him overtime for some 10 or 20 minutes. Alternatively, the patient might refer to an experience at a party in which someone had cornered him and wouldn't let him leave for an extraordinarily long time. These latter two associations would be viewed as derivative or encoded representations of the adaptive context of the therapist's extension of the patient's hour. As such, they facilitate an interpretive-like response known as the play back of selected derivatives organized around an indirectly represented intervention context.

In summary, then, the adaptive context is an extremely important aspect of the listening-formulating-intervening process. For each session, a therapist reviews the known contexts, identifies their main implications, seeks out manifest representations of these contexts, or in their lack, explores the patient's material for similarly disguised encoded representations. These efforts are made relatively automatically, and from time to time in each session, the therapist will pause and attempt to sum up his impressions in this critical area.

The search for indicators and for adaptive contexts tends to be concentrated on the manifest content level. These efforts also tend to be relatively straightforward. As a result, a therapist will spend much of his or her listening-formulating efforts in the search for derivative or encoded meanings contained in the patient's material – in a quest for an understanding of the patient's unconscious communications. In general, each and every association from a patient is a potential carrier of latent or derivative meaning. However, some of these associations prove to be rich conveyors of encoded implications, whereas other associations prove to be flat and relatively barren (e.g., symptoms tend to be poor carriers of specific derivative meaning, as is also true of intellectualized associations). On the whole, the most meaningful associations from patients take the form of narratives and images, rich stories that carry with them the potential for encoded expression.

In practical terms, the search for derivative meaning involves the identification of those specific themes that are shared by the manifest and latent images. This particular search is always shaped by the implications of the activated context. A given segment of associations may be rich with implications, but it is a matter of therapeutic skill to use the meanings of an adaptive context as a guide for identifying those themes that are most pertinent to the manifest and latent expressions contained in the material from the patient.

A major communicative finding is pertinent here. It has been shown with great consistency that the patient's initial and basic unconscious response to an intervention by a therapist is that of *selected encoded perceptions*. Thus, the patient's derivative material contains first and foremost a series of highly selective unconscious perceptions drawn from the universal implications of the activated intervention context. This derivative material is therefore a product of two basic inputs: (a) the qualities of the therapist's intervention and (b) the nature of the patient's inner madness—his or her unconscious fantasies, memories, and other mad propensities. Indeed, it is the patient's inner psychopathology that is the single most important patient-factor in the selection of encoded meanings from the universal implications of an intervention by the therapist. It is in this way, through dealing with encoded perceptions of the therapist, that the patient's psychopathology comes into play. It also follows that an intervention from the therapist, which identifies his or her own prior adaptive context and then moves on to the patient's selected unconscious perceptions of the implications of this context as it illuminates an expression of patient-madness, states in the most comprehensive fashion possible the true implications of the material from the patient. Such a statement touches upon the madness (or sanity) of the psychotherapist as well as the madness of the patient. Therefore, it meaningfully illuminates this madness in a fashion that permits fresh nonpathological adaptation.

Once a series of encoded perceptions of the therapist in light of his or her interventions has been registered outside of awareness within the patient, there follows a series of *selective reactions to these encoded realizations*. Among these responses, the most important are: (a) gross behaviors; (b) the stimulation of conscious and unconscious fantasies and memories; (c) subsequent distortions and misperceptions; (d) encoded efforts to help and even cure the therapist, especially in the form of models of rectification; (e) efforts to harm and disturb the therapist. Here, too, the communicative approach has shown that many of these responses to encoded perceptions are conveyed by the patient in derivative form.

There follows an essential principle of technique: An *encoded perception* is any derivative (disguised or symbolized and displaced) expression that is consonant with the known implications of an intervention context, whereas a *reaction to a perception* is typically characterized by an image that is different from such implications. Further, in carrying out this type of decoding process, it is essential to keep in mind that the latent or raw image (the disturbing or dangerous and anxiety-provoking image) is always an unconscious perception of the therapist. Thus, manifest material from the patient that alludes to other individuals and to themes other than therapy may consistently be viewed as disguised expressions of latent perceptions of the therapist. The symbolization and displacement are always from a raw encoded image of the therapist to some other type of communication. Only rarely will a patient use manifest material related to the therapist as a way of encoding other, more dangerous images of the treating individual. In fact, the most useful means of disguising threatening perceptions of the therapist lies in alluding to the patient himself.

As can be seen, this particular listening-formulating process takes into account many manifest factors, but it stresses the patient's unconscious communications and, in particular, his or her unconscious perceptions of the therapist, selected in terms of patient-madness as responses to the universal implications of particular interventions by the therapist. It is this interaction within which the patient's madness and its meanings are conveyed. The therapist who wishes to identify the unconscious implications of patient-madness has no choice but to interpret in these terms. It follows as well that the therapist must assign each segment of the patient's associations to one or more possible communicative functions: that of expressing an indicator, of representing an adaptive context, and/or of conveying derivative meanings; such an effort is inherent to a comprehensive application of the listening-formulating process. The complexities of this process are a reflection of the many implications of the communications from the patient. Any effort at comprehending in-depth the meanings of a patient's behaviors and associations must entail this particular type of effort.

Still, it is important to stress again the feasibility of mastering this particular listening-formulating process. Although it is true that these efforts require a significant measure of resolution in respect to one's own therapist-madness, on a cognitive level it is relatively easy to identify manifest indicators and direct representations of intervention contexts. Thus, much of the work in listening and formulating involves the identification of themes that bridge manifest from latent—decoding a disguised communication about someone other than the therapist as it connects to an encoded and unconscious perception of his or her interventions. Therefore, it is sensitivity to metaphor, to bridging themes, to the guiding influence of the implications of intervention contexts, and to in-depth self-knowledge that facilitates this type of listening and formulating as it promotes the development of truly valid interventions.

Observations from the communicative vantage point have revealed *seven dimensions of all human and therapeutic interactions*. These areas constitute the substance of the patient's adaptive and communicative efforts, and they are extensively interrelated. Each involves a need or motivational system, as well as an area of adaptation. From time to time in each session, the communicative therapist pauses to evaluate exactly which of these dimensions the patient is working over. He or she always does so in light of an intervention context. Further, it is recognized that the patient's communications in each of these spheres represent the actualities of the therapeutic interaction and their unconscious implications as their primary meanings and that fantasy connections are always secondary. The recognition of these dimensions serves as a second-order guide for the therapist's interventional efforts. Each of these formulations is eventually funneled into the basic listening-formulating schema.

Although these seven dimensions are indeed quite complex, they do not prove to be unwieldy in the clinical situation. For the communicative therapist, an interpretation involves a *synthesis* of the patient's material—organizing what the patient has offered in scattered form—through which a statement is created in regard to the conscious and unconscious implications of the stimulus of the therapist's interventions as they cause and unconsciously illuminate the patient's madness. In principle, the communicative therapist utilizes only the material of a given hour in creating such an interpretation. He or she adds virtually nothing to these interpretive efforts, making almost exclusive use of the patient's material in shaping an interventional effort. Both interpretations and managements of the ground rules are carried out in this fashion, primarily in terms of—and at the behest of—the patient's encoded or derivative expressions. Because of this, the communicative therapist automatically deals with those areas that the patient is working over at a given moment. The guidelines offered here are designed mainly to sharpen the therapist's thinking, to provide a perspective on possible issues and correlations, and to serve as a background tool which a therapist may use from time to time in a given hour in order to sort out more carefully the patient's ongoing associations. In brief (see Langs, 1982a, in press b), the seven dimensions are as follows:

The therapist's most critical interventions involve *the manner in which he or she constitutes the therapeutic setting and relationship and provides the patient with a set of clear-cut ground rules and boundaries for this experience.* It is through this means of intervening that the therapist establishes the basic therapeutic symbiosis or selfobject mode of relatedness essential to the treatment experience. The efforts in this sphere express a great deal in regard to the therapist's own inner capacities as well as offering the patient a core mode of relatedness and a sense of basic trust, holding, and containment that is essential to the ideal therapeutic interaction. Through derivative validation, communicative studies have identified the ideal secure frame; departures from this ideal are experienced as dysphoric and create many issues for both patient and therapist alike.

The ideal set of ground rules is constituted by a set fee, length of sessions, frequency of hours, and time of sessions. It involves the placement of the patient on the couch with the therapist behind him or her and out of sight. The patient is advised to utilize the fundamental rule of free association, and the therapist maintains evenly hovering attention. In addition, the therapist maintains neutrality (the use of appropriate silence, interpretation–reconstructions, and constructive framework-management responses exclusively), total privacy, relative anonymity, total confidentiality, and a one-to-one relationship. There is an absence of physical contact except for a handshake at the beginning and end of the treatment, and a number of other implied ground rules and boundaries.

Those treatment situations that are constituted in terms of these ideal ground rules may be termed *secure frame psychotherapies.* Those situations in which one or more basic deviations exist in regard to these tenets may be termed *deviant frame psychotherapies.* Although the secure frame therapy paradigm is relatively ideal, some measure of effective psychotherapeutic work can also be carried out under deviant conditions.

In essence, the secure frame provides the patient with a sense of basic trust, clear-cut interpersonal boundaries, and a sound sense of reality testing (the therapist behaves in a manner that is in keeping with his assigned role and functions). Further, the secure frame provides positive attributes to the other dimensions of the therapeutic interaction. The therapist capable of establishing this type of frame for the patient's psychotherapeutic experience is unconsciously seen as sane, capable of managing his own inner mental world and interpersonal relationships, and able to offer a strong sense of hold, healthy narcissistic reinforcement, and containment.

In addition to these powerful positive attributes, the secure frame also creates danger situations for both patient and therapist. These center around claustrophobic anxieties experienced in terms of the sense of entrapment and claustrum created by these particular tenets. Within the claustrum, the patient fears annihilation by the therapist, desertion and abandonment to the point of starvation, and disintegration as well as an uncontrolled upsurge of violent and sexual impulses, wishes, and fantasies in both him- or herself and the therapist. It is these anxieties, centered around Melanie Klein's paranoid-schizoid-phobic position and anxieties, that create the unconscious motivation within the patient to carry out therapeutic work designed to resolve his or her immediate madness in the treatment experience. Thus, the secure frame, which provides the patient with the ideal mode of relatedness and holding condition for treatment, also leads to the creation by the therapist of a claustrum that creates an anxiety-provoking danger situation for the patient.

As for the deviant frame, its basic attributes involve a mistrust of the therapist, a view of him or her as incapable of ideal, healthy, narcissistic reinforcement, holding, and containing, as well as a blurring of interpersonal boundaries and disturbances in reality testing in the patient's view of the therapist and his or her own subjective experience. The deviant frame creates disturbances in the other dimensions of the therapeutic interaction and unconsciously conjures up an image of the therapist as mad and unable to contain and manage his or her own inner mental and interpersonal difficulties.

Despite these powerful negative attributes, the deviant frame offers the patient (and therapist) certain pathological gratifications and defenses. Among these, pathological mirroring and idealization, manic-fusion defenses, counterphobic defenses, and the undoing of separation anxieties loom large. It is these pathological defenses and gratifications that have made deviant frame therapy so attractive for patients and therapists alike (Langs, 1982b).

In the clinical situation, it is the goal of the communicative therapist to maintain the ideal frame at the behest of the patient's derivative communications. Although many patients will consciously request alterations in the ideal ground rules, all patients consistently support the secure frame on a derivative level. Furthermore, the communicative therapist is highly sensitive to all interventions in this sphere, both deviant and those directed toward securing the frame, because each patient is most sensitive himself to interventions in this sphere. Virtually all meaningful communicative psychotherapy is carried out in light of intervention contexts constituted by the patient's efforts to alter the ground rules or to otherwise impinge upon this aspect of the treatment, as they lead to interpretive and framework securing interventions by the psychotherapist. In substance, then, communicative psychotherapy is ground-rule psychotherapy; further, efforts of this kind are virtually the only means through which the interactional truths of the patient's madness can be illuminated and modified.

Second, there are three possible *modes of relatedness* in the psychotherapeutic relationship, with many variations in regard to each. The ideal treatment relationship is constituted by a *healthy (therapeutic) symbiosis* in which the therapist secures the ground rules of treatment and adopts a basically interpretive approach. The patient, for his or her part, accepts these conditions of treatment and, if he or she wishes to alter them, is prepared to explore and analyze the ramifications of such efforts. *Pathological symbiosis* is constituted by deviant gratifications for the patient and/or therapist, much of it involving noninterpretive interventions and framework alterations.

Healthy autism emerges for the therapist when there is no need for interpretation or ground-rule management in light of the patient's immediate material. For the patient, healthy autism is expressed when there is no activated adaptive context for the patient to work over, and his or her material is functionally meaningless (i.e., the patient, for the moment, is lying fallow). On the other hand, *pathological autism* is reflected in a therapist when he or she fails to interpret or manage a ground rule in the face of meaningful material from the patient, or does so erroneously (i.e., based on his or her own inner needs). Pathological autism exists in a patient when there is indeed an activated intervention context, and he or she responds with functionally meaningless associations (i.e., a failure to represent the activated adaptive context and/or a failure to provide a meaningful and coalescing derivative complex). Finally, *pathological parasitism* occurs when either patient or therapist exploits the other party to the treatment for destructive and selfishly pathological needs.

As noted for all of the spheres of human interaction, the patient's associations will from time to time touch upon images related to modes of relatedness. It is critical, however, for the therapist to recognize that the representations by the patient initially reveal unconscious perceptions of the therapist himself in light of the actualities of the treatment relationship; only rarely are fantasies and wishes expressed in these areas.

Next, there are two basic *modes of cure:* that of *true insight* (understanding in light of adaptive contexts and derivatives) and that of *action-discharge-merger.* The former mode is, as noted, constituted only by adaptive context-oriented interventions—interpretive and framework management. The latter is a factor in all other interventions by a psychotherapist, even those that are seemingly interpretive and/ or verbal. Patients will from time to time portray such modes of cure, the former in allusions to efforts to understand and resolve problems in constructive fashion, the latter in images of impulsivity, action, self-serving exploitation, and the like. When these latter images appear in the patient's material, it is critical for the therapist to discover the intervention context that has led to an unconscious perception of him or her in such light.

In addition to an analysis of the patient's material in terms of the listening-formulating schema, the therapist attends to images related to openness of *communication*, its disturbance, concealment, and the like. Through such images, he or she gets in touch with his or her own communicative resistances, as well as those within the patient.

The next sphere touches upon the usual classical psychoanalytic considerations of issues in several areas. The therapist attends to all *representations of intrapsychic conflict, dynamic problems, and genetic allusions*. However, he or she must maintain the principle that the patient is initially representing selected unconscious perceptions of the therapist in light of his or her interventions, as well as suggesting genetic implications of these interventions for the therapist. It is through unconscious activity and condensation (the patient's material, along the me–not me interface, alludes to both therapist and patient) that the same associations upon the patient's own dynamics and genetics as well. Perhaps the most important technical principle in this regard is the necessity of waiting before intervening for the patient to represent issues of instinctual drives and difficulties, especially sexual, in a meaningful, coalescing derivative complex. The absence of such material suggests an incomplete representation of the unconscious dynamic issues within the treatment interaction. Observations indicate that sexual issues, whatever their underlying meanings and functions, are among the most significant causes of madness in patients and therapists alike.

In the next area, patients represent concerns with regard to the *cohesiveness of identity, the need for narcissistic mirroring and idealization, and issues of tension regulation, self-cohesion*, and the like. All of the considerations of self psychology fall into this realm. However, in keeping with communicative principles, it is essential that the therapist recognize that the first level of all such representations involves selected unconscious perceptions of the therapist himself in this area. It is this unconsciously perceptive dimension of narcissistic and identity issues that has been almost entirely neglected in the psychoanalytic literature.

Finally, the therapist monitors allusions to *madness* in terms of gross contradictions, loss of control, erratic behaviors, and other signs of insanity. Similarly, *sane behaviors and sensible actions* are considered in this area as well. The category owes its importance to the finding that madness and sanity have their own forms of contagion and their own vicissitudes. Most notable among these is the realization that in those situations where a therapist expresses his or her madness, the patient will respond in generally sane fashion and submerge his or her madness under that of the therapist. This finding has important consequences in the understanding of material from patients in psychotherapy.

These, then, are the dimensions of the therapeutic interaction. In a given session, a patient will shift from issues in one sphere to those in another. A truly meaningful and coalescible derivative complex involves selected encoded perceptions of the therapist in light of his or her interventions in three or more of these areas of human experience. The presence of such material speaks for the likelihood of interpretive intervention.

As a highly condensed illustration, we may study a young man in twice weekly psychotherapy for depression and an aimlessness to his life, who is being seen at a reduced fee. The therapist had refused his check for her fee because the patient had failed to pay for a session he had missed toward the end of August; this had occurred because the patient was uncertain whether the therapist had returned from her vacation for that hour. The therapist, in recent sessions, had been intervening in a manner that suggested movement toward rectification of the reduced fee (the patient was now earning more money and could afford her usual fee) and responsibility for the missed session.

The patient began his hour by talking about his efforts to develop a small business as an independent trucker. He had been having trouble renting trucks. The owner of the rental agency had suggested that the patient lease a truck so that he would always have a vehicle available; in the long run, he could earn more money. Under pressure, the patient finally gave in, but then became anxious over the additional responsibility and worry.

The patient revealed that a woman had given him some "speed" at a bar and that he was coming off the drugs in the session; hence he was having trouble free associating. He was thinking of going to school to become a social worker. He had gotten into a hassle with his girlfriend over money that he borrowed from her and had failed to return. He always had it pretty easy with money. When his grandmother died, she left him an inheritance, and his father sends him a check every month. He had missed the check that month, which reminded the patient that he still owed the therapist some money, though he wasn't sure just how much. He was still uncertain about whether he should pay for the session in August because he wasn't sure that the therapist was in her office. He had called his father about the money, but the patient felt bugged about having to press him. His father's way of keeping his claws in him and controlling him was through money and giving him things. His mother kept it that way as well.

The therapist intervened and indicated that the patient was having trouble talking freely because of the influence of the drug and felt that he was rambling. His difficulty seemed related to some of the other things he had talked about. Money seemed very much on his mind, particularly the thought of being pressured to spend his own money in order to lease something that would bring with it more responsibility. He had connected that money to the money he owed the therapist, and he had thought about being charged or not being charged for a session. He had then thought of his father as well as his mother, and how they always used money and gave him things to control him and get their claws in him. The therapist suggested that the way she had been handling the financial arrangements may have had the same effect—that she has been very inconsistent about money and his payments and that the patient seemed to sense that she might well be doing the same thing as his parents (i.e., using money to keep him under her control).

The patient responded that he was aware of being seen by the therapist at a low fee. His parents had always done that to him. They offered to pay for his graduate school, but he would rather not go to school at all than do it that way. Every Christmas his parents would give him all these presents he didn't ask for, and then think they could run his life. He was reminded of the apartment in which he lived, where the rent was extraordinarily low. He had been given a special deal, treated with favoritism. The apartment was supposed to be saved for low-income people, but the landlord liked him because he had promised to fix up the apartment. He didn't really like living there because he had to worry about things falling in the halls and rats and roaches and such. He probably would never live like that again. Other people do live better, and the patient wondered why he didn't care.

The therapist suggested that the patient was now adding something more about the fee arrangement. It seemed to repeat the situation with the apartment where somehow he was getting something at a low price, a special deal that was meant for people with more financial difficulties than himself. He seemed to feel that it was a matter of special interest and was not really right. He had enjoyed this kind of arrangement, but on a deeper level, he seemed to wonder if there was really something wrong with the whole situation, including its basic structure because it was damaged and infested.

The patient now thought of his friend who believed that wherever you live is important. This man had gone out and gotten a really good job, and he really had made good use of his great talents. He did not remain in a limited position like the patient. The patient realized that he was bright himself, but this guy was at a much higher level and really made good use of his capabilities. Anyhow, the friend paid a lot of money for his apartment and lived really well.

As the hour drew to a close, the therapist suggested that in light of what the patient had said about payment and some of the possible meanings of those things that do not cost very much, they should open up the question of the patient's fee and see where it goes. She then added that the patient had asked about payment for the session in August. She told him that she had indeed been there for the session and that the patient was responsible for any session that he has missed. The therapist then realized that she had extended the session some 2 or 3 minutes in making her last intervention. The patient made note of this extension and then said that he would pay for the additional (August) session the following hour.

This material illustrates two relatively sound communicative interventions. In analyzing the hour, we begin with the patient-indicators. Here, they involve the patient's request for a low fee and his coming to the session while still high on drugs. There is also the patient's failure to pay for the missed hour. All of these are gross behavioral resistances (frame breaks), though the drug intake may also be seen as symptomatic. It would be the therapist's goal in this session to intervene in light of her own intervention contexts as reflected in the patient's material, as a way of revealing the unconscious meanings of these particular expressions of patient-madness.

The main adaptive contexts for this hour include the low fee charged by the therapist, the check that was left out for the patient to take back because of its insufficiency in light of the number of hours for which the patient was responsible, and the otherwise secure conditions of treatment. In the hour, the patient represents the two main intervention contexts—the low fee and the refusal to accept his check—on a manifest level by alluding directly to each. As noted, this type of direct representation facilitates interpretive and framework-mangement intervention.

To review the main highlights of this hour briefly in terms of the seven dimensions of the therapuetic interaction (with the implication that the primary level of meaning involves selected encoded perceptions of the therapist, actual implications of her interventions), we may note the following. The efforts to develop a small business as an independent trucker is a representation of the insightful mode of cure (based on the adaptive context of the therapist's previous valid interpretive and framework-management interventions). The truck owner's suggestion that the patient lease a truck may well reflect a healthy symbiotic mode of relatedness (the relatively secure frame and the therapist's recent constructive interventions). On the other hand, the woman who gave the patient "speed" would represent a pathological mode of symbiosis and parasitism (based in all likelihood on the therapist's offer of a low treatment fee). Also involved is an action-discharge-merger mode of cure, as well as the possibility of a representation of a narcissistic disturbance in the pathological use of a selfobject. In addition, there is a sense of violation of the frame (the drug is illegal), dynamics and genetics suggesting oral conflicts, and a subsequent allusion to disturbances in communication. Finally, there is also a sense of madness to the drug offer and intake, as well as to the patient's rambling in the session.

As can be seen, quite early in this session the patient's material is rich in encoded and direct imagery related to virtually all of the dimensions of the therapeutic interaction. This quality suggests the likelihood of the existence of material for interpretive and framework-management responses by the therapist.

The failure to return the money that he owed to his girlfriend reflects some measure of a frame break (the patient violated an agreement), a parasitic mode of relatedness, an action-discharge-merger mode of cure, a disturbance in communication, aggressive dynamics, the pathological use of the girlfriend as a selfobject, and the possibility of irrationality or madness. The images that follow may be similarly classified; space limitations makes it necessary to leave further efforts in this direction to the reader.

All these qualities of the patient's material would, as suggested earlier, be funneled into the listening-formulating processes. In the main, they would guide the therapist in organizing the patient's selective derivative perceptions of her in light of her interventions—in terms of both the nature of the deviant and frame-rectifying interventions at hand and the madness within the patient that leads to his particular selection of images of the therapist.

In the main, the early image of taking on responsibility for one's business suggests an unconscious perception of the therapist as attempting to rectify the frame both in regard to the low fee and the payment due to her. On the other hand, the images of the money lent to the patient and not returned, the patient's inheritance and checks from family members, and their use as a way of controlling and keeping his parents' claws in him touch upon the pathological effects of the low fee. There is also a possible image of the therapist to the effect that should she not charge the patient for the missed hour, she would be lending him money that he would never return and providing him with gifts that are ultimately self-destructive and self-serving—a misuse of the patient as a pathological narcissistic selfobject.

With the adaptive context of the therapist's expectation that the patient would pay for the missed session in August portrayed manifestly and in the presence of a rich derivative complex, the therapist intervened in a manner that attempted to understand the unconscious basis for the patient's resistance in coming to the session under the influence of drugs. She attempted as well to touch upon some of the encoded perceptions related to both the low fee and the issue of the payment due for the missed hour. The intervention is structured as a sound interpretation in that it attempts to explain these indicators in light of adaptive contexts and the patient's consequent derivative perceptions. The therapist correctly uses a nontransference model in suggesting that her behavior in these areas is an actual repetition of pathogenetic interactions with the patient's parents (rather than a distortion based on transference), again adhering to the sound principle of defining selected valid perceptions before attempting to recognize any subsequent distortions.

Perhaps the main failing in this particular intervention involves the therapist's avoidance of the patient's clear corrective and model of rectification, and a failure to propose at this point that the patient is pointing to a need to correct some issue in regard to his fee. These models are proposed in the patient's allusion to leasing a truck so that he can always have one available (i.e., this could be translated into the patient's suggesting that he pay the full fee so that he has his own therapeutic space). An additional corrective is implied in the patient's wish to be independent of obligations to his parents because of their misuse of such indebtedness.

Despite these limitations to the intervention, the therapist obtains striking indirect (encoded) validation of her efforts. The patient alludes directly to his low fee – a representation of a previously omitted critical intervention context. He then offers another powerful model of rectification, stating that he would rather not go to graduate school if his parents were to pay his way. Other images add to the implications of the destructive qualities of the low fee and the nonpayment for the missed hour. There is a portrayal of the potentially damaging and disease-producing qualities of the deviant conditions of treatment as well – the therapeutic space is sick rather than healthy and promotes illness rather than cure and growth. Each of these derivative images add in some significant fashion to the therapist's intervention, while on the surface, the patient clearly continues to work through the various fee issues. This type of surface working through, accompanied by clear, unique, derivative communications that extend the therapist's intervention, constitutes an ideal type of validating reaction in a patient to an interpretation of the therapist.

With the additional material, the therapist then extended her interpretive efforts by showing the patient his additional encoded perceptions and his proposed models of rectification. Here too, the therapist falls short of definitively indicating that the patient seemed to be proposing the need to increase his fee, though her caution in this regard is to be respected.

The intervention is once more validated through a combination of surface working through and unique derivative expressions. Here, there is interpersonal validation through an allusion to a very bright male friend–an encoded perception of the constructive functioning of the therapist. There is also cognitive validation in the patient's representation of a really nice apartment–therapeutic setting–that the patient would have if he paid higher rent–a higher fee.

At this point in the hour, the therapist herself regressed and made several errors. She failed to identify the patient's proposed models of rectification clearly, directly answered the patient's question regarding payment for the August session (instead of waiting for his own derivative answers), and extended the hour by 2 or 3 minutes. As noted elsewhere (Langs, in press a,b), these failings reflect a relatively universal dread within psychotherapists with regard to making valid interpretations and with respect to the secure frame. In this instance, it was possible to trace this sense of danger in the therapist to anxieties regarding the patient's sexual perceptions of and fantasies toward herself, as well as additional but secondary issues. Still, for present purposes, this excerpt and brief analysis have been offered to illustrate the manner in which communicative therapists, such as myself, listen and intervene in an actual therapeutic setting.

The communicative approach extends and revises present-day psychoanalytic and psychotherapeutic techniques. It adds to the self psychologists' focus six other dimensions of the therapeutic interaction, which must consistently receive the therapist's empathy and attention. It points especially to the function of the patient's manifest material as a container of derivative images that involves selected but valid perceptions of the implications of the therapist's interventions. It provides the classical psychoanalyst, who tends to focus on dynamics, genetics, and perhaps to some extent on mode of relatedness (though virtually never the mode of relatedness between analyst and patient), with some five or six additional dimensions that require conceptualization as they pertain not only to the patient, but again to the analyst as well.

The approach brings to the field in general a comprehensive view of the manifest and latent implications of the material and behaviors of patients and offers a full sense of the complexities of the ongoing conscious and unconscious communicative interaction between the two participants of treatment. Although its basic tools (the listening-formulating-intervening schema and the seven dimensions of the therapeutic interaction) are relatively complex, their mastery is certainly possible.

However, the therapist who wishes to interpret and identify the true unconscious meanings of the material from his or her patients consistently has no choice but to master these techniques in order to achieve this goal.

Finally, it is important to note that the communicative approach is based on the single premise of a conscious and unconscious adaptive communicative interaction between patient and therapist; it remains quite open to addendum, refinement, and revision. Once psychoanalysts and psychotherapists have absorbed the findings of the communicative studies to this point, it is greatly hoped that they will be able to further extend the techniques so derived.

REFERENCES

Langs, R. (1982a). *The psychotherapeutic conspiracy*. New York: Jason Aronson.

Langs, R. (1982b). *Psychotherapy: A basic text*. New York: Jason Aronson.

Langs, R. (in press-a). Making interpretations and securing the frame: Danger situations for psychotherapists. *International Journal of Psychoanalytic Psychotherapy*.

Langs, R. (in press-b). *A workbook for psychotherapists: Vol. II. Listening and formulating*. Hillsdale, NJ: New Concept Press.

5 An Analyst at Work in Sweden

Bo Larsson, M.D.

According to Freud (1937), "It almost looks as if analysis were the third of those 'impossible' professions in which one can be sure beforehand of achieving unsatisfying results. The other two, which have been known much longer, are education and government" (p. 248). In my practical work, however, I have come to consider it as a most gratifying profession. Moreover, if the nature of psychoanalysis is looked upon as a hermeneutic experience rather than a healing procedure, I am not even sure that its results are as unsatisfactory as Freud, with his high ambition and keen self-criticism, seems to have thought.

As we all know, psychoanalysis has changed a lot since Freud discovered or invented it. Many analysts prefer to look upon these changes as an enormous increase in psychoanalytic knowledge and a growing sophistication of our theories and techniques, but to my mind, it is questionable whether this is true. I am of course neither original, nor necessarily correct, in claiming that Freud is still surpassed by none in the depth and integration of his understanding of the human mind, and that we had consequently better stick to most of what he taught us.

An important difference between modern analysts and Freud and his contemporaries lies in the amount of formal training analysts are receiving today. Theoretically, uniform training should have led to some uniformity concerning basic principles. After having read the answers to a questionnaire about the selection and function of the training analyst in preparation for the precongress on training before the Helsinki Congress in 1981 (Cabernite, 1982; Larsson, 1982; Orgel, 1982; Sandler, 1982; Weinshel, 1982), it has, however, become even more obvious to me how differently psychoanalysts think and work in different parts of the world. This is not necessarily a drawback but could, on the contrary, be a challenge to all of us, if we are willing to communicate openly about how we work. Hopefully, the present paper provides an example of such an effort.

First, I would like to say a few words about my own theoretical background. When I was a candidate, Thomas Szasz was widely read by members of the Swedish Society. The Swedish analyst, Carl Lesche, developed his "metascience" of psychoanalysis during that time, and besides the standard literature, these two authors were important to my first impressions of psychoanalytic theory.

Szasz (1961) thought that mental illness was a myth, and he regarded it as something fundamentally different from somatic illness. In spite of all exaggerations, some of his reasoning seemed to the point. He believed that "psychotherapy is an effective method of helping people – not to recover from an 'illness,' it is true, but rather to learn about themselves, others and life" (1961, p. xi). If you substitute the word "psychoanalysis" for "psychotherapy," he is, to my mind, perfectly right. He wanted "to present an essentially 'destructive' analysis of the concept of mental illness and of psychiatry as a pseudomedical enterprise" (p. x), and in spite of his "destructiveness," this analysis still appears to be well founded. He then tried "to offer a 'constructive' synthesis . . ." (p. x) to fill the gap by presenting a semiotical, a rule-following, and a game-model analysis of behavior. Although these do represent steps in the direction toward an *understanding* of behavior, or rather of the field of interest of clinical psychoanalysis, the philosophical basis of the attempt appears rather meager, which may possibly account for his later development (Szasz, 1971, 1973, 1978) toward more "destruction" and less "construction."

Nevertheless, another of his books (Szasz, 1965) has also had a rather large influence on the teaching of psychoanalysis in Sweden during the late 1960s and early 1970s. In that book, he proposed "to describe psychotherapy as social action, not as healing. So conceived, psychoanalytic treatment is characterized by its aim – to increase the patient's knowledge of himself and others and hence his freedom of choice in the conduct of his life; by its method – the analysis of communications, rules and games; and, lastly, by its social context – a contractual, rather than 'therapeutic,' relationship between analyst and analysand" (pp. viii–ix). He preferred to call this method "autonomous psychotherapy." Szasz (1965) did not think it could be practiced in totalitarian countries and also felt pessimistic about its possibilities in a welfare state because: "In mid-twentieth-century America, welfare has displaced liberty, and the

Autonomous Individual has become the Superfluous Man, the Remnant" (p. ix). It should be added that autonomy is what, in Szasz's view, should be the aim of psychoanalysis.

Sweden being the welfare state par excellence, it is no wonder that these views struck a resonant note among Swedish analysts. As the responsibility left to the individual has steadily decreased in Sweden since then, the problems to which Szasz addresses himself are more and more poignantly felt. Whether the solutions he offers to these problems are correct, possible, or convenient seems to be dubious.

Anyhow, I am an analyst who tried to look upon psychoanalysis with the critical eyes of Szasz and tried to follow some of his recommendations. Gradually, I have given many of them up because they are scarcely tenable to a psychoanalyst in a welfare state. Some of them do not seem suited for any state, except for Utopia. But sometimes one gets an uneasy feeling that perhaps Szasz was not completely wrong when he saw a fundamental contradiction between psychoanalysis and the welfare state, even if psychoanalysis is somehow still possible and successfully practiced in a country like Sweden. Only the future can tell whether this will continue to be the case. As to contemporary psychoanalysis, some of the impact of the Swedish social security system on psychoanalysis is described later in this paper. To my mind, this impact is too important to be neglected, and it can be foreseen to become still more important.

Lesche, the other author who was essential to my initial outlook on psychoanalytic theory, has tried to grasp the essence of psychoanalysis. In his "metascience," developed from the ideas of German philosophers like Apel and Habermas, he has reached conclusions that are strikingly similar to some of those of Szasz (1961, 1965), Ricoeur (1965), and Schafer (1976, 1978). He thinks that natural science, because of its obvious technical successes, has become so prestigious that it has almost completely forced its paradigm on all other sciences, to the detriment of the humanities or the human sciences (*Geisteswissenschaften*). To simplify a very complicated matter, one could say that natural sciences are concerned with the "explanation" of invariances, with causal connections, and with prediction of phenomena in "nature," whereas human sciences are concerned with "understanding" the meanings of human acts, or the results of them. We often tend to assume that there are causal or other invariant connections between body and soul, between matter and acts. According to Lesche, there are no such connections. You cannot "translate" anything from the "extensional language" of natural science to the "intensional language" of human science. It is not possible with cross-explanations between "body" and "soul." (For a compara-

tively basic discussion of this, see Schafer, 1976, 1978; for more elaborate discussions, see Brentano, 1874/1973; Husserl, 1925–1928/1968,
1936–1937/1976; Lesche, 1962, 1973, 1978, 1979, 1981).

According to Lesche, none of the *concepts* of natural science are or can
be used in psychoanalysis in their original meaning. *Words* borrowed
from natural science (e.g., cause, cathexis, discharge, energy, etc.) are
just *metaphors* that have lost or should lose the meaning they had in the
natural science. Lesche calls them quasi-naturalistic because they only
seem similar to the concepts of natural science, but they actually pertain
to the meaning and motivation (not cause) of human acts. Psychoanalysis is a human science with a hermeneutic (interpreting) and emancipa-
tory aim. It has nothing to learn from the natural sciences and vice
versa.

The last statement might be difficult to accept. When reflecting on
natural science, you will always find that an abstraction from the subject and from all acts of a subject is made "use of" in order to get "objective" knowledge (Husserl, 1925–1928/1968). The subject matter of
psychoanalysis is, however, nothing but the subject and its acts. How
could you possibly say anything about something you have already decided not to take into consideration? That is, how could natural science
have anything to say about the human subject and its acts when these
are not allowed into any of its concepts?

It is not possible to go into detailed argumentation here. Suffice it to
say that this view of psychoanalysis as a human science has important
consequences for many psychoanalytic theories. I mention only one
here. Psychopathological states cannot be regarded as illnesses any
more than they can in the thinking of Szasz. They should rather be
looked upon as life styles, "pathological" or "abnormal" life styles if you
wish to stress that we regard them as *in-sane* or deviating from the
norm. This is not to say that the ordinary psychopathological concepts
could not be useful for descriptive purposes. It is still meaningful to talk
about an obsessional life style, a perverse life style, and a psychotic life
style. What is important is that you can never expect to find the invariances or "natural laws" that you find in natural sciences, and hence it is
not possible to make predictions. There are as many life styles as there
are human beings. The aim of clinical psychoanalysis is to understand
the life style of each person being studied, as one uniquely lived by him,
and to make the analysand understand his life style in a life-historical
perspective, in order to make emancipation from remaining infantile
misconceptions possible. In a way, you could say that it is not possible to
arrive at a "diagnosis" until the analysis is terminated.

With this background, I would now like to turn to my daily work as an
analyst. For the time being, working in Sweden as an analyst, at least if

you are a medical analyst, is economically possible. It is socially quite gratifying, and you have no problems getting analysands. Unofficially, psychoanalysis has become more and more accepted by certain psychiatrists, psychologists, social workers, and psychotherapists, but officially, the attitude is ambivalent, to say the least. We do not know how much this is due to the traditions in these professional fields, to our own ambivalent attitude toward *them*, to the general development of Swedish society, or to the attitude of the authorities. With the assistance of the International Psychoanalytic Association, we are trying to scrutinize our situation at the moment. What I intend to do in this paper is to give a subjective and honest description of my own work and the principles that govern it. I leave it to the reader to judge which influences are the most important and the degree of coherence of the principles I adhere to.

As an (unintended) consequence of social reforms in Sweden, psychoanalysis with medical doctors has recently become practically free of charge. A less conspicuous effect of social ideology on psychoanalysis is that it has gradually become almost self-evident that if you need anything, perhaps especially from a doctor, you are entitled to get it. Paradoxically, most medical analysts have such long waiting lists that most patients must accept a considerable delay from the moment they first see their future analyst to the point when their analysis can begin. Of course, this can function as a test of motivation, but some patients who might have been analyzable when they first saw their analysts are not so any more when they are offered to start analysis many years later.

As medical analysts are called upon by many more patients than they can accept, they have to choose between them for reasons other than strictly psychoanalytical ones, whatever criteria you use for judging analyzability. Over the years, I have become more and more convinced that the correlation between analyzability and traditional diagnoses is rather low. Even if I still find basically sound the habit of using psychopathology as a rough classification of different life styles, rather than of nosological entities, I do not think classical diagnoses are very helpful for the selection of suitable analysands. More and more, analysts seem to abandon Freud's (1913) recommendation to start with a trial analysis, but I think it is a worthwhile undertaking for several reasons. It strikes a note of seriousness and emphasizes that psychoanalysis is a large task for analyst and analysand alike. Accordingly, in the initial interview, I stress that the trial is reciprocal. When Freud (1913) stated that it is impossible to judge analyzability without trying to analyze, he was of course concerned with the problem of diagnosis. I would prefer to think in terms of the possibility for me and that unique analysand to work together in order to reach the specific psychoanalytic goals, which makes the distinction of indications, suitability, and analyzability rather superfluous (Tyson & Sandler, 1971).

The pertinent question is not the psychiatric diagnosis, but rather a person's motivation, his capability to sustain the unavoidable sufferings which are part of psychoanalysis, his practical possibilities to carry through an analysis, and last but not least, whether he values or will be able to value the specific psychoanalytic goals. It has been argued that it is almost impossible to get a valid judgment on these issues during a trial analysis because the patient will become so scared and obedient that you will, after all, not get a good evaluation of his analyzability. I do not think this is true. Of course, the insecurity has an impact on the analysand, but keeping that in mind, I think you can nevertheless pass a fairly good judgment on whether an analysis will be possible or not. The effects of the trial period can in most cases be analyzed after its termination.

If the analysand is accepted, I inform him that I may be the one who decides to terminate the analysis, but I promise not to stop it against his will, without giving notice 6 months or 1 year before. The length of both trial period and the time I oblige myself to continue the analysis after a notice of termination varies according to the character of the case. I try to make the trial period as short as possible, sometimes just a week, but in certain cases (e.g., with obsessional character neuroses) it can be extended over several months. One important reason for my taking care to be so explicit is that some analysands would like to stay in analysis forever in our system where it costs them next to nothing. Another reason is that the more explicitly stated and strict the frames of the psychoanalytic setting are, the more secure will the analysand feel inside these frames. The same is probably true for the analyst.

The aim of our training analyses is traditionally agreed to be not only, as Freud first thought, to acquaint us with our own unconscious, but also to have our symptoms and "pathological" character traits analyzed. Without denying the importance of these traditional goals with their emphasis on "normality," the hermeneutic view implies a slightly different outlook. The essential thing for an analyst is not whether he complies with some psychological norm or other but rather whether he possesses a good self-knowledge and freedom both from inner peremptory instinctual impulses and superego commands. According to Loewald (1981), "it becomes difficult to continue thinking, with Hartmann (1939), in terms of an average expectable environment . . . or, with Anna Freud (1976) in terms of an average expectable 'mental equipment.' What is expectable, in the two senses of 'to be anticipated' and to be 'achieved as being expected from you,' is no longer clear and unmistakable. What is, or ought to be, the average is in doubt" (pp. 41–42).

Over the years I have learned that patients generally feel very confident in me and stick with me, even if I just see them for one consultation. I have asked myself if I seduce patients into analysis and, consequently, felt somewhat relieved when I learned that Willi Hoffer is supposed to have said that the first thing you have to do is to seduce the patient into analysis. Of course, I try to use as little seduction as possible, but I think I have to accept a certain amount of seductiveness as an inevitable – but not unanalyzable – ingredient in my contact with prospective analysands. Every analyst, by the way, must accept certain character traits as part of his own analyzed personality, to be accounted for rather than to be treated as nonexistent.

When I started my analytic practice, I was convinced that the explicit and detailed information of a contract was very important. I was taught so by my teachers, and I was not only influenced by them and Szasz but also by Menninger (1958). Though I still think it is important to be outspoken about what is demanded from the analysand, I am not as elaborate today as I was at the beginning, partly because when you become more experienced you do not need so many rules to bolster up self-confidence. Also, it would be hypocrisy to put too much stress on such ingredients of the psychoanalytic relationship as autonomy and mutual responsibility when the insurance system has actually taken over all economic responsibility. I am obliged to write a separate bill for each session to the insurance authorities, and I still hand the copies of these bills over to the analysand at the end of each month, mostly because the law requires me to do so but also to remind both the analysand and myself of the invisible third party of the psychoanalytic situation. Sooner or later in an analysis, it will become absolutely necessary to analyze this state of affairs, even if the analysand does not bring it up himself. In Sweden, the dependency on authorities is quite openly accepted by the majority of people, and I think the risk that analyst and analysand collude in avoiding the subject is rather large.

Still another effect of the insurance system is that I loose my fee when the analysand cancels a session. Consequently, I cannot allow a person to stay in analysis if he cancels too many sessions, and I make that clear as part of our contract. Most analysands find it reasonable. This sort of contract is, of course, a far cry from Freud's (1913) principle of leasing a definite hour. The hour does not belong to the patient, if he does not turn up, and he is not liable for it, if he does not make use of it. What impact such a practice may have on the psychoanalytic situation and on the psychoanalytic process is very hard to judge. The changes have been gradual, and analysts belonging to our society adapt themselves gradually, too. Nevertheless, at least theoretically, there exists a conflict between a state, which takes over more and more responsibility for the individual, and the psychoanalyst, who wants to promote the responsibility of the individual. But as it has turned out, the Swedish medical psychoanalyst is the agent both of his individual analysand and of the social insurance system. Hopefully, this will be only in theory, because as yet the only way the state interferes with the strivings of the analyst is economically. As long as analysts are not obliged to promote the value of the state in their professional activities and as long as analysts do not openly challenge the values of the state, psychoanalysis is still possible. It may, however, be a symptom of an insecure and uneasy situation that most heated debates among medical analysts in Sweden concern economy.

Freud's (1913) famous metaphor of psychoanalysis as playing chess is, to my mind, somewhat misleading. As a matter of fact, I think you can—and must—begin an analysis in an indefinite number of ways, depending on the personality of the analysand and that of the analyst as well. Furthermore, the analysand is likely to know only a small part of the rules of the game, to say nothing of its implications. The lack of symmetry in the outlook of the two players will persist until the end of the analysis, even if one tries to be very explicit and uses the opening phase (Glover, 1955) to teach the analysand the rules, especially the fundamental rule. If, for example, an analysand tells me that he does not know what to say in the beginning, I explain to him that he should say anything that comes to his mind. Later on, I just answer that he knows very well what he should say, the only exception being when nothing really seems to come to his mind. In that case, as Freud (1912) told us, the analysand is generally preoccupied with some transference thoughts, but this is not likely to happen until quite a bit of preparatory work with the fundamental rule has been done. It is quite common that the analysand pauses because he regards some of his thoughts as nonthoughts, as it were, and it often takes some time before he understands what is really meant by claiming that all thoughts should ideally be communicated. I tend to be very insistent throughout an analysis on the analysand's obedience to the fundamental rule, and more often than not, I intervene when it becomes clear from the context that the analysand is withholding some thought. This emphasis on the fundamental rule functions practically as one of the frames of the psychoanalytic situation.

However, the analysand is obviously not required to speak from the moment he enters the consultation room until the moment he leaves, and the next thing he must learn is that psychoanalysis consists of more than free association. When I interpret, or intervene in some other way,

I obviously expect the analysand to pay attention to what I am saying. The analysand is also encouraged to make self-observation and self-reflection become part of his life during and outside the sessions. This requirement can, especially if a strict superego is transferred onto the analyst, be misinterpreted as a commandment to be slavishly followed. In that case, it is necessary to call the analysand's attention to the fact that he has misunderstood your intentions, and in due time, you must analyze the meaning of his particular way of misunderstanding, be it connected with his character, a transference manifestation, a defense, or a simple misunderstanding.

I have always wondered what could possibly be meant by the "neutrality" of the analyst. In certain phases of an analysis, as I explain later, I find it neither possible, nor desirable, to maintain an attitude of total emotional abstinence. As to my personal values, I think it has been amply demonstrated by philosophers (e.g., Gadamer, 1960/1975; Habermas, 1968) that there is no such thing as a value-free scientific activity, and I see no reason to conceal to the analysand that I value certain strivings, which are the very essence of psychoanalysis (i.e., a constant seeking for truth and an effort to understand as much as possible about mental life).

Concerning the handling of the transference in the early stages of an analysis, it is not easy to understand what Freud (1913) intended with his recommendation: "*So long as the patient's communications and ideas run on without any obstruction, the theme of transference should be left untouched*" (p. 139). The difficulty lies in the fact that almost no analysand's stream of communications will run on more than a few minutes without interruption, and if it does, the continuous talk is generally an intellectualized defense, which should be interpreted as resistance. Actually, what such an analysand thinks during his rare pauses is often closer to free association than all of his talk.

In my view, which sort of interventions should be made during the beginning of the treatment and which should not differs widely with different analysands. The analyst's most urgent task during the opening phase is to make it possible for a "working alliance" to develop (Greenson, 1967). (I prefer that term to the similar "treatment alliance," Sandler, Holder, & Dare, 1970, because it has no medical connotations.) If the patient is very regressed, I think it is important first to help him progress. This generally is not very difficult when the transference gratification, which every analysand gets merely by having four or five sessions a week, is combined with an attitude of considering the patient a responsible adult. Of course, it is necessary at the same time to demonstrate some empathy for the patient's situation. If my general analytic attitude does not suffice to promote progressing, I try to interpret in such a way that the level of anxiety decreases, and I let the analysand know that it certainly will be much easier for him to handle his problems if he understands his unconscious wishes, thoughts, and feelings, which is precisely what can be attained in psychoanalysis. There is no need to go into detail concerning the different technical devices you could use to allay a deep regression, but if you cannot find any reasonable ego to cooperate with, you cannot establish a working alliance, and thus cannot analyze, no matter how much a patient needs or wants your help. Only under the controlled regression which an established working alliance makes possible, can analytic work be done.

If the analysand has already developed an intense transference before analysis was started, which is rather common with patients who have been on a waiting list for years, I think it is necessary to analyze some of the transference early in analysis. If you succeed, and you generally do, you may see catharsis-like part regressions, sometimes with true reliving of infantile situations. In this case, one had better leave the material in peace and address the adult parts of the analysand's ego. Such a situation will, by the way, provide a good opportunity to demonstrate the difference between the experiencing and the observing ego, and thus it can be one of the most effective ways of establishing a working alliance.

In the beginning, I try to analyze patients who begin their analysis less dramatically in the same way as when a deep regression has been allayed or an intense transference has been handled. I teach the fundamental rule in practice, I encourage establishing the ego split necessary for a working alliance, and I do my best to analyze transferences to significant persons outside the analytic situation. Most analysands have created some kind of transference situation with persons in their environment before they enter analysis, and generally, it is not too difficult to identify the persons with whom the analysand has chosen to play the roles of his or her early childhood family. At the same time, you have an opportunity to demonstrate the psychoanalytic way of thinking. If this initial bit of analysis is successful, most analysands will next begin to create a transference neurosis just because this is the most effective resistance (Freud, 1912), but as we all know, it is also what is needed to recover what has been labeled the infantile neurosis. Several authors have recently pointed to the fact that the infantile neurosis is not identical with the neurosis that the analysand had as a child (e.g., Lebovici, 1979). If you take a hermeneutic view of psychoanalysis, you need neither undertake nor read about longitudinal studies (e.g., Provence, 1966) in order to realize that no one can make an "identical" copy of himself as he was at an earlier age. Suffice it to point to the famous dictum of Heraclitus that it is impossible to dive in the same river more than once.

In considering the river an adequate metaphor for the stream of consciousness, I am completely in accord with Schafer (1976, 1978), though I do not think this view implies the necessity of creating a special action language and doing away with metapsychology in Freudian terms. It is certainly true that we study mental acts, not things, as Schafer points out, but when you stop experiencing and begin to reflect on your own acts and mental acts, it is necessary to reify them temporarily. Thus, depriving us of adjectives and nouns as Schafer wishes would impoverish our descriptions of how acts are experienced.

I look upon psychoanalysis as a dialogue, although a very special one in which the analysand does most of the talking. What should be promoted in this dialogue is self-reflection, primarily in the analysand, secondarily in the analyst. The aim of the dialogue is to make possible the revelation of hidden meaning. When taken seriously, this view has implications for your technique (e.g., just as you can talk about an optimal level of anxiety, you can also talk about an optimal level of communicativeness, which is different for different analysands and also different during changing phases of a single psychoanalysis). It is well known that analysands interpret our talking according to their neurosis, most often as oral and narcissistic supplies, and that they interpret our silences in different ways too, but usually as rejection. I think that you should ideally try to find out what your talk, as well as your silences, mean to the analysand at any moment and, as it were, dose your quantity of speech in order to balance gratification and frustration. I am convinced that it is impossible to understand any desires of the analysand except when they are frustrated. But you can certainly also frustrate so much that no understanding becomes possible. That is why I prefer thinking in terms of an optimal level of frustration rather than in terms of abstinence. When and how you should frustrate is, among other things, a question of timing.

What motivated Freud to formulate the rule of abstinence is, I believe, that psychoanalysis, in its pursuit of the hidden meaning of mental acts, also has to take into account the "dialectics of desire" (Ricoeur, 1965). One reason I tend to decrease my number of interventions during an analysis is that most analysands feel the analyst's interventions as gratifying in one sense or another, and if you want to understand the content of the wishes you gratify by your interventions, you will have to stop gratifying them. As we know, similar principles hold true of other types of gratifications that the analyst administers within the psychoanalytic setting.

How active I am is also determined by another consideration. The analyst will inevitably interact unconsciously with his analysand, but I think I differ somewhat from many colleagues in the way I use my countertransference. Analysts with a "totalistic" view of countertransference (Kernberg, 1965) appear to have a keen eye on their countertransference and use it very skillfully to understand what is going on in the patient. I think there can be a danger in placing too much stress on the importance of countertransference (Pöstényi, 1979, 1980), but still there is a kernel of truth in these analysts' preoccupation with it (e.g. Heimann, 1950; Joseph, 1978; Little, 1951; Racker, 1957). Most psychoanalytic insight is reached by what one analyst has called "scenic understanding" (Lorenzer, 1970, 1974). His idea is that analysands arrange childhood scenes and try to induce the analyst to play the part either of one of the significant objects or of himself in a certain situation. I wonder if all analysts take at least some part in these scenes, whether they advocate the "classical" or the "totalistic" approach to countertransference. If Lorenzer is right in holding that all specific psychoanalytic understanding is arrived at by play-acting, it is of course neither advisable nor possible to avoid completely playing the parts the analysand wants you to play. On the contrary, you should permit yourself to act in accordance with at least part of your "objective countertransference," to use Winnicott's term (1949).

It is a widely accepted rule that the best thing you can do when you do not understand what is going on in the psychoanalytic situation is to keep silent. However, I am not sure this is the best way to increase understanding. That is why I most often allow myself to interact verbally and, to a certain degree, emotionally with my analysands, until I become aware that I am acting in a play with the analysand as both director and coactor. What has happened is that, either preconsciously or unconsciously, I have identified with the part the analysand wanted me to play. When I realize that I am involved in playing a scene, I stop the interaction. After that, I have to do some self-analysis to exclude that I really acted out some of my own unconscious conflicts because, if this is the case, it is certainly necessary to keep silent and try to find out what it was about. But, if my reaction was "objective," or to use a better term, adequate, whether it was preconscious or unconscious, it has to be scrutinized in order to understand what happened and to interpret the scene to the analysand. If this is done in a systematic way, I often grow so acquainted with the roles the analysand wants me to play that I recognize them at an early stage.

It may be fruitful to go on play-acting for a while, even if I realize that that is what I am doing because, more often than not, it means that the analysand is trying to understand a new aspect of some of his inner representations. (I agree completely with Schafer, 1978, that "imagos are necessary ones own ideas . . . ," p. 124). The danger of this technique is, of course, the temptation to act out one's own conflicts and the risk of changing psychoanalysis into some sort of psychodrama. The first risk is always immanent, but I am not sure that it is really increased by this special technique. On the contrary, it may be that with a rather constant eye on your own transference and countertransference, you give yourself a better chance to detect your acting out of your own unconscious conflicts.

As to the second risk, I can only say that what I do is very distantly related to psychodrama. It is probable that I talk somewhat more than French analysts are supposed to, but probably not more than English analysts. I do not think that my arguments in favor of "scenic understanding" are rationalizations, making it possible for me to escape the dullness and passivity of the analyst's work. I have tried to work this way with some analysands at the same time that I have worked in a more conventional, restricted way with others. My experience was that I was able to understand the analysands better and more effectively when I did not at all costs avoid playing the parts they allotted to me. To avoid misunderstandings, I should add that I use this technique only during the transference neurosis, and only part of the time. An analysis of course comprises much more than interpretations based on transference–countertransference interaction and "scenic understanding." Even if "the work of analysis involves an *art of interpretation . . .*" (Freud, 1925, p. 41), it also involves many other components which should, ideally, promote the superordinate goal, that of understanding. Some of these components constitute what is often called the "setting." To illustrate my views on the setting as subordinate to understanding and, as it were, in the service of the specific psychoanalytic goals, the use of the couch may serve as an example.

According to my experience, the couch is very useful and promotes the psychoanalytic process during the longest periods of most analyses. But it is not unusual that the couch is used for defensive purposes, thus promoting a goal contrary to that of psychoanalysis. If the couch is misused in that way, I try to interpret its resistance implications. If this does not result in any changes, the analysand should be encouraged to sit facing the analyst. It then often becomes clear that what the analysand has been doing is fantasying away the analyst. After 1 or 2 weeks of face-to-face analysis, this is usually no longer a problem. The analysis gets a fresh start, and stalemates (Glover, 1955) or chaotic situations (Reich, 1933) can often be avoided. The use of the couch is thus no sine qua non for psychoanalysis. In practice, it is more a rule than an exception that I analyze face to face, at least during 1 or 2 weeks of every analysis, and whether the analysand should ideally sit in a chair or lay on the couch, is determined by the dynamics of the analytic process, not by the psychopathology of the analysand.

Another important area in which I have the impression that my technique differs from that of many of my colleagues is dream interpretation. To my mind, Freud's (1900) dictum, *"The interpretation of dreams is the royal road to a knowledge of the unconscious activities of the mind"* (p. 608) deserves to be taken seriously. Dream interpretation is a most rewarding part of analysis. Furthermore, I agree with Ricoeur (1965), who points out that the interpretation of dreams is the paradigm for all other psychoanalytic interpretations, like those of parapraxes, neurotic symptoms, art, and society. Because of both the inherent and the didactic value of dream interpretation, I tend to spend a comparatively large amount of time on it in my analyses. I am, of course, aware of the warnings of Freud (1911) and others that dreams could be used by the analysand for defensive purposes, but I do not think that this is a difficult problem to handle technically. In my opinion, the greatest risk today is that classical dream interpretations will fall into oblivion, and I think that Langs (1980) is right in presuming that quite a few contemporary analysts often interpret dreams from their manifest content only, without taking the time to ask for associations.

In his technical paper on dream interpretation, Freud (1911) admonishes "that dream-interpretation should not be pursued in analytic treatment as an art for its own sake, but that its handling should be subject to those technical rules that govern the conduct of the treatment as a whole" (p. 94). But in the same paper we find that, somewhat astonishingly, he almost takes for granted that many analysts come "from dream-interpretation to analytic practice . . ." (p. 91), a path that probably is hardly ever taken by modern candidates in analytic training. The reason the art of dream interpretation seems to be lying fallow to some extent may perhaps be sought in a general tendency to regard early psychoanalysis as outdated. It could also have something to do with ego-psychological studies of manifest dreams (e.g., Erikson, 1954) or just be a bad habit borrowed from Kleinian technique. Anyhow, I think it is still important to try to interpret dreams following Freud's (1900) guidelines. Personally, I never give a dream interpretation without having first subdivided the manifest dream into dream elements and asked for associations to most of them. If day-residues appear during the dream analysis, they indicate that the analysand is associating "convergently." If you do not get any day-residues, it generally means that the analysand is in a phase of resistance, and under these circumstances, interpreting the dream should be given up.

In most cases, I start teaching the technique of dream interpretation as soon as the analysand begins to produce dreams. Some analysands will learn how to approach a dream rather quickly, others will never learn it. When an analysand is able to tell the dream, to divide it into dream elements, and to associate to these, he can usually go through most of the procedure without me doing anything but eventually reminding him of some dream element he might have forgotten. Which aspect of the latent content I choose to interpret in the end naturally depends on what I think suits the psychoanalytic situation and promotes the psychoanalytic process. If the analysand has already tried to interpret his dream before the session, I nevertheless take care to ask for associations, and it is very rare that his own interpretation turns out to be correct. It may be so on a certain level, but you will generally get more material from deeper levels when you work with associations to a dream.

What has been said about dream interpretation applies to several other aspects of psychoanalytic work. Analysands learn to follow the fundamental rule more or less conscientiously depending on their personality. As already mentioned, I think that learning the fundamental rule is really a learning experience, and something similar could be said about the psychoanalytic way of first producing, then observing, and then working with, associations in order to understand parapraxes, character traits, defenses, symptoms, and affective reactions. You first have to listen to the analysand and observe if a phenomenon is ego-syntonic or ego-dystonic. If it is ego-syntonic, I usually ask the analysand if he has noticed that he acts (in Schafer's broader meaning) in some way or other, hoping just to make him aware of and curious about the phenomenon. If there are signs of resistance, I generally point to the fact that the matter we are talking about seems to be emotionally charged and thus important to him. If he does not accept that as a reason for trying to understand, I drop the matter for the moment and return to it later. If I have succeeded in arousing his curiosity or if the phenomenon is ego-dystonic from the start, I ask him to give associations just as if it were a dream. More "talented" analysands will learn the whole procedure of observing, associating to, and reflecting a phenomenon within a reasonable time and begin to use the same method by themselves. This is, of course, highly desirable and lays the foundations of a lifelong, ongoing, self-analysis. Before that point is reached, however, there is always a good deal of analysis of resistance to be done. But even this part of the psychoanalytic process can ideally be learned by the analysand in about the same way as has just been described. According to my experience, a reasonable number of my analysands actually approach the ideal of being able to practice self-analysis, even if it may require a rather lengthy analysis with some of them.

If analysis is successful, the analysand gradually replaces his former more or less conscious dialogue with different introjects by a silent dialogue with me as an analyst. In the ideal case, this dialogue is conscious and preconscious rather than unconscious, and it gradually becomes increasingly independent of the actual experience of the analysis. The analyst becomes more and more an "instance," belonging partly to the ego, partly to the superego and the egoideal. He is remembered as the instigator of that instance rather than identified with it. Thus, what was accomplished during the actual analysis can transcend its termination. Finally, I would like to return to my initial remarks on the results of psychoanalytic work. If the goal of psychoanalysis is "structural changes," whatever is meant by that, Freud was probably right when he grew more pessimistic in regard to the "therapeutic" efficacy of psychoanalysis over the years. In *Analysis Terminable and Interminable* (1937), he ascribes the limitations of clinical psychoanalysis to two main types of obstacles, namely, the death instinct and factors of a physiological or biological nature. Whether it is possible to disarm the manifestations of the death instinct or not by psychoanalysis remains an open question (Bégoin & Bégoin, 1979; Grunert, 1979; Pontalis, 1979; Sandler, 1979; de Saussure, 1979; Spillius, 1979). But biological and physiological factors would, according to the view of psychoanalysis put forward in this paper, be outside the territory of psychoanalytic interest and influence. These factors are studied by natural sciences, and it is not possible to "translate" their concepts, which are always pertaining to invariances of nature, into those of psychoanalysis, which are always concerned with meaning. Consequently, a change of biological and physiological factors can never be aimed at by psychoanalysis. As already stated, my view is that psychoanalysts have to strive for the more humble (and more profound) goal of increasing self-knowledge and furthering emancipation from what Freud called illusions. Inside this field, I think psychoanalysis is rather efective and challenged by no other science or technique.

REFERENCES

Bégoin, J., & Bégoin, F. (1979). *The negative therapeutic reaction, envy and catastrophic anxiety.* Paper presented at the Third Conference of the European Psycho-Analytic Federation, London.

Brentano, F. (1973). *Psychology from an empirical standpoint.* London: Routledge & Kegan Paul. (Original work published 1874)

Cabernite, L. (1982). The selection and functions of the training analyst in analytic training institutes in Latin America. *International Review of Psycho-Analysis, 9,* 398–417.

Erikson, E. H. (1954). The dream specimen of psychoanalysis. *Journal of the American Psychoanalytic Association, 2,* 5–56.

Freud, A. (1976). Changes in psychoanalytic practice and experience. *International Journal of Psycho-Analysis, 57,* 257–260.

Freud, S. (1900). The interpretation of dreams. *S.E.,* 4 and 5.

Freud, S. (1911). The handling of dream-interpretation in psychoanalysis. *S.E.*, 12 (p. 91).

Freud, S. (1912). The dynamics of transference. *S.E.*, 12 (p. 99).

Freud, S. (1913). On beginning the treatment. *S.E.*, 12 (p. 123).

Freud, S. (1925). An autobiographical study. *S.E.*, 20 (p. 7).

Freud, S. (1937). Analysis terminable and interminable. *S.E.*, 23 (p. 216).

Gadamer, H-G. (1975). *Wahrheit und Methode*. Tübingen: J. C. B. Mohr. (Original work published 1960)

Glover, E. (1955). *The technique of psycho-analysis*. London: Baillière, Tindall.

Greenson, R. R. (1967). *The technique and practice of psychoanalysis*. London: Hogarth Press.

Grunert, U. (1979). *The negative therapeutic reaction as a reactivation of a disturbed process of separation in the transference*. Paper presented at the Third Conference of the European Psycho-Analytical Federation, London.

Habermas, J. (1968). *Erkenntnis und Interesse*. Frankfurt am Main: Suhrkamp.

Hartmann, H. (1968). *Ego Psychology and the Problem of Adaptation*. New York: International Universities Press. (Original work published 1939)

Heimann, P. (1950). On counter-transference. *International Journal of Psychoanalysis, 31*, 81–84.

Husserl, E. (1968). *Phänomenologische Psychologie*. Den Haag: Martinus Nijhoff. (Original works are unpublished manuscripts, 1925–1928)

Husserl, E. (1976). *Die Krisis der Europäischen Wissenschaften und die Transzendentale Phänomenologie*. Den Haag: Martinus Nijhoff. (Original work published 1936, unpublished manuscripts 1934–1937)

Joseph, B. (1978). Different types of anxiety and their handling in the analytic situation. *International Journal of Psychoanalysis, 59*, 223–228.

Kernberg, O. (1965). Notes on countertransference. *Journal of the American Psychoanalytic Association, 13*, 38–56.

Langs, R. J. (1980). *Interactions: The realm of transference and countertransference*. New York: Jason Aronson.

Larsson, B. (1982). The selection and function of the training analyst. *International Review of Psycho-Analysis, 9*, 381–385.

Lebovici, S. (1979). *L'expérience du psychanalyste chez l'enfant et chez l'adulte*. Paris: Presses Universitaires de France.

Lesche, C. (1962). *A metascientific study of psychosomatic theories and their application in medicine*. Copenhagen: Munksgaard.

Lesche, C. (1973). On the metascience of psychoanalysis. *The Human Context, 5*, 268–284.

Lesche, C. (1978). Some metascientific reflections on the differences between psychoanalysis and psychotherapy. *Scandinavian Psychoanalytic Review, 1*, 147–181.

Lesche, C. (1979). The relation between psychoanalysis and its metascience. *Scandinavian Psychoanalytic Review, 2*, 17–33.

Lesche, C. (1981). The relation between metapsychology and psychoanalytic practice. *Scandinavian Psychoanalytic Review, 4*, 59–74.

Little, M. (1951). Countertransference and the patient's response to it. *International Journal of Psychoanalysis, 32*, 32–40.

Loewald, H. W. (1981). Regression: Some general considerations. *Psychoanalytic Quarterly, 50*, 22–43.

Lorenzer, A. (1970). *Sprachzerstörung und Rekonstruktion*. Frankfurt am Main: Suhrkamp.

Lorenzer, A. (1974). *Die Wahrheit der Psychoanalytischen Erkenntnis*. Frankfurt am Main: Suhrkamp.

Menninger, K. (1958). *Theory of psychoanalytic technique*. New York: Harper & Row.

Orgel, S. (1982). The selection and functions of the training analyst in North American institutes. *International Review of Psycho Analysis, 9*, 417–434.

Pontalis, J.-B. (1979). *The negataive therapeutic reaction: An attempt at definition.* Paper presented at the Third Conference of the European Psycho-Analytic Federation, London.

Pösténdyi, A. (1979). Tacit assumptions, countertransference and psychoanalytic technique: Part One. The influence of tacit assumptions on theory. *Scandinavian Psychoanalytic Review, 2*, 159–172.

Pöştényi, A. (1980). Tacit assumptions, countertransference and psychoanalytic technique: Part Two. The influence of countertransference on theory and technique. *Scandinavian Psychoanalytic Review, 3*, 29–36.

Provence, S. (1966). Some aspects of early ego development: Data from a longitudinal study. In R. M. Loewenstein, L. M. Newman, M. Schur, & A. J. Solnit (Eds.), *Psychoanalysis – A general psychology* (pp. 107–122). New York: International Universities Press.

Racker, H. (1957). The meaning and uses of countertransference. *Psychoanalytic Quarterly, 26*, 303–357.

Reich, W. (1933). *Charakteranalyse.* Wien: Sexpol Verlag.

Ricoeur, P. (1965). *De l'interprétation.* Paris: Éditions du Seuil.

Sandler, A-M. (1982). The selection and function of the training analyst in Europe. *International Review of Psycho-Analysis, 9*, 386–398.

Sandler, J. (1979). *The negative therapeutic reaction: An introduuction.* Paper presented at the Third Conference of the European Psycho-Analytical Federation, London.

Sandler, J., Holder A., & Dare, C. (1970). Basic psychoanalytic concepts: 2. The treatment alliance. *British Journal of Psychiatry, 116*, 555–558.

de Saussure, J. (1979). *Narcissistic elements in the negative therapeutic reaction.* Paper presented at the Third Conference of the European Psycho-Analytical Federation, London.

Schafer, R. (1976). *A new language for psychoanalysis.* New Haven, CT: Yale University Press.

Schafer, R. (1978). *Language and insight.* New Haven, CT: Yale University Press.

Spillius, E. (1979). *Clinical reflections on the negative therapeutic reaction.* Paper presented at the Third Conference of the European Psycho-Analytical Federation, London.

Szasz, T. (1961). *The myth of mental illness.* New York: Dell.

Szasz, T. (1965). *The ethics of psychoanalysis.* New York: Basic Books.

Szasz, T. (1971). *The manufacture of madness.* London: Routledge & Kegan Paul.

Szasz, T. (1974). *Det andra syndafallet* [The second sin]. Stockholm: Aldus.

Szasz, T. (1978). *Psykoterapi – en myt* [The myth of psychotherapy]. Stockholm: Alba.

Tyson, R. L., & Sandler, J. (1971). Problems in the selection of patients for psychoanalysis: Comments on the application of the concepts of 'indications,' 'suitability' and 'analysability.' *British Journal of Medical Psychology, 44*, 211–228.

Weinshel, E. (1982). The functions of the training analysis and the selection of the training analyst. *International Review of Psycho-Analysis, 9*, 434–444.

Winnicott, D. W. (1949). Hate in the countertransference. *International Journal of Psychoanalysis, 30*, 69–74.

Analyzing Sequences from Unresolved Shame and Guilt Into Symptom Formation

6

Helen Block Lewis, Ph.D.

My technique of conducting psychoanalysis has changed radically since my first case under "classical" Freudian supervision in 1945. The kernel of my present technique is a focus on the sequelae of unresolved states of shame and guilt into symptom formation. Freud's original discovery was that neurotic symptoms develop out of forbidden sexual longings. My focus on shame and guilt picks up on the "forbidden" aspects of experience. It relies heavily on Freud's description of primary process transformations – symptoms and dream content – that are created under the press of forbidden longings. In its microscopic analysis of patients' streams of consciousness, my technique is thus very classical, but in other respects, it is quite unorthodox.

Elsewhere (Lewis, 1981, 1983) I have detailed the changes in Freud's theoretical formulations that I consider necessary in order to account for new information. I list these here only very briefly. (a) I have abandoned Freud's metapsychology because it rests on a mistaken concept of primary human narcissism. This is contrary to our newer information about infants' extraordinary sociability. (b) I have replaced Freud's narrow theoretical framework with a broader theory that assumes the cultural or social nature of human beings. This is more consonant with anthropological evidence that human beings are everywhere organized into societies governed by moral law. (c) I have adopted the hypothesis that human culture is our species' evolutionary adaptation to life. Moral law is thus immanent in human life. (d) In this new framework, the self, however narcissistic or egotistical it appears, is a quintessentially social phenomenon. (e) Sex differences in the organization of the self are inevitable as a result of differences in socialization experiences. (f) I assume that shame and guilt are the affective-cognitive signals to the self that its basic affectional ties are threatened. (g) Symptoms arise when both shame and guilt are evoked and cannot be appropriately discharged. (h) Differences in symptom formation depend on whether shame or guilt is to the fore in the person's experience.

This chapter is divided into three parts. In the first part, I offer a brief account of the phenomenology of shame and guilt and I describe the changes in technique that are involved in a focus on the sequelae of two states. In the second, I discuss the empirical evidence that supports the focus on shame and guilt in the formation of neurotic symptoms. In particular, I sketch the evidence on the interrelation of cognitive style, sex, proneness to shame or guilt, and proneness to depression and paranoia. In the third part, I present some case material that illustrates how I work.

I.

My focus on sequences from states of undischarged shame and guilt is based on a phenomenological study of the two states (Lewis, 1971). An important source for this phenomenological study was 180 transcripts of psychotherapy sessions collected from "pairs" of extremely field-dependent and extremely field-independent patients in treatment with the same therapist (Witkin, Lewis, & Weil, 1968). My listening technique in psychoanalysis is now focused on identifying the patient's states of shame and guilt and on tracing the sequelae from these undischarged states into symptom formation.

From the fact that it is necessary to identify states of shame and guilt and their sequelae, it is obvious that both states involve considerable gaps in awareness. In this respect, I follow Freud's description of the superego as partly unconscious. In particular, states of shame and guilt often exist without being correctly identified by the patient. In addition, shame is often unacknowledged because it is extremely painful and perceived as irrational. There is also a state I call "bypassed" shame, in which events that might evoke shame are registered or noted by a "wince" or "jolt" to the self. Ensuing ideation then takes the form of thinking about what negative (shaming) thoughts the therapist would have about the patient. The ideation following bypassed shame is often difficult to distinguish from guilty ideation. Acute unidentified or unacknowledged shame is often hard to distinguish from its rapid transformation into depressive ideation. Unidentified guilt is usually experienced in transformation as obsessive worry or fear (dread) of specific happenings.

This focus on evoked, undischarged states of shame and guilt and their sequelae is very different from my earlier mode of listening for echoes of the past in the context of the "timeless unconscious." The focus sharply distinguishes between the transference and the patient-therapist relationship. Not all the events that occur in the patient-therapist relationship are transferential, because shame and guilt are being evoked in almost every session. The focus thus intensifies the analysis of the patient-therapist relationship. This vigilance in pursuing the patient-therapist relationship makes it easier to retrieve and rework illuminating transferences from the past. Even more important, it helps prevent symptom formation as a side effect of treatment itself.

It has been my experience that patients benefit from this guided tour through their own "superego" upheavals. A particular therapeutic boon is that the focus makes it easier for patients to see that it is he or she who is being judgmental, not the therapist. The therapeutic situation becomes less painful because the therapist is experienced as more accepting and supportive of the self than is the patient. The inevitable shame evoked by this contrast is itself a fruitful source of insight into the sequence from shame into humiliated fury and thence into guilt for "unjustified" hostility. It has been my experience that patients who do not have the prior expectation that treatment should last several years have been able to terminate in a relatively short time. I now routinely practice a form of dynamic focused psychotherapy that often, although not always, turns out to be short term. Professional therapists in training with me are one exception to this description. The endless demand on one's shame and guilt which being a therapist entails requires a more rigorous code of self-understanding than most nontherapists need. For the rest, although I am not in a hurry to terminate, I am much more receptive to patients' suggestions that they are ready than I used to be when a 2-year stretch seemed the irreducible minimum that could be useful.

The phenomenology of shame and guilt involves an examination of these two affective states with respect to the position of the self in the field of experience. Three aspects of the concept of the self are involved in a comparison of the states. These are: the self as an "identity"; the self as a "boundary"; and the self as a "localization" of experience "inside" or "outside" the self.

The self refers to a registration of experience as belonging to one's own *identity*. In this respect, shame and guilt are both registered as one's own experience. Shame, however, involves more self-consciousness and more self-imaging than guilt. The experience of shame is directly about the *self*, which is the focus of a negative evaluation. In guilt, it is the *thing* done or undone that is the direct focus of negative evaluation. We say, "I am ashamed of *myself*" and "I am guilty of having *done* (or *not done*) *something*." Because the self is the focus of awareness in shame, "identity" imagery is usually evoked. At the same time that this identity imagery is registering as one's own experience, there is also vivid imagery of the self in the other's eyes. This creates a "doubleness of experience," which is characteristic of shame. This double experience is a frequent basis for what Freud called the "internal theater" of the self in its own and other's eyes that is so characteristic of hysterical patients.

A second aspect of the self is that it has *boundaries* that distinguish the self's experiences and the "other's" experiences. The boundaries are often routinely and safely crossed when one has a vicarious experience with someone emotionally close. Even when two people have not been previously close, the self may function vicariously. In experiments involving the Zeigarnik effect, it could be demonstrated that when two people were working cooperatively, there was no difference in recall between those tasks personally completed and those actually completed by the cooperating partner (Lewis, 1944; Lewis & Franklin, 1944). Shame is the vicarious experience of the other's negative evaluation. In order for shame to occur, there must be a relationship between the self and the other in which the self cares about the other's evaluation. This is a particularly important point because shame is often given the narrow meaning of either "fear of getting caught" or else a "narcissistic" reaction. The other is also an important figure in the shame experience, usually in the position of being admired. Fascination with the other and sensitivity to the other's treatment of the self renders the self more vulnerable to shame. Shame is actually close to the feeling of awe. It is also the feeling state in which one is susceptible to falling in love.

Guilt also involves the self in vicarious experience. But it is the experience of the other's harm, injury, or suffering. By implication, the self *is able, has done*, or *has not done* something. At the moment of shame, in contrast, the self *is unable* to avoid the vicarious experience of the other's negative evaluation of the self. In guilt, vicarious experience involves a more intact self; in shame, vicarious experience involves a self suffering the (admired or beloved) other's disapproval or scorn.

A third aspect of the self is that it is a perceptual product that *localizes experiences* as originating "out there" or "within the self." Both localizations, however, are registered as one's own experience. Shame, which involves more self-consciousness and more self-imaging than guilt, is likely to involve a greater increase in feedback from all perceptual modalities. Shame thus has a special affinity for stirring autonomic reactions, including blushing, sweating, and increased heart rate. Shame usually involves more bodily awareness than guilt, as well as visual and verbal imaging of the self from the other's point of view. Shame is thus a more acutely painful experience than guilt. Because the self is involved in imagery of itself in relation to others, it can appear as if shame originates "out there," whereas guilt appears to originate "within." This characteristic makes shame appear to be a more primitive or irrational reaction than guilt. Both states, however, involve the self in trying to maintain affectional ties to significant others. Shame is the experience of losing self-esteem in one's own and others' eyes. It is the experience of failure. Guilt is the experience of injuring others or things and requires that one make appropriate reparation.

There are intrinsic difficulties in the states of shame and guilt that can impede their resolution or discharge. These may be grouped under three headings. First, difficulties in recognizing one's own psychological state can arise from the fact that shame and guilt are often fused and therefore confused. Shame and guilt may both be evoked simultaneously by a moral transgression. The two states then tend to fuse as the experience of guilt. The dictionary confirms this observation by defining shame as an acute or "emotional" sense of guilt (Lewis, 1971). Shame of oneself is thus likely to be operating underneath guilt for transgression.

The self-reproaches that are likely to be formed as guilty ideation develops might run as follows: How could I have *done that*? What an injurious *thing to do*. How I have *hurt* so-and-so. What a moral lapse that *act* was. What will *happen to* (or *become of*) him or her? How should I be *punished*? What must I *do* to make *amends*? *Mea culpa!* Simultaneously, shame ideation says: How could *I* have done that? What a *fool* — what a *bad person* — not like *so-and-so*, who does not do such things. *How worthless I am. For shame!*

When shame and guilt are evoked simultaneously by transgression, the shame or personal failure component, although acute, can be buried in guilty ideation and remain active even after appropriate amends have been made. This is a frequent source of unresolved obsessive dilemmas.

A second difficulty in the resolution of states of shame and guilt arises from the fact that the stimulus to shame can be twofold: Either a moral transgression or a failure can evoke shame. Ausubel (1955) has drawn attention to the twofold stimulus evoking shame, distinguishing between moral and nonmoral shame. When nonmoral shame is evoked, it readily connects with moral shame. For example, under the press of shame for competitive defeat or sexual rebuff, one can begin an immediate search for the transgressions that make sense of the injury one has suffered. Thus, shame has a potential for a wide range of associative connections between failures of the self and its transgressions.

There are many varieties of shame phenomena that need to be accurately identified. Mortification, humiliation, embarrassment, feeling ridiculous, chagrin, shyness, and modesty are all different psychological states, but with the common property of being directly about the self and overtly involving the other as referent in the experience. As a beginning to the study of these states, I treat them as variants of the shame family, but with different admixtures of pride and of self-directed hostility. Humiliation, for example, is experienced either in one's own or in the other's eyes and can involve rapid shifts of position of the self from one stance to the other. Embarrassment, to take another example, involves the self in a feeling of temporary paralysis or loss of powers in relation to the other. Mortification, in contrast, has a clear element of conscious, wounded pride and involves the self in a more distant relationship to the other.

Most important for the appropriate discharge of the shame state is the awareness that shame can be discharged in good-humored laughter at the self and its relation to the other. After all, shame is "only about the self." This is an observation that Freud (1905) first made in his remarkable study of the way jokes dissolve humiliation (for a fuller treatment, see Lewis, 1983). Because shame responses are so florid and so painful, however, there has been a tendency to regard them as pathological regressions, a view that coincides with the patient's shameful imagery of himself or herself. One is ashamed of being ashamed, thus compounding the difficulty of finding a rational solution in some gentle ridicule.

Guilt, in contrast, is about *things*. It therefore has an "objective" quality (Heider, 1958). It is this objective quality that has led theoreticians to regard guilt as a higher order response than shame. It is often difficult, however, to assess the degree of one's responsibility or to assess the degree of punishment that is appropriate. When guilt is evoked, it can thus merge into a "problem" of the rational assignment of motivation, responsibility, and consequences. As the person becomes involved in these problems, it can happen that guilty affect subsides, whereas ideation about how to make amends continues. Guilt thus has an affinity for "insoluble dilemmas" in which the self is active, self-contained, but unable to stop thinking about what to *do*. (The Rat-Man is a classic example of the profound connection between unresolved guilt, bypassed shame, and insoluble obsessive dilemmas; see Lewis, 1971.) In addition, the unconscious gratification of being in a morally elevated state of guilt sometimes keeps the state active beyond the time of restitution or expiation.

A third difficulty intrinsic in both shame and guilt is encountered in discharging the hostility that is naturally evoked in both states. In shame, hostility against the self is experienced in the passive mode, as emanating from the other. (Indeed, in many instances, this perception is accurate.) When shame is evoked by personal betrayal or by unrequited love, the self feels crushed by the rejection. The self feels not in control but overwhelmed and paralyzed by the hostility directed against it. One could "crawl through a hole," "sink through the floor," or "die" with shame. The self feels small, helpless, and childish. So long as shame is to the fore in consciousness, it is the other who is experienced as the source of hostility. Hostility against the rejecting or betraying other is almost simultaneously evoked. But it is humiliated fury, or shame-rage, which is simultaneously being processed as "inappropriate" or "unjust" fury. To be furious and enraged with someone because one is unloved by him (or her) renders one easily and simultaneously guilty for being unjustly enraged. Evoked hostility is readily redirected back upon the vulnerable self in the form of more shame and guilt. Evoked shame-rage, moreover, inevitably produces retaliatory feelings that "turn the tables" on the other. But so long as the other continues to be loved or valued, the awareness of one's humiliated fury is muted, and it is "turned back upon the self" transformed into depression.

When hostility is evoked in connection with guilt, what is experienced is righteous indignation, which is considered an "appropriate" reaction. The consciousness of guilt and its appropriateness may actually be a quiet source of gratification in being morally elevated. Righteous indignation requires the correct assessment of blame, and the ideation that develops is busy determining responsibility both of the self and of others. The position of the self as the initiator of guilt puts the self "in charge" of the allocation of blame and of the assessment of happenings in the field. The active role of the self in guilt opens the possibility that hostility may be directed not only against the self but against the other and against forces in the field, thus creating an affinity between guilt and the projection of hostility. The affinity between guilt and the necessity to do something to make amends creates a readiness to transform guilt into obsessive ideation. The projection of hostility outward creates the familiar transformation of guilt into paranoia.

Table 6.1 summarizes the phenomenological description of shame and guilt and the working concepts that emerge.

II.

Over the years as a practicing psychoanalyst, I became slowly convinced that unanalyzed shame in the patient-therapist interaction is a

TABLE 6.1
Summary of Phenomenology of Shame and Guilt

	Shame	Guilt
Stimulus	Disappointment, defeat, *or* moral transgression	Moral transgression
	Deficiency of *self*	Event; *thing* for which self is responsible
	Involuntary; self *unable*, as in unrequited love	Voluntary; self *able*
	Encounter with "other" *or* within the self	Within the self
Conscious Content	Painful emotion	Affect may or may not be present
	Autonomic responses: rage, blushing, tears	Autonomic responses less pronounced
	Global characteristics of self	Specific activities of self
	Identity thoughts; "internal theater"	No identity thoughts
Position of Self in Field	Self passive	Self active
	Self focal in awareness	Self absorbed in action or thought
	Self-imaging and consciousness; multiple functions of self	Self intact, functioning silently
	Vicarious experience of other's negative view of self	Pity; concern for other's welfare
Nature and Discharge of Hostility	Humiliated fury	Righteous indignation
	Discharge blocked by guilt and/or love of "other"	Discharge on self and other
Characteristic Symptoms	Depression; hysteria "affect disorder"	Obsessional; paranoid "thought disorder"

Shame Variants: humiliation, mortification, embarrassment, chagrin, shyness

Guilt Variants: responsibility, obligation, fault, blame

frequent source of what is euphemistically called 'negative therapeutic reactions" or, more bluntly, therapeutic failure. These observations have been detailed more fully in some of my other publications (see Lewis 1971, 1981, 1983). I have the hunch that some of the cases Kohut (1971) and Kernberg (1975) call "narcissistic" personality are cases in which shame has been ignored or bypassed in the patient-therapist interaction with surprising and often very florid sequelae into symptoms (Lewis, 1980).

A second source of my focus on shame and guilt in neurosis was my work over the years with H. A. Witkin on field dependence (Witkin et al., 1954). These years studying the differing organization of the self in field-dependent and field-independent cognitive styles were also years in which I was trying to identify the sources of unexpected therapeutic failures. Field dependence is a construct that we pursued partly because it was congenial to a psychodynamic view of perception. The idea that personality style might be reflected in characteristic modes of orienting oneself in space was developed as part of the "New Look" at cognition that characterized the psychology of perception in the late 1940s and early 1950s. Field dependence is a cognitive style that catches the self in relation not only to its physical surround but in relation to significant others. It should also be noted in passing, that the Gestalt psychologist, Wertheimer, whose work we were extending, had a working concept of the self as early as 1912. Similarly, Freudian revisionists during the 1940s and 1950s, principally Horney and H. S. Sullivan, were also developing a working concept of the self. It is thus somewhat ironic that self psychology has only recently been rediscovered by Kohut and others as a necessary addition to classical psychoanalytic thinking.

During the 1960s, Witkin, Edmund Weil, and I (Witkin et al., 1968) planned and executed a study in which we predicted that field-dependent patients would be more prone to shame than to guilt in their first therapeutic encounters, whereas field-independent patients would be more prone to guilt than to shame. The transcripts of the first two psychotherapy sessions of "pairs" of field-dependent and independent patients in treatment with the same therapist were assessed for their implied affective content by Gottschalk and Gleser's (1969) reliable and valid method. As predicted, field-dependent patients showed significantly more shame anxiety than guilt anxiety, whereas field-independent patients showed significantly more guilt than shame. The success of these predictions encouraged me to undertake my phenomenological study.

Our study of field-dependent and field-independent patients also yielded evidence that, as one might expect on an introspective basis alone, shame and self-directed hostility occur in conjunction with each other. This finding was subsequently confirmed (Safer, 1975; Smith, 1972). Guilt, in contrast and surprisingly, occurred in our transcripts in conjunction with hostility directed outward and inward with about equal frequency.

Once the results on shame and field dependence and on guilt and field independence were in place, several other well-known facts could be assembled to form a network of connections for predicting forms of psychopathology, including sex differences in proneness to depression and paranoia (Lewis, 1976, 1978). Robust evidence now connects field dependence and depression (Crouppen, 1976; Levenson & Neuringer, 1974; Newman & Hirt, 1983; Witkin, 1965; Witkin et al., 1954). Field independence, as might be expected, is linked to paranoia (Johnson, 1980; Witkin, 1965; Witkin et al., 1954). The well-established sex difference in field dependence neatly parallels the sex differences in proneness to depression and paranoia. Women are more field dependent and more prone to depression. Men are more field independent and prone to paranoia, especially between the ages of 15 and 35 (Lewis, 1976, 1978). This congruence between sex differences in cognitive style and in forms of pathology may be connected to shame and guilt as possible mediators of the differences. Smith (1972) predicted and confirmed a connection between shame and depression. Izard (1972) has good evidence for the existence of shame in the emotion profiles of depressed patients. The projection of guilt in paranoia has been an accepted clinical observation since Freud's (1911) unraveling of Schreber's delusions. The empirical evidence, however, for the connection between guilt and paranoia is less well developed than the evidence for a connection between shame and depression.

Evidence from cognitive and behavioral approaches to depression strongly suggests the usefulness of considering shame as a major component of depression (Lewis, in press). In a reformulation of learned helplessness theory, for example, Abramson, Seligman, and Teasdale (1978) suggest that depression is the end product of a faulty attributional style in which people focus on their personal helplessness. Specifically, learned helplessness theory assumes that people who ascribe the causes of "bad events" to "internal," "stable," and "global" personal traits (ISG attributions) are likely to be depressed.

In a further refinement of ISG style, Peterson, Schwartz, and Seligman (1981) have found that depressed women undergraduates were more likely to blame their *characters* for bad events than they were to blame specific *behaviors*. (If anything, blame for behaviors was negatively correlated with depression.) If we equate blame of the self for its character with shame and blame for behaviors with guilt, we may glimpse a convergence of evidence from behavioral and psychoanalytic sources suggesting the role of shame in depression. Indeed, the most hopeful sign of fruitful collaboration between behavior theorists and psychoanalysts is the evidence provided by Peterson, Luborsky, and Seligman (1983) that depressive mood can be predicted from ISG attributions.

Behavior theorists have described a cognitive paradox in depression: If depressed people are as helpless as they feel, logic dictates that they should not also feel self-reproaches (guilt) for what they are unable to do (Abramson & Sackeim, 1977; Peterson, 1979; Rizley, 1978). This paradox vanishes, however, if we assume that depressed people are helpless to change the vicarious experience of another's negative feeling about the self–(i.e., to get out of a state of shame). Humiliated fury won't do it; expressing such fury is likely to get the self into even more trouble with the other, especially as humiliated fury is felt by the self to be inappropriate and blameworthy, leading to guilt as well as shame.

One small finding of a behavioral study (Lamont, 1973) from more than a decade ago seems to capture the essence of the connection between shame and depression. In this study, the following cognitive message was demonstrated to have a strong positive effect on dysphoric people. It read: "We don't have that much control over other peoples' feelings [no shame at loss] and we don't have to feel responsible for how other people feel [no guilt]" (p. 320; the brackets enclose my interpolations).

III.

A brief reinterpretation of an acknowledged "mistake" by a distinguished psychoanalyst can be used to illustrate the difficulty of correctly identifying a patient's state of guilt. Overt shame, although often unacknowledged, is somewhat easier to identify because there are more nonverbal signals of it. Malan (1976) describes an incident early in his work with brief dynamic psychotherapy in which an ill-chosen interpretation may have contributed to a worsening of the patient's condition. Here is the incident:

> A man walked into a hospital where I was casualty officer, complaining of the fear that he might kill his wife. Questioning revealed that while he was serving abroad in the Army during the war his wife had an affair with another man and had had a child. Being inexperienced and full of enthusiasm for the power of interpretation, I said to him: "So you have good reason to want to kill your wife." He made no clear response to this and went off. Two days later he came back in an exalted state, demanding of everybody: "Do you believe in the Lord?" He was clearly psychotic and had to be admitted as an emergency patient.

Malan's interpretation had sympathized with and probably increased the patient's humiliated fury. It did not pick up on the patient's more *proximal* complaint: that he was *afraid* he would kill his wife. The patient was, without being aware of it, in a state of *guilt* for what he wanted to do to his wife. Translating "I am afraid I will kill her" into "You must be in a state of guilt for wanting to kill her" is not only accurate, but it reminds the patient of his own good judgment. Although the patient's guilt state is unrecognized by him, its existence is nevertheless the source of his fear of what he might compulsively do: commit a crime and an injustice in the name of bringing justice to his wife. Guilt clearly rests on the humiliated fury or shame-rage that the patient has been harboring and simultaneously recognizing as unjust. His psychotic symptom can be understood as a condensation of his scorn or ridicule of the therapist who tacitly gives him permission to kill as if he (and the therapist) were the Lord.

I now describe in very condensed form the course of my treatment with two young men, one of whom was an obsessional, the other a depressive-hysterical personality. Both were roughly the same age, from the same cultural background, and equally caught in fairly serious trouble. Both young men, as it happened, had mysterious childhood illnesses when they were about 7 years old. These illnesses were clearly related in the patient's mind to masturbation. Patient X had a very field-independent cognitive style. Patient Y had a less field-independent cognitive style, although it was not extremely field dependent. Their cognitive style is mentioned in passing only as a reminder of the association that has been noted between field independence and obsessional defenses and between field dependence and depression. Patient X came to treatment for relief of a 4-year-long potency failure. He was seen three times a week for 100 hours. Patient Y came to treatment in an acute depression. He was seen three times a week for 2 months and twice a week for another 2 months before termination. (Both of these cases are described at greater length in Lewis, 1971, a book which also contains many detailed tracings of symptom formation from evoked and undischarged shame and guilt.)

Patient X opened his first consultation session by saying: "It's embarrassing for a man, but I'm impotent." He reported that the last time he had been sexually potent was some 4 years ago with the woman who had been his fiancée at the time. He then described numerous failures in the subsequent years. At this first session, the analytic task was set at finding the feeling source that issues in a recurrent inhibition of the patient's sexual arousal. Without specifically naming shame and guilt as the sources that issue in the inhibition, I offered help in tracing the sequence that evokes doubt and anxiety whenever intercourse begins.

The chain reaction by which the embarrassing symptom itself evokes anxiety and doubt, and thus reproduces itself, was also indicated. It is important to note that setting the analytic task as the analysis of sequences does not focus on the reconstruction of childhood events. These are by no means unwelcome or unimportant, but they are not the central goal of the analytic work.

The patient was visibly relieved by the formulation of the analytic task, which although obvious, had not occurred to him in quite this way. The identification of anxious and doubting thoughts as one of his present troubles made his potency symptom seem more mundane and more manageable. As became clear in later sessions, it was a very specific relief of the thoughts he had been entertaining as to the reasons for his impotence. These had included terrifying (unidentified) shame images of his symptom as a reflection of some underlying deep-seated character deficiency. The patient, who was sophisticated psychologically, was caught up by the many characterological descriptions with which psychoanalysis abounds and was applying these to himself. For example, one idea he entertained was that he was "really a homosexual." That he had felt like refusing some homosexual offers that had been made to him could be evidence that he was repressing his homosexuality; the same interpretation could be given for the fact that men did not attract him sexually, whereas women did. Identifying the work of psychoanalysis as the analysis of sequences from evoked feelings into symptoms thus keeps the analytic work away from pejorative characterological descriptions and focuses on feeling states and their cognitive content. It is my belief that this focus helped to speed the recovery.

In response to the patient's opening remark: "It's embarrassing for a man, but I'm impotent," I had replied: "Yes. I should think it would also be infuriating." The patient had spoken of his embarrassment without at the moment appearing in any way embarrassed. Nonetheless, I wished particularly to acknowledge the "natural" place of embarrassment or shame in his difficulties. I also made a mental note that my patient needed at some time in our work to introspect fully the affective-cognitive state of embarrassment and its aftermath. My reply, directing his attention to his fury, served to make a first connection between the state of embarrassment and humiliated fury. The latter affective state is likely to give way to guilt.

It should be noted that the patient's anxiety and doubt were not "ego-alien." The patient was not suffering from "crazy" ideas about his potency; these he would have been able to identify more clearly as obsessive. That perfectly rational thoughts about one's own situation are nevertheless sometimes primary process transformations of bypassed shame and guilt is another important point of technique. In this instance, the patient's persistent anxiety about his potency was first shown to be obsessive. The patient had been vaguely aware that it would be better for him if he were not anxious about his potency. He had, in fact, spent some 4 years trying to persuade himself that the "next time" he would be without anxiety and therefore successful. He was, however, unable to banish his anxious and doubting thoughts because they were obsessive thoughts carried by a current of bypassed shame. This same bypassed shame was identifiable in subsequent sessions as the precipitating stimulus to his first potency failure.

The reality or correctness of a patient's self-description is always difficult to assess. What the therapist (and the patient) can be sure of is the immediate feeling state out of which the self-description emerges and the negative or positive feeling state which the self-description thus reflects. Freud (1917), it will be remembered, had difficulty assessing the "reality" of the depressive patient's self-reproaches. On the one hand, he wondered "why a man has to be ill before he can be accessible to a truth [viz., that he is] . . . petty, egoistic, dishonest, lacking in independence, one whose sole aim is to hide the weakness of his own nature" (p. 246). On the other hand (and on the next page), Freud takes the view that there is "no correspondence, so far as we can judge between the degree of self-abasement and its real justification. A good, capable, conscientious woman will speak no better of herself after she develops melancholia than one who is in fact worthless . . ." (p. 247). The therapist is clearly on firmer ground if he or she does not take a position on the content of the patient's self-reproaches, but rather calls the patient's attention to his or her state of shame or guilt. My technique thus minimizes the danger that the therapist will get caught up in analyzing the content of the patient's (often rational) self-reproaches, without first calling the patient's attention to his or her implicit state of shame or guilt.

The patient had somewhat startled me in his first session by observing, shortly after his first remarks about his impotence, that he felt "well-adjusted otherwise" (i.e., apart from his symptom of potency failure). He pursued this theme of being well-adjusted otherwise by voicing the hope that he would not need to undergo an intensive, long-term analysis leading to a character reorganization. He wished that his potency symptom could be removed and that he would be left unchanged. I remember being on the verge of explaining to him (what I then believed) that symptoms cannot be directly attacked because they have their origin in character organization, except that some combination of kindness and unwillingness to dispute with him made me forbear. I felt he had enough trouble, without getting more "bad news." In looking back on the hour, it seemed to me that the request was reasonable enough if the patient felt content with himself, as he was. Why should a patient not request symptom relief without character reorganization? Perhaps it could not be done. But why could the therapist not undertake to trace a symptom (i.e., to trace the incidence and subsidence of "primary process" transformation or symptom formation in the stream of consciousness) and leave it to the patient to see if, after symptom relief, he wished to pursue analysis further? The patient could always resume treatment if other symptoms occurred.

The likelihood was that the sequence from the affect source into anxiety had been formed in his childhood and had many parallels in his life pattern. The therapeutic issue the patient had really raised was: How many of these parallels did he have to see before he could feel reasonably in control of the sequence? This is an empirical question, without any fixed answer in terms of psychoanalytic theory or any other theory.

It was Freud's use of psychoanalysis as a method of research into development and as a method of treatment that resulted in a confound between finding the origin of an illness and finding a method for its treatment (see Lewis, 1981, for a fuller treatment of this point). It should be noted that my focus on sequences from evoked undischarged shame and guilt into symptoms is not a focus on direct removal of symptoms. It differs from cognitive and behavioral approaches which assume that symptoms arise out of faulty cognitions and which therefore arrange cognitive and behavioral programs designed directly to remove the symptom by a relearning or deconditioning process. In contrast, what happens during my sessions is close attention to the patient's stream of consciousness in pursuit of unconscious sequences from shame and guilt. However, because these states are cognitive as well as affective in their structure, patients also do learn about their own processes. What they learn is something more than ways of identifying misperceptions of the present because of its similarities to the past. There is, moreover, greater attention to hidden affective states as they actually occur than there used to be when pursuit of the past was a more central focus.

Like classical psychoanalysts, I recommend the use of the couch as an aid to relaxed free association and as means of speeding the process of treatment. I recommend it, however, only if the patient decides to come for treatment more than once a week and only after several weeks of face-to-face confrontation in which shame and guilt evoked in the patient-therapist relationship have been analyzed. The couch is used, it should be noted, with the expectation that it will shorten treatment by catching sequences more quickly and not as a signal for a long-term undertaking.

In the case of Patient X, for example, he inquired about using the couch after treatment was in progress for 3 weeks. In response to my recommendation that he use it, he replied that he "doesn't like being a thing" and "prefers to see my face." He was thus conveying the potential humiliation that he might experience if he were treated as a "thing": his preference for seeing my face reflected his vigilance against the scorn, located in the other, which might be experienced against himself. The patient was surprised when he realized that he was expressing shame ideation about lying on the couch; he was also surprised that there was an actual feeling of shame in these ideas. A few sessions later, he agreed to try the couch — it was more "sportsmanlike," he said, to follow my recommendation. He chose to do so at a time when he was beginning to be plagued by hostile thoughts about me. The absence of face-to-face confrontation saved him from the potential embarrassment of witnessing my reaction, and his own reaction to my reaction, to his wish to humiliate me. Needless to say, vigilance against leaving this sequence unanalyzed is necessary whether the patient uses the couch or not.

The patient had successful intercourse for the first time in his life when he was 21 years old with the woman who was then his fiancée and with whom he was passionately in love. He had successful intercourse with her several times thereafter; they lived in different cities, however, and could see each other only infrequently. Their engagement had been broken some months after their first intercourse. The patient had been unwilling to marry immediately because he could not support himself. He had some time before become dissatisfied with the well-paying career he thought he wanted and had prepared for in college, and changed to a riskier but intellectually more attractive career in the arts. This meant that he would be unable to support a household in the immediately foreseeable future. His fiancée had not wanted to postpone marriage, and therefore, they agreed to part. Shortly after they broke up, she married someone else.

Before his first sexual intercourse, Patient X had many hesitations and scruples about it. He had great difficulty in controlling his passion for her but had felt very guilty about his wish for intercourse because he was sure he was not able or willing to marry immediately. (His fiancée had been previously betrayed by a man "without scruples"; the patient was determined not to hurt her.) On the evening when success in his new work made it seem more likely that he would have a career as an artist, he overcame his guilty scruples and allowed himself to have intercourse for the first time.

It was in connection with this first occasion of sexual intercourse that Patient X received a psychic blow. His fiancée said, after intercourse, that she had worried about his potency because he had been so tardy in taking her to bed. In a sudden reorganization of the patient's perceptual field with regard to himself, hesitations that the patient had understood as a result of a principled conflict became an indication of cowardice: fear of impotence. The patient's prior ethical struggle and his efforts at self-control of his sexual urge were an indication of impotence in his beloved's eyes. What the patient had been processing as guilt, she had understood as something shameful.

The patient was not aware of any feeling of anger or of hatred toward her at the time they first had intercourse. He had registered, only peripherally, that he had received some kind of psychic blow. That his scruples had not been appreciated, but on the contrary, had been interpreted as inadequacy, was a mortification that he experienced not with the full affect of shame, but rather as a jolt or "jar." In an instant, however, the self was cast down from the relatively elevated position it had occupied as the protector of her welfare to the humiliated position implied in her view of him – afraid he might not be potent in intercourse and blind to his own motivations. This shift of the self from an elevated position in his own eyes to a mortified one in her eyes, from a scrupulous man to a man of doubtful potency, had taken place without any awareness of the affects of rage and shame that were involved, except the experience of a "blow." We are assuming that the rage evoked in conjunction with the shift in position of the self was trapped by its origin in his own previously unconscious "being pleased with himself" for being ethical. Rage was thus transformed into shame about his having been such a "fool." It was also trapped against the self in guilt for being in a rage at her. The patient experienced considerable bitterness in describing retrospectively his scruples about intercourse: He spoke scornfully of himself as a "moral prig" or a "minor-league mystic."

The patient remembered that when he left her that night he was thinking there must be something wrong with his "capacity to love" because he did not feel as rejoicing as he had expected he would feel after having made love. He also had a very vivid recollection of hearing her say: "I was worried about you," as he saw "the semen running down her thighs." It became apparent that this vivid recollection of seeing the semen running down her thighs functioned as a reassurance to him that he had actually ejaculated on this occasion. As he had gone over the experience of her remark over and over in his mind, he had actually wondered if they did have intercourse. The doubt was very transient and always ended in the certainty that they had. But it was thus apparent that doubt (obsessive doubt) had made its appearance in the aftermath of their first intercourse, stirred by a current of guilt for bypassed humiliated fury at his beloved's doubting (and unconsciously cruel) remark.

The patient had intercourse again with his fiancée the next night and remembers that he again felt guilty about rejoicing less than he should.

He remembers again thinking that there was something wrong with his capacity to love. As indicated previously, their engagement was terminated by mutual consent some months after the events described. Thereafter, to the patient's growing concern, he found himself with potency loss on attempting intercourse with other women even though he was very much attracted and aroused to the point of erection.

Let us examine more closely the process by which the woman's doubt about her lover's potency became the patient's doubt about it, an obsessive doubt which ultimately inhibited erection. Consider, first, Patient X's state of recently overcome guilt about having intercourse with his fianceé without being certain of their plans for marriage. It was inevitable that Patient X should be in a background state of guilt toward his fiancée, specifically for wanting to have intercourse with her without being perfectly committed to marriage. This guilt, which can seem excessive to an observer, is compelling to the protagonist. The guilt is not just for having intercourse – an event easily brought into harmony with the mores of sexual freedom – but for the implied personal betrayal in his doubts about marriage. These doubts placed him in a position in which he was practicing hypocrisy if he did not take his girl into his confidence. Patient X was thus in a background state of guilt for hypocrisy or deceit. He could not explain his scruples because this meant acknowledging to his girl his reservations about their future. As it turned out, this psychic state unconsciously reproduced X's state of "guilt for deceiving" after childhood masturbation.

Another reason he suffered a "mortification in silence" from her remark was that he was in love with her. (This itself was a reason for his having withheld his scruples from her, for fear of losing her.) In the state of being in love, the full mortification of her thinking he was impotent was intolerable. It would have involved him in hating her for thinking so little of him. Because he loved her, his hatred was trapped and could find expression only against himself. The patient's being in love thus made him more vulnerable to a shaming remark from his beloved.

X thus began to think that there might be something wrong with his capacity to love. The content of his self-reproach in his background state of guilt was that he had taken her to bed without loving her enough. His self-reproach thus involved his capacity to love in a figurative sense. The content of her reproach to him was literal: that he had not been man enough to take her to bed sooner. Although the content of the two reproaches was thus different in meaning, the feeling of deserving reproach for some omission was picked up by the patient from her remark and "took hold" of his thoughts in the form of a doubt. The doubt is a comparison formation fusing his idea that he had taken her to bed when he should not have with her idea that he had not taken her to bed when he should have. As a result of his self-doubt, his girl remained (almost) untarnished as a love-object in his eyes. He was the fool, a "minor-league mystic," who perhaps did not realize, as she did, that he was afraid of being impotent.

If, now, in addition to the two immediate factors of being in a background state of undischarged guilt and of being in love, we add some predisposition from traumatic childhood experience to undischarged guilt connected with the shame of sexuality, we may understand how his beloved's remark, which might have been a trivial occurrence to some other man, was a powerful force toward symptom formation for Patient X.

The main events of the patient's biography were described by him in the early sessions; other events of psychological importance became apparent as analytic work progressed. His parents were separated when he was 3 years old, reunited when he was 4, and divorced when he was 5. The patient knew by family legend rather than by personal recollection the emotional turmoil that actually characterized his early childhood. At a point when he was contemplating termination of his analysis (against my advice), he found himself asking his mother about the events of his earliest years and was very much moved by her account of how desperately unhappy she had been when he was an infant. His mother told him that she had been close to suicide. He also learned then that he had cried incessantly during the first "terrible" year of his life.

His mother married again when he was 6, to the man who helped create a stable, loving household in which the patient grew up. The patient loved his stepfather, a kind, sensitive man who in turn loved him as if he were his own son. A sister was born when the patient was 7, and except for a childhood illness lasting a year, which occurred at about this time of the patient's life, the rest of his development was uneventful.

The childhood illness was a mysterious one, finally diagnosed as an allergy for want of some better explanation. The illness, however, which was characterized by fever, shortness of breath, vomiting, and malaise, kept the patient in bed for most of 1 year, coinciding with the year after his sister's birth. There had been a suspicion of rheumatic fever and heart enlargement. The patient remembered this time of his life with a mixture of pleasure and guilt. He remembers enjoying being "pampered" and also the conscious guilt that he experienced at making his mother wait on him. He remembers with particular pleasure that he spent long hours in bed fantasying—making up stories—and enacting them either with toys or else just in his head. Although the chronology of his illness clearly indicated some connection, if only in time, between his illness and the birth of his sister, the patient experienced doubt that the two events were at all connected, even with respect to time. He found the admission of some connection between the two events disturbing – specifically, the idea that his illness might have been an emotional one was humiliating.

A "sensible" pediatrician, one among many consulted over the course of this year, suggested to the child's mother that he might be suffering from "too many fathers" and suggested that the illness be more or less ignored. The child was returned to school. With this routine, or else spontaneously, the illness disappeared; however, it left behind extra anxiety about his physical functioning.

The patient's father was the image of villainy for him during his childhood and into adulthood: Father was thought to be a contemptible, dishonest, inconsiderate, "bad" man, who made mother suffer and was to be hated for it. The patient remembers that he was "not sorry" when he stopped seeing his father, only relieved. The patient was unaware that his background affect was guilt in this self-observation that he was "not sorry," only "relieved" not to see his father anymore. The guilty affect had found its expression in his observation about his "real" as opposed to "expected" feelings. He was, however, troubled by the obsessive thought that father would return to "spoil" his own (the patient's) special occasions. He remembers having the idea that father would come uninvited into his bar mitzvah, thus embarrassing both the patient and his stepfather. He also had the identical obsessive thought in connection with celebrations of his recent success in work. (Actually, the patient had recently met his father, by arrangement, after a lapse of many years and judged him to be a weak, "hypocritical," sorry figure of a man, whom the patient had no further wish to see.)

In this biographical sketch, we can observe two special sources of chronic guilt connected with sexuality: (a) the patient's illness and accompanying fantasy life and (b) his "justified" hatred of his father. Guilt that develops out of a conscious wish not to be like a contemptible father is likely to be strong. The contrast between the "good father," who made mother and child happy, and the "bad father" was very strong. The child's own lapses from goodness, his tendencies toward selfishness, weakness of character, inconsiderateness, and so forth thus contained the threat of the child's being as guilty (contemptible) as his father.

The patient's long and mysterious childhood illness was also a fertile time for guilt, specifically guilty fantasy about the self and the other. The patient remembers masturbating at this time. He was readily able to connect his conscious guilt for making his mother wait on him with guilt about "what he was doing in bed." As is almost always the case, guilt feeling for masturbation took the concrete form of self-critical ideas about "doubleness" or "hypocrisy" and "deceit." The (shameful) pleasure of fantasying about what the self and the other are thinking about and doing with each other is followed by guilt about the "deceptions" involved in the "private theater."

The patient's earliest childhood recollection was given spontaneously in the course of his biographical account. It is as follows: He was being taken care of by his maternal grandmother, his mother having absented herself in connection with separation from father. The incident occurred in a park when he was about 3 years old. A child asked him: "Are you Jewish?" He answered, "Yes." The child hit him, and he came crying to his grandmother, who said, "You should have said, 'I don't know.'" He remembers that he was surprised at her reply. That his grandmother should have counseled "hypocrisy," and made a virtue of cowardice, seemed to the patient a measure of the extent of influences in his family life that were opposed to his growth as a courageous man. I think it may also be regarded as a reflection of how occupied he was with guilt—in this instance, his grandmother's—and specifically with guilt about "hypocrisy."

It should also be noted that the patient's childhood illness was followed by a long interval of uncertainty about his physical health, specifically about the activities he might not be able to sustain. If we suppose that he made an emotional connection between masturbation fantasy and his illness, specifically a connection between guilt for masturbation and his illness, then we may understand that his girl's doubt about his potency connected, via his guilt, with earlier, "real" doubts about his "performance."

One analytic hour illustrates how the analysis of obsessive doubt about the time of the hour that developed in the transference was used to illuminate the development of doubt about potency. In the third week of his analysis, the patient phoned very early one morning to check on the time of his afternoon hour. (This followed a missed hour the week before, the result of the patient's having misheard the time; this slip had not been at all interpreted.) Although the patient had a clear recollection of our both repeating the correct time for the coming hour, he had awakened on this particular morning and found himself in sudden doubt about whether the hour was 3 o'clock (the correct time) or an hour earlier. His doubt was strengthened by the recollection of his previous mistake. His "instinct" told him it was 3 o'clock, but I "doubted my instinct," he said.

He also was aware that morning that he had "very little to say" in the coming hour. This felt to him like a shortcoming of some sort, a blank or empty mind. The patient was unaware that his having very little to say had any connection to the sudden appearance of doubt about the time of the hour. He gave me an amusing account of his general irregularity and sloppiness with respect to time. He had the thought and dismissed it that he might not have wanted to come to the session. He remembered that he had skipped dessert at a very pleasant luncheon before the preceding hour in order to make that one on time. I wondered whether this rush could have taken place without some resentment. He agreed that there might have been some trivial resentment at the inconvenience of interrupting lunch. He said he was also aware of some resentment at having to pay for sessions, when, in fact, the work involved has to do with his feelings and is therefore "priceless." But he knew that this cannot be helped. I agreed that analysis is an "anomalous situation." I also pointed out that trivial or inappropriate resentment may be even easier to bypass than justified resentment.

At this point, he remembered having had some thoughts about me "sitting there listening." These thoughts had occurred the previous night as he was getting ready for bed. He remembered being gratified that he had made me laugh during the preceding session. He had been giving thought to what I am thinking about as "I sit and listen": what kinds of "real" reactions I have in addition to professional ones; what I "really" think of him; what I am "really" like. This was also embarrassing, because he knew all this was "none of his business."

I pointed out that thinking about what I am thinking about him and telling me about it is embarrassing. Embarrassment evokes resentment; both are quickly buried in his guilty thought: "none of his busness." By some "psychic alchemy," I say, bypassed shame and resentment are transformed into "nuisance" thoughts connected with the hour. Doubts about whether his thought about the time of the hour is correct are somehow the product of his guilt, resentment, and embarrassment over his thoughts about what I am thinking during the time of his hour. He agreed that the thoughts this morning about the time were a "nuisance." In fact, he realized that he was really ashamed to call me to check the time and had to overcome this feeling before calling. "I really didn't want you to know – my pride wouldn't let me tell you I had forgotten the hour. It was really silly, since I'm always so sloppy about time."

I suggested that the structure of feeling underlying "nuisance" doubts about the time of the hour is the same as the structure of feeling underlying nuisance doubts about intercourse. Should I or shouldn't I call? Should I or shouldn't I try to have intercourse? Will I or won't I mistake the time? Will I or won't I be potent? Infuriatingly, once doubt starts it is very difficult to allay. The doubts about the time of the session originated in some bypassed embarrassment-resentment connected with my view of him. Doubts about his potency seem to have originated in bypassed shame-rage at his girl's shaming view of his scruples about intercourse. The patient saw the parallel and began to laugh. I had the impression that he was actually embarrassed by seeing the parallel.

Let us pause for a moment to see the parallels between the patient's situation in this analytic hour and many previous occasions in his life. His (embarrassing) thoughts about what I am thinking about him as I "sit there and listen" are parallel to fantasy (essentially sexual) about what the other thinks about the self. That the patient entered this kind of state with respect to me was a transference phenomenon of the most ordinary kind. The loss of awareness, which came with the transference sexual fantasy state, somehow involved a loss of awareness of certainty that he could trust his thoughts about the correct time. We may fill in the missing content: a loss of certainty that he could trust his thoughts about (what he was thinking about me and what I was thinking about him) the time of the hour. It is as if the material in parenthesis dropped out of awareness, leaving behind only the self's doubt that it knows the time of the hour. The shame involved in thinking of what I am thinking about him during the time of the hour has lost its connection with the self; the thoughts about the time of the hour remain, but in uncertain connection with self—in doubt.

The patient's very next set of thoughts after his seeing the parallel to doubt about intercourse took him to his own "inappropriate smile." The other day, as he had the task of telling a colleague some "bad news" at work, he had difficulty suppressing his own smiles at his colleague's histrionics. I understood his shift of thought as a relief of his own embarrassment of the moment. He remembered a time when he was a witness to the other's discomfiture. He felt guilty for his own inappropriate smile, as if he could help the "doubleness" of his feeling. In this self-reproach, I was also, by implication, included, with particular reference to my "gratifying" (maybe inappropriate?) laughter of the previous session. I did not analyze this sequence with him on this occasion. On many others, however, the sequence from his own embarrassment or shame with respect to me, into thoughts about the opposite position of the self as witness to my humiliation (my discomfiture as he sees me in unprofessional conduct, inappropriate behavior), and thence into guilt for pleasure in his enjoyment of being witness (his "sadism") could be analyzed in detail. Specifically, guilt feeling about fantasies of humiliating me could be shown to express itself in "back-and-forth" insoluble obsessive dilemmas resulting from what he thought I thought about him. If he thought I was thinking scornful thoughts, he would be offended, but also gratified by my guilt (like his) for feeling scorn. If he thought I was thinking admiring thoughts about him, he would be gratified, but also uncertain of my ability to remain objective. The dilemma was between thoughts of guilt and impotence (shame).

Part of the analytic process in this connection involved the spelling out of the way in which guilt ideation reflects guilty feeling. The patient opened an hour some months later by saying that he had trouble waking up and then went back to half-sleep. I asked if it is dreamless sleep. The patient said, "No," it is partly interrupted by (hypnagogic) fantasy. He wondered if this is "normal." I said he must be worried that it's "wrong." He slapped his hand to his head at his own blindness and agreed that his worry is a guilt product. But somehow, he said, he could never escape the feeling that indulging in sexual fantasy leads downhill (to shame).

After 5 months of treatment and potency successes, the patient began to experience a strong wish to terminate treatment. I counseled against this course on the ground of caution. The patient agreed that continuing would be wiser, and the next time he attempted intercourse, he found himself "self-conscious" and with a loss of erection. That night he had the following dream: He was with a woman, with a white body, seen only from behind. Her face was not visible. A man was also there, who gave the okay to go ahead with sex. The patient then "buggered" the woman, and she got up and started walking around town with his penis inside her anus. He could not withdraw his penis, so they went about their business this way.

The patient remembered that he had felt a little disappointed and a little bit put down at his decision to continue treatment, but on the whole, he was pleased with a "wise decision." His associations to the dream led him to thoughts about an older woman whom he met the night before and whom he despised because she made advances to him in the presence of her husband. This woman reminded him of me. The man in the dream was the woman's husband who, in reality, does not stand up to his wife.

A shift in position of the self into the position of the other was contained in the dream's first image of the woman seen from behind. The dream image turned things around (i.e., it is I who sit behind the patient). The patient realized that his dream about the woman with the white body was a dream about me. (This image was the same as in his first dream in treatment.) The fury that was underneath a "put down" became available to him from the content of the dream. We were able to understand that what had been evoked was retaliatory scorn of me for siding with his doubts. The image of us "stuck," and walking about the town for all to see our disgrace (?) was "double." I was disgraced; but was I not unshameable? He was disgraced; but it was his big penis that couldn't lose its erection. The patient saw the sequence between his put-down reaction and the "self-conscious" moment before intercourse. He understood that his potency failure was the byproduct not only of his slight conscious humiliation, but of guilt for unconscious, "unjust," throttled rage.

In the consultation hour, Patient Y stated the reason for seeking treatment as follows: I am totally self-destructive. That's what Q says [the wife of one of his closest friends, who had urged him to treatment], and she's right. I used to be a leader. Now I'm withdrawn in a corner, not myself, brooding, depressed. I know what the trouble is: I'm jealous. I need a job that gives me more scope. If I thought that getting a better job would make me happy, I wouldn't go into treatment. But I know better.

In this account by the patient of his difficulties, we find a sweeping negative generalization about himself. The patient feels he is so self-destructive that even if he got a better job, he wouldn't be happy and would need treatment.

It is tempting for the therapist to get caught up in the cognitive content of the patient's shameful and guilty ideation. For example, one could set the analytic task as finding the childhood reasons for why Y is so jealous and so self-destructive. Instead, it is important to point out to the patient that he is in an acute state of being ashamed of himself and guilty, as well, for jealousy.

The patient is also dissatisfied with himself for "jealousy"; his idea about it is that jealousy has transformed him into a brooding, depressed person. Although he is quite aware of the feeling of jealousy and is guilty about it, he is not aware that he is ashamed of this feeling and, moreover, that being in a state of jealousy (more accurately, envy) is a feeling of being somehow inferior to the other (i.e., ashamed). That rage accompanies this feeling, and that humiliated fury finds the self as its principal target, is what needs to be unraveled so that the sequence between feeling "jealous" (shame) and feeling depressed does not automatically occur.

In this first consultation session, the problem was set as "finding the sequence" that leads to depression. It was also possible to convey to the patient that he felt as guilty about his jealousy as if it were a "voluntary" reaction instead of a "natural" or inescapable reaction. The sweeping generalization implied in his remarks about himself was thus made more specific.

The patient was the eldest child of a prosperous professional family. He had a competent, devoted father and a nervous, devoted mother. His childhood and adolescence were entirely uneventful, except for a mysterious childhood illness when he was 7, which took the form of "seizures." There were suspicions of epilepsy or some other neurological disorder, which led to hospitalization for observation. But no neurological disorder could be found, and the seizures vanished after an interval. The patient did not remember this episode of his childhood until some weeks after treatment had begun. During a session when an acutely depressed weekend, culminating in a sleepless night, was being analyzed, he reminded himself of it.

It became apparent in the first week of treatment that the patient was suffering acutely from the breakup of his first and only love affair, which had been "on and off" for several years and was now most likely ending in his girl's marrying someone else. He was currently in the suspenseful state, waiting to hear of this marriage. This was the first girl with whom he had fallen in love; he wanted to marry her. She had at first refused him, but they continued to see each other. Some months later, after a pregnancy scare, she changed her mind and wanted to marry him, but he had suffered a loss of feeling for her. She then left the country, and he found himself utterly bereft in the ensuing year. There were emotional outbursts during which he couldn't stop weeping over his failure to have prevented her from leaving him. He had made it clear to her that he wanted her back, and they spent the next summer together. But he was not really sure she loved him, nor was he sure about why he was not more decisive about insisting that they marry.

This was the emotional background against which he judged himself "totally self-destructive," in agreement with his happily married friends. It was also apparent to the patient that although he loved his friends very much, he was now all the more envious of their happiness and particularly envious of the man who, by comparison with the patient, seemed so decisive and certain about his love for his wife.

The session after the patient described his terrible emotional outbursts after his girl had left (his fourth session) was marked by irritated feeling on his part about the analytic procedure. "I'm impatient," he said, "with this whole process." He found it unpleasant "not knowing what was going on" and particularly unpleasant to "see the wheels turning in my head." It was possible to show him that he had been embarrassed at describing his emotional storms, in which he reminded himself of his nervous mother. His irritability was a natural concomitant of embarrassment and was directed at the process that had evoked it.

In the next session, he reported an "awful weekend" in which he had been terribly depressed and unable to sleep. The sequence of events that preceded it was as follows: Y remembered that he had "felt badly" after the preceding session, although it was an "interesting one." That afternoon, moreover, he had been turned down for the better job that he was seeking. He experienced only a slight reaction, something like: "Too bad. They could have used me." But as the weekend progressed, he found himself growing more and more depressed and feeling more like the way he had felt when he couldn't stop weeping. "This must go very deep," he said, and remembered another woman friend of his who was "worried about him" (i.e., about his sanity). At that point in the hour, the

recollection of his childhood seizures came to him, and he described
these childhood events.

It was possible in this session to suggest that the disappointment in
failing to get a better job had joined with his embarrassment during the
preceding analytic hour to produce a feeling of shame, which Y experienced as depression. The disappointment over the job was "rationally
trivial" and had been experienced in that way. At the same time, an unavoidable feeling of "unrecognized merit" ("they could have used me")
was evoked. There had been sweet fantasies of getting the job so that
not only he but his friends would be pleased with his triumph. That
these feelings were in contradiction to his rational views would make
them easily bypassed with only a slight, conscious reaction. When, in addition, a feeling of shame evoked in the preceding hour was also present
and, specifically, shame before a woman, he might readily feel "awfully
depressed." He would remember that another woman friend had
"worried about his sanity" and remind himself of his seizures in childhood, which must have been very worrisome.

In the next session, the patient recalled additional details about his
childhood seizures. His account of them began: "It never happened in
public." He remembered, for example, that once when some cousins
were baby-sitting for him, he awoke and had a "seizure." He went to the
head of the stairs and realized that they "didn't see." He then went back
to bed and fell asleep. The patient readily appreciated that the "in public" aspect of his account bespoke his shame of seizures. The remainder
of this session was devoted to introspecting how envious and hateful he
can feel toward his friends, with the guilty question: Why do I feel so
jealous and hateful? I once again pointed out that he was feeling guilty
about a natural reaction of envy. I also suggested that the envy might be
less likely to be evoked if he felt surer that all the good things that happened to his friends were likely to happen to him (less guilty and therefore surer).

The patient missed his next hour because of the flu, but in spite of
being ill with a high fever, he had a "fantastically clarifying" insight. As
he went away from the preceding hour, wondering why he didn't feel
more confident that fate would also treat him kindly, he realized that he
had been carrying "a guilty secret" around with him for years. He had,
when he was an adolescent, once masturbated in public. He realized
over the weekend, as he recollected also the shame of his "seizures," that
he had felt tremendous shame over the occasion when he masturbated
in public. Actually, he does not know whether anyone saw him on that
occasion; he remembers only that he "came to" and found himself
masturbating on the street. He understood, he said, that although he
did not feel guilty about masturbation, because he knew it is universal,

he did feel ashamed of it and continued to feel ashamed of it. He always had the nagging thought, always immediately denied, that he had somehow damaged his potency. This must have accounted, he now realized, for some of the "sturm and drang" that had accompanied the breakup of his affair with his girl. Although he had never been impotent, he must have been terribly worried about himself (i.e., ashamed of himself "underneath"), as if he carried a stigma that he himself could not face. He felt that the insight he had over the weekend was "liberating." In fact, the patient had seen the connection between shame and obsessive ("nagging") thoughts about his sexuality.

In the following session, it was possible to trace with the patient the workings of embarrassment over telling me what "he never told anybody, and felt he never could." The evoked shame state expressed itself in some intrusive thoughts about what a girl with whom he walked to the bus would think about his walking her to the bus. (Would she think he was flirting with her?) In the subsequent hour, the patient announced that he felt calm and fine, and raised the possibility of his terminating the treatment. "Where do we go from here?" he asked and then worried that I would think him "too ebullient" or maybe that he was some kind of manic-depressive. The ideational route of hostility evoked in connection with shame vis-à-vis the analyst, and back from the analyst as target and onto the self, could be shown. The thought that I must think he was only unready to stop treatment, but a manic-depressive as well, was a boomerang from the impatient thought: What else has she got to say ("Where do we go from here?")?

The ideational components of depressed feelings were restored to the patient's awareness before he terminated analysis. Specifically, it was possible to show him that when he spoke of himself as "depressed," the language describing his emotional state involved a description that "fused" how he felt and how he must appear to the other. So, for example, he understood that humiliated fury, to which he did not feel he was entitled (i.e., he felt guilty), expressed itself as feeling "glum," "reticent," "withdrawn," "in a corner," "faceless," or "like a nobody there." All these subcategories of depressed feeling had in common thoughts about what the other might think about him. There was a fusion of how he felt and how the other felt about him. In this way, the fusion of the self and the other, which is the phenomenological characteristic of both depression and shame, could be shown to create the close similarity of feeling states in both experiences.

Emphasis on tracing the sequence from overt, unidentified shame into depressed feeling had two specific therapeutic advantages in this case. The patient became more aware of the episodic nature of his depression. Times when he was not depressed were recognized and rescued from the global self-dissatisfaction that tended to obscure other times in his first consultation session. The shame of having been depressed tends to evoke ideation in which the patient thinks of himself as "too ebullient" or "manic-depressive" when he is not depressed. The idea that depressed feeling is only about the self and only about some unidentified shame is also a therapeutic aid. The patient voiced this understanding when he said, "Is that all?" after the session in which he understood the connection between his guilty secret (shame of masturbation) and nagging thoughts about his sexual attractiveness and prowess. "Is that all?" tends to deflate analysis; it can also subtly deflate the analyst who may respond by reemphasizing the importance or gravity of the patient's symptoms. In addition to carrying deflating affect, however, "Is that all?" reflects the patient's perception of a characteristic of neurotic symptoms, namely, that they are only about the self. From this perception, there can come an increase in the ease with which the self rights itself and resumes its quiet functioning.

REFERENCES

Abramson, L., & Sackeim, H. (1977). A paradox in depression: Uncontrollability and self-blame. *Psychological Bulletin, 84,* 838–857.

Abramson, L., Seligman, M., & Teasdale, J. (1978). Learned helplessness in humans: Critique and reformulation. *Journal of Abnormal Psychology, 87,* 49–74.

Ausubel, D. (1955). Relationships between shame and guilt in the socializing process. *Psychological Review, 62,* 378–390.

Crouppen, G. (1976). *Field dependence in depressed and normal males, as an indication of relative proneness to shame and guilt and ego functioning.* Unpublished doctoral dissertation, California School of Professional Psychology.

Freud, S. (1905). Jokes and their relation to the unconscious. *S.E.,* 8.

Freud, S. (1911). Psychoanalytic notes on an autobiographical case of paranoia (dementia paranoides). *S.E.,* 12.

Freud, S. (1917). Mourning and melancholia, *S.E.,* 14.

Gottschalk, L., & Gleser, G. (1969). *The measurement of psychological states through content analysis of verbal behavior.* Berkeley: University of California Press.

Heider, F. (1958). *The psychology of interpersonal relations.* New York: Wiley.

Izard, C. (1972). *Patterns of emotion: A new analysis of anxiety and depression.* New York: Academic Press.

Johnson, D. (1980). *Cognitive organization in paranoid schizophrenics.* Unpublished doctoral dissertation, Yale University, New Haven, CT.

Kernberg, O. (1975). *Borderline conditions and pathological narcissism.* New York: Jason Aronson.

Kohut, H. (1971). *The analysis of the self.* New York: International Universities Press.

Lamont, J. (1973). Depressed mood and power over other people's feelings. *Journal of Clinical Psychology, 29,* 319–321.

Levenson, M., & Neuringer, C. (1974). Suicide and field dependency. *Omega, 5,* 181–185.

Lewis, H. B. (1944). An experimental study of the role of the ego in work: I. The role of the ego in cooperative work. *Journal of Experimental Psychology, 34,* 113–126.

Lewis, H. B. (1971). *Shame and guilt in neurosis.* New York: International Universities Press.

Lewis, H. B. (1976). *Psychic war in men and women.* New York: New York University Press.

Lewis, H. B. (1978). Sex differences in superego mode as related to sex differences in psychiatric illness. *Social Science and Medicine, 12,* 199–205.

Lewis, H. B. (1980). "Narcissistic personality" or "shame-prone" superego mode. *Comprehensive Psychotherapy, 1,* 59–80.

Lewis, H. B. (1981). *Freud and modern psychology: Vol. I. The emotional basis of mental illness.* New York: Plenum Press.

Lewis, H. B. (1983). *Freud and modern psychology: Vol. II. The emotional basis of human behavior.* New York: Plenum Press.

Lewis, H. (in press). The role of shame in depression. In M. Rutter, C. Izard, & P. Read (Eds.), *Depression in children: A developmental perspective.* New York: Guilford Press.

Lewis, H. B., & Franklin, M. (1944). An experimental study of the role of the ego in work: II. The significance of task-orientation in work. *Journal of Experimental Psychology, 34,* 195–215.

Malan, D. (1976). *The frontier of brief psychotherapy.* New York: Plenum Press.

Newman, R., & Hirt, M. (1983). The psychoanalytic theory of depression: Symptoms as a function of aggressive wishes and field articulation. *Journal of Abnormal Psychology, 92,* 42–49.

Peterson, C. (1979). Uncontrollability and self-blame in depression: Investigations of the paradox in a college population. *Journal of Abnormal Psychology, 88,* 620–624.

Peterson, C., Luborsky, L., & Seligman, M. (1983). Attribution and depressed mood shifts: A case study using the symptom-context method. *Journal of Abnormal Psychology, 92,* 96–104.

Peterson, C., Schwartz, S., & Seligman, M. (1981). Self-blame and depressive symptoms. *Journal of Personality and Social Psychology, 41,* 253–260.

Rizley, R. (1978). Depression and distortion in the attribution of causality. *Journal of Abnormal Psychology, 87,* 32–48.

Safer, J. (1975). *The effects of sex and psychological differentiation on response to a stressful group situation.* Unpublished doctoral dissertation, The New School for Social Research, New York.

Smith, R. (1972). *The relative proneness to shame and guilt as an indication of defensive style.* Unpublished doctoral dissertation, Northwestern University, Evanston, IL.

Witkin, H. (1965). Psychological differentiation and forms of pathology. *Journal of Abnormal Psychology, 70,* 317–336.

Witkin, H., Lewis, H., Hertzman, M., Machover, K., Meissner, P., & Wapner, S. (1954). *Personality through perception.* New York: Harper & Row.

Witkin, H., Lewis, H., & Weil, E. (1968). Affective reactions and patient-therapist interactions in more and less differentiated patients early in therapy. *Journal of Nervous and Mental Disease, 146,* 193–205.

7 The Heuristic Approach to Psychoanalytic Therapy

Emanuel Peterfreund, M.D.

It has been my conviction that very disparate and incompatible approaches to psychoanalytic therapy and psychoanalysis have been and are being practiced, all under the name of Freudian. Here, I believe, lies what may be the fundamental scientific problem in our discipline, a basic source of difficulty and confusion. In a recent work (Peterfreund, 1983), I attempted to delineate some of the basic characteristics of the spectrum of approaches now being practiced. Many of the approaches, ones I refer to as *stereotyped*, have in common the fact that they view the patient as but an example of an assumed body of *clinical theory*. In clinical theory I include such concepts as conflict, defense, mental representations, infantile sexuality, Oedipus complex, castration anxiety, penis envy, primal scene trauma, and the like. These are concepts used to order, organize, and explain psychoanalytic findings.

In contrast to these stereotyped approaches is one that focuses on the *therapeutic process*. A theory of the process refers, first, to the mode of psychoanalytic inquiry or investigation – the source of psychoanalytic understanding – and second, to the method of treatment. It includes the concepts of resistance, transference, interpretation, working through, and so on, concepts already familiar to psychoanalytic clinicians. But unfortunately, this theory is still in its infancy. With the aid of such basic concepts as working models and strategies, I have therefore attempted to further the development of the theory of the process. My efforts are based on what I call a *heuristic approach* to psychoanalysis and psychoanalytic therapy (Peterfreund, 1983) – heuristic because that word stresses the principal purpose of the process, which is to *discover*. The heuristic approach has long been practiced; it is not at all a new form of therapy. But it has remained largely unrecognized amid the many forms of treatment usually referred to as Freudian. The heuristic approach allows new awarenesses and understandings to emerge about an individual patient.

Because clinical theories stemming from Freud have played a dominant role, most stereotyped work has been based on his theories. For many years, therefore, case after case in the literature has been reported and discussed in terms of penis envy, castration anxiety, primal scene, Oedipus complex, and other such concepts. Of course, any clinical theory can be used as the basis for a stereotyped approach. In recent reports of stereotyped work, the terms have changed in keeping with the "newer" clinical theories. Thus, in addition to the concepts familiar to us from the 1940s through the 1960s, we now read about selfobject, grandiose self, infantile omnipotence, symbiotic phase, rapprochement subphase, splitting, narcissism, narcissistic rage, idealizing transference — the list is endless.

Common to all reports of stereotyped work is that they generally give us little understanding of the patient's personal psychology, the meanings and motivations that are unique to him. Instead, the patient is hammered onto the scaffolding of some clinical theory, and the unwillingness of any patient to being so impaled is all too often explained as a manifestation of resistance. In case reports, the patient is presented to us in the jargon of the clinical theory. But by and large, we are told virtually nothing about the therapeutic process—how the analyst arrived at his findings. And we are given equally little evidence for the clinical ideas presented—why, for example, one explanatory clinical hypothesis was selected instead of another. Furthermore, we are very often presented with the analyst's dynamic formulations but given no idea of whether they were accepted by, or had any meaning for, the patient.

Psychoanalysts have tended to write as though the term *analysis* spoke for itself, as if the statement "analysis revealed" or "it was analyzed as" preceding a clinical assertion was sufficient to establish the validity of what was being reported. An outsider might easily get the impression from reading the psychoanalytic literature that some standardized, generally accepted procedure existed for both inference and evidence. Instead, exactly the opposite has been true. Clinical material in the hands of one analyst can lead to totally different "findings" in the hands of another (see Peterfreund, 1983, chap. 1).

The analytic process—the means by which we arrive at psychoanalytic understanding—has been largely neglected and is poorly understood, and there has been comparatively little interest in the issues of inference and evidence. Indeed, psychoanalysts as a group have not recognized the importance of being bound by scientific constraints. They do not seem to understand that a possibility is only that—a possibility—and that innumerable ways may exist to explain the same data. Psychoanalysts all too often do not seem to distinguish hypotheses from facts, nor do they seem to understand that hypotheses must be tested in some way, that criteria for evidence must exist, and that any given test for any hypothesis must allow for the full range of substantiation/refutation.

Many of the characteristics of stereotyped analytic thinking can be seen in detailed reports of interactions between patient and analyst or in case summaries based on stereotyped work. I have used both methods elsewhere (Peterfreund, 1983). The first method is preferable, but the psychoanalytic literature surprisingly lacks such detailed reports of interactions with patients.

To highlight how rooted much analytic work is in an assumed body of clinical theory and the lack of interest in evidence and method, let me quote a case report I read when I was a candidate in training. At that time (it was in the mid-1950s), psychoanalysis wielded enormous influence and enjoyed unprecedented prestige. Its potential seemed unlimited. The case report I am about to cite differs from those found in the current literature only in superficial aspects (i.e., in the clinical theory it stresses and in the jargon it employs). The basic scientific problems inherent in this type of analytic work and case reporting remain unchanged.

The paper was entitled "Notes on Oral Symbolism" (Arlow, 1955) and includes the following case report:

A female patient had in common with her father an intense fear of fire, specifically that the fire would get out of control and do tremendous damage, killing people. The father had suffered mutilation of one of his limbs through an accident when he was a very young child. The patient identified herself with the castrated image of her father, nurturing unconscious fantasies of obtaining revenge for him and for herself and achieving at the same time restitution of the corresponding missing organs. She had entertained similar fantasies in childhood and during adolescence concerning the individual who had been responsible for the father's mutilation. These fantasies became associated in her mind with her envious feelings about her older brother. As a little girl she wanted very much to have dark curly hair like his and she had been told by her mother that if she ate lots of raw carrots her hair would curl, an anticipation in which she was sorely disappointed. A compulsion to stare at the genital region of men was analyzed as a displacement into the visual sphere of an oral wish to devour and incorporate the phallus.

During her treatment the patient's husband failed in a crucial professional competition. Through identification with him the patient again felt herself castrated. The analyst now represented to her the smug, successful victor in professional competition and, within this context in the transference, the wish to retaliate by castrating the analyst became very strong. While the patient was raging, and attributing her husband's professional setback to Jewish competitiveness and favoritism, she had the following dream.

> There was a tremendous crematorium furnace. It had a huge oval-shaped opening into which the people had been thrust and two smaller round glass windows through which she could see the flames destroying the victims.

She connected the two round windows with her eyes and with her need to stare at the genitals of men. The huge aperture represented a devouring mouth after the fashion of the well-known posters advertising the Steeplechase. During the session the patient complained of excessive salivation, her stomach 'growled,' and she felt, as she put it, an intense 'angry hunger.' The fire in the furnace thus symbolized her consuming oral rage against her husband's castraters and her own. (pp. 64–65)

My chief objection to this case report and the approach it reflects is that we hear of one conclusion after another but are given little if any evidence for these conclusions; we do not know how possible alternative interpretations of the data were ruled out. Apart from the implication that the analyst uses dreams, we have little idea of the nature of the therapeutic process; we have no way of knowing if the patient understood and accepted any of the formulations—or if they were offered. We know nothing about the patient's ability to work in a process, to explore experiences in depth and verbalize them, and so on. The case report is rooted in the clichés and jargon of the era, and we learn little of the patient's experience.

To be more specific, if a father was mutilated, why does it *necessarily* mean that he was seen as castrated? Perhaps this hypothesis is correct, but no evidence is given. We are told that the compulsion to stare at the genital region of men "was analyzed" as a displacement into the visual sphere of an oral wish to devour and incorporate the phallus, a statement we must accept on faith, for no evidence is given. Similarly, we are not given evidence for the statement that the husband's failure in a crucial professional competition is a "castration" in the patient's mind.

At only one point are we told something of what the patient is supposed to have understood or "connected" on her own, when she presumably connected the two round windows of the dream with her own eyes and with her need to stare at the genitals of men. But even here we are entitled to be skeptical. We know little of the mode of investigation; we do not know how she worked in the treatment process. Did she realize that she had the right to disagree completely with her analyst? Conceivably, this patient may well have learned her analyst's favorite themes and may possibly have learned to think (and perhaps even to dream) accordingly – a situation that, unfortunately, is all too common.

Arlow's understanding of the case may indeed be accurate. But he does not tell us how he arrived at his conclusions, nor does he distinguish his thinking and formulations from the patient's understanding. In every other discipline that makes some claim to scientific validity, conclusions are buttressed by evidence and a delineation of method. In any scientific discourse, we have every right to know something about the mode of investigation that led to the conclusions claimed. And if the method of investigation is not revealed or if it is faulty, we have every right to question and even dismiss the conclusions offered.

Any doubts about whether the example just given is typical can easily be put to rest by a perusal of the psychoanalytic literature. Indeed, I have found it bewildering that the fundamental problems concerning the process and the issue of evidence have received so little attention in a discipline whose members are, for the most part, medically and scientifically trained. What would we think of reports claiming the discovery of a new basic enzyme, a new neurotransmitter, a new drug useful for depression, or a new cure for cancer that did not detail the evidence or the nature of the investigation that led to the conclusions but merely stated that the issues "were scientifically investigated"?

In *The Process of Psychoanalytic Therapy* (Peterfreund, 1983), I led up to a description of my approach by defining and illustrating the strategies I advocate and what I call working models.[1] I presented case histories and many individual hours and clinical vignettes. In contrast to stereotyped approaches to analytic therapy, the heuristic approach, which I strongly advocate and to which I now turn, does not focus on an assumed body of clinical theory from which quick "answers" or understanding may be derived. It focuses on a *method of investigation* from which "answers" may hopefully emerge. It is rooted in a patient's experience, and it attempts to discover the unique nature of that patient's inner life. It emphasizes evidence and scientific constraints; hypotheses are open to substantiation or refutation. And it insists that the patient is an *equal partner* with the analyst in establishing the truth of what may

---

[1]"Working models" is a dynamic term borrowed from Bowlby (1969). It is closely related to the term "schemata" used in cognitive psychology. For a more detailed description of working models see Peterfreund (1983, chap. 6).

be going on in him. Finally, its "answers" are hard won, and no claim is made for any ultimate truth. Uncertainty characterizes its work and provides a basic motivation for further investigation.

To illustrate the heuristic approach in the space at my disposal, I am focusing on one event in order to show how the heuristic therapist struggles to understand the patient over a period of time. I hope to show how, even with patients for whom reasonable success can be anticipated, we stumble, fumble, muddle along, struggle with many hypotheses, and often wonder if we are getting anywhere.

I therefore selected what seemed to be an important "simple" event in the life of an analytic patient capable of reliable introspection and capable of establishing and maintaining a working therapeutic relationship. I decided to follow some aspects of the analytic process that I expected would center around the event or be related to the event. The situation was limited by time because a vacation was scheduled to interrupt analytic work within 6 weeks. I did not take notes when the event to be followed was initially reported. Only later, when I recognized the possibility of using the event for this occasion, did I try to reconstruct it. Subsequently, I took some rough notes during the hours, but for the most part, I reconstructed the sessions and my own thinking immediately after the hours. The reader should understand that I cannot present entire sessions, but only fragments. Also, to make the material readable, I have taken the liberty of presenting my reconstructions of what the patient said as though they were direct quotes.

This method has many obvious disadvantages. Certainly, it is hardly acceptable as formal research. But it also has advantages. I would be reporting from notes taken at the time. I would not be presenting material from preselected hours, ones that could easily be reinterpreted in light of subsequent events. Clearly, I would not know where the case material was leading or how successful the process was going to be as I went on from hour to hour. The case material is presented only to illustrate some aspects of the heuristic therapeutic process itself, some of my own inferential steps, the strategies employed, the difficulties in understanding even a "simple" event, how evidence emerged, and the presence of error correction by the patient. In brief, the case is presented to illustrate some aspects of analyst and patient at work.

But there is another reason for presenting the case in this way. I believe that if psychoanalysis is to be taken as a serious science and if its conclusions or findings are to be assigned any truth value, its practitioners will have to stop reporting without supporting evidence and without specifying the nature of the process that generated the findings claimed. The approach I am taking—presenting vignettes from a sequence of hours to demonstrate the unfolding of the process—is but one way of approaching this general problem.

The following event became a focus for analytic work over several weeks and is central to this discussion. A young man in his early 20s spoke of having been puzzled by his behavior on the previous day. As I understood the situation, he had been having an affair with Helen, a slightly older divorced woman who had a child. Helen had apparently acted affectionately on that day, expressed her love for him, talked of marriage, and indicated that she would be willing to have a child by him if he wished. He was puzzled by his almost immediate, sharp change in attitude toward her. He found himself flirting with another woman that very night, in Helen's presence; he recognized that Helen suddenly seemed old, even ugly, and that some of the profound sexual passion he always felt for her had lessened.

Given the fact that this young man was an able analytic patient capable of detecting and verbalizing his subjective emotional states, what inferences can reasonably be made about the material and what can the therapist do with these inferences?

One could begin to think along "classical" lines. One could say that the patient was involved in an incestuous conflict. Helen, older and already a parent, was "obviously" a mother figure. Incest conflicts and castration anxiety could explain the data. Thus, as soon as the fulfillment of his Oedipal wishes became a distinct possibility, the patient unconsciously defended himself. Helen became undesirable, even repulsive. Or we can find other formulations based on other clinical theories to account for this patient's reaction: fears of attachment, fears of closeness to another person, and the like.

Although many of these formulations seem plausible and reasonable, I tend to opt for minimal assumptions and formulations. I invariably choose to work very closely to the data and, to borrow a phrase Otto Isakower used when he was my teacher, "to remain unknowing." I attempt to keep open as many options as possible and to focus on the process. I allow the process to generate my understanding, wherever it may "naturally" go. And basic in this process is the need to enter the patient's world of experience.

In truth, I felt that I did not at all understand what had happened to the patient. I did not have any context to help me, and I could not follow his experience. He himself was aware of a conflict: He was obviously running away from what seemed to him a fulfillment of important wishes—he had always wanted Helen to respond to him with open affection. As I attempted to follow his experiences and get into his world, there was a gap, a discrepancy, between her affectionate words and behavior, her speaking of possible marriage and children, and his subsequent reactions. I had no idea of what had been evoked in the patient to explain his changed attitude toward her. I felt that because so much was unknown and uncertain, the best strategy was to suggest to the patient that he try to fill in the gap, if possible, to give both of us some sense of the continuity of his experiences. I therefore suggested that he go back and try to recapture the moment. What had happened to him while Helen was speaking and acting affectionately and referring to marriage and children? What did he feel, think, experience? I was, in effect, asking him for additional relevant information to reduce the uncertainty.

In response, in subsequent hours, he was gradually able to capture some aspects of what had happened. He recognized that he had become extremely angry at Helen when she spoke of the possibility of having children. (I had not even recognized the possibility that her talking of children was perhaps the sensitive issue for him. If I had any very tentative ideas about the event, they were for the most part related to the attachments of marriage and what they would mean for this man.) The patient then recalled an incident when he became extremely upset after a very casual sexual relationship with a woman named Doris, fearing that he had impregnated her and therefore, somehow, for the rest of his life might have to pay for what he had done were she indeed to have a baby. I knew of the incident, but it had not come to my mind until the patient spoke of it. The incident had taken place while he was on vacation and had never been understood by either of us, though I knew that he was extremely panicky and even dysfunctional for a brief period. But the patient's recognition of the relation of the past vacation incident to the current one lent support to his focusng on Helen's speaking of children as possibly being *the* most dangerous issue for him on the day of the event in question.

I might add that I know of no general, simple, clinical theory that could have given me this understanding. I might have had a tentative hypothesis about the significance of having children in the event being studied had I initially recalled the earlier experience with Doris. But I did not recall it at the time; the general emotional contexts of the two experiences were quite different. But most important, my understanding, as elementary as it may be, emerged from the process as a result of the patient's work. Some uncertainty about the event being studied had been reduced.

In a subsequent session, the patient told of feeling "smothered" by Helen after she spoke, and then added that "it was more like being flattened out, as though there was no space and the world had become two dimensional." The experience now reported was unusual and unique; I could never have anticipated it. I verbalized to him exactly what I understood he was trying to tell me, something I often do to check on whether I have caught the essential nature of an experience. This strategy allows the patient an opportunity to correct my understanding. As I verbalize the experience, I attempt to enter the patient's world and to experience exactly what is being reported. I was especially interested in getting this reported experience accurately because it was so unusual, even odd. It is a good strategy to attend carefully to such experiences. What is a two-dimensional world, described as "one where there is no space in front of you" – no third dimension? As I tried to capture in myself this odd experience, I felt as though I couldn't move; I was paralyzed, immobile, and I said to the patient that no movement seems possible in this kind of world. He agreed unhesitatingly. Immobility was a basic issue. One is "caught in place," he noted. He then told of how nice it feels at night when, on going to sleep, he first lies on his back until he gets drowsy and then rolls over and falls asleep lying on his stomach. Being able to turn over, having the freedom to move, is particularly satisfying. Obviously, in a two-dimensional world such movements would not be possible.

Note what has happened in the sessions reported. There was a genuine interactive experience. Initially, he spoke of an incident that puzzled and worried him. I pointed to a discontinuity in the experiences reported. He was eventually able to add some highly relevant experiences and memories to partially fill in the gap: The issue of having a child now seemed to be crucial. He added other important experiences. I caught sight of what seemed to be an important aspect of these experiences, one that he had not mentioned: the immobility. He confirmed this understanding by saying that it felt as though he was "caught in place" and also by pointing out how especialy pleasurable it is at bedtime to experience a sense of having full mobility, of not being in a smothered, flattened, two-dimensional world.

But now that we had learned that the talk of children seemed to have triggered anger, an altered representation of Helen, and an experience described as a two-dimensional world, a host of new problems presented themselves. What were these experiences all about? Why did having a child upset him so, and where did the odd two-dimensional-world feeling come from? In regard to the latter, I wondered what could conceivably give a person that type of anxiety. Some early traumatic experience perhaps? I know that my thoughts frequently flashed back to what I knew of his early life (my working model). He had suffered from recurrent croup, a very serious problem when he was young. Could such recurrent incidents leave an infant with a feeling about the world of the kind he reported? I truly didn't know.

Later, the patient recognized that when he spoke of "feeling flattened" he had the sense that Helen was very close to his face, as though "stuck" to him. His implication was that he would be attached or "stuck" to her in some pathological way. He added that when upset about possibly impregnating Doris during his vacation, he feared being "tied to her forever," never being able to escape from her if she had a child by him.

Subsequently, much emerged about his fear of death, present since early in his life. He had fears of being in a coffin, and when young, he resolved that he would be cremated lest he wake up after being buried and find himself "stuck," unable to move, immobilized, and helpless. At this time, he told of a recurrent dream:

> I am in a gigantic dark place; great pillars are there. I can't see the ceiling or the ends of the pillars. I am walking, and I hear the sound of footsteps, my own or those of someone else. I hear a male voice saying 'too big.' I felt small in an infinite space.

He then spoke of his great fears of small spaces as a child. Sometime when he was between the ages of 5 and 10, he became panicky when going up the Statue of Liberty. He had been afraid of being trapped in the narrow stairway, caught in the crowd of people with no possibility of escape should the need arise. Apparently, he actually did get upset and began to scream.

He also told of some games he played when young. In one game that he played with his mother, he was an astronaut wearing a helmet. He would pretend to be injured and then run to his mother to receive assurance from her that "all is okay, your head is not cut off." In a typical game with a friend, each would alternately pretend that he was "trapped" – often in a closed box – and then be rescued by the other. The patient said that there was something "very physical," perhaps even sexual, about these games – not surprising in view of the many masturbatory fantasies that he had later in life during which he was tying up someone or being tied up himself.

A few days later, after a weekend, he told of his profound discouragement. Everything was wrong; his new job was not living up to his expectations. He belittled his abilities on the job, wondered if he knew anything and even if he was suitable for any demanding professional work. Helen did not want to be with him on the weekend. He felt low and confused.

I asked if he could detect in himself what had most likely evoked his mood, what had troubled him the most. He replied, "I don't know, maybe it was the stuff we talked about last week, maybe it is the job, maybe it was because of Helen's attitude this weekend. I don't know. I feel that I don't know anything. I can't see anything; I can't see a thing."

For reasons almost totally inexplicable to me at the time, I registered very strongly his words "I can't see anything; I can't see a thing." I echoed them back to the patient. Only later did I realize that as he was talking I had been flashing back to the material of the previous week: the fear of being smothered and also the recurrent dream. Smothering had a blindness aspect, and darkness and not being able to see were prominent aspects of the recurrent dream.

I said to the patient that I realized that he was trying to say that he couldn't understand the many difficult life situations that he was talking about. But I wondered if his whole mood was perhaps in itself a historically determined state—one of bewilderment, of feeling that nothing made sense, of feeling that he knew and understood nothing, of feeling incapable of productive work—and, I added, that perhaps not seeing was actually part of the state. He replied that my remarks had caught his mood, and he then pointed out that fear of blindness had always been his greatest fear, followed by fears of death.

I then said that in the recurrent dream mentioned the week before, there had been an important aspect of darkness and of not seeing. He replied that at that very moment he had been thinking of the dream. He added that in the previously mentioned games he played with his mother, anxiety about blindness was an important aspect. He tried to deal with the "not seeing" aspect of other fears—the fear of being flattened, for example—but came up with nothing conclusive.

My attempt to view the patient's general mood as historically determined may not have been an optimal approach. He frequently had such moods of "I know nothing, understand nothing, and everything is bewildering." This was my first effort to approach the mood as perhaps an analyzable state itself. I had some vague thoughts that perhaps trauma, possibly related to the early croup incidents, might have left a residue consisting of such states. In other cases, I have been successful in my attempts to approach general confused moods as historically determined "relivings" of some aspect of a traumatic situation. But obviously, my strategy was not altogether successful in this hour, and I might have done better had I allowed the patient to sort out some of his confused feelings about many of the things that had been disturbing him. The work nevertheless did enable me to get a glimpse of at least one important issue—his fear of blindness.

In one session shortly afterward, the patient connected some of his problems concerning Helen with those he had always had with his parents. A quarrel with his father was the context that brought the particular relationship to the fore.

He had a problem with father about money and about getting a car. The patient said he needed a car to get to his analytic sessions. Father suggested that he could use public transportation, which realistically was an impossibility for the patient because of the nature of his job. In the course of the conversation, father said, "You will have to grow up."

The patient was infuriated. He thought of giving up the idea of getting a car as well as treatment and living on his own salary. His father, recognizing how upset the patient was, asked him to come to his office. It turned out, according to the patient, that father "was not quite the asshole," he thought he was. Father did realize that his suggestion about using public transportation was not very wise.

The patient then went on to talk of Helen and wondered if what has been happening with Helen was in some way related to arguments with his father, of which the incident he had just described was typical. He then added:

> For so long Helen was indifferent, and then she talked of marriage and of having babies – a totally different attitude from what she showed in the past. And 2 weeks ago she indicated that she didn't mean a word of what she said that night; she was reacting from anxiety. I get very angry when someone feels a certain way and can't admit it. I feel lied to, and it is hard for me to grow up when a woman can't trust herself to say that she is in love. For just a moment it was uncovered [her feelings of love for him], then it is covered again. And if I respond to the now uncovered moment, then she is different and no longer feels that way. It is like seeing something at one moment, and then it is denied the next.
>
> Both of my parents do this kind of thing in their own way. Father is too weak and frightened to admit that he is frightened. He gets angry, and if you try to talk to him about it, he denies it. And mother diverts a conversation and gets very intellectual. When I told her about my argument with father and how it may mean stopping treatment, she asked why I want to stop treatment, when that is not the point! I don't want to stop; the problem is with my father, and if that is not straightened out, I may have to stop.
>
> When my parents act that way, there is no one in the room to talk to . . . [the patient was also obviously indicating that when Helen doesn't admit to her feelings or denies them, there is also no one in the room to talk to]. I realize more and more that parents are not a different class of people.
>
> If I had strangled father the other night in his office, it wouldn't have been the one I wanted to strangle, not yesterday's father, the enraged man who slammed doors and called me names and seemed so big and overpowering. I wonder if I ever thought then that I would grow up and be as big as he is, if not bigger. Now I can really kill him, as he sat there. Now I am bigger and I can get revenge, but he really is not the father of 25 years ago, and that part of him that is still the father of 25 years ago is not all there is to him. I almost felt sorry for him.

In this session, the link between Helen and his parents had to do with denied feelings. Father could not recognize his own fears and angers, and mother tended to misunderstand and intellectualize emotional situations. Helen, he felt, was denying her true feelings and her genuine emotions when she told him that she didn't mean a word of what she said when she spoke of marriage and having his child. In such situations, there is no one for him to talk to. Note that this session was certainly related to the original incident, which is the focus of our attention. But the patient did not deal with the main issue of that event, *his* sudden change in mood and feeling toward Helen. Of course, it would have been grossly intrusive had I pointed this out to the patient because it was irrelevant in the current session.

I also learned in this session that I had misunderstood something important about the initial event. The patient corrected my understanding. Helen had never spoken of being in love with him, as I had thought; she had only acted very affectionately and then spoke of possible marriage and children. This distinction was important for the patient because he always wanted her to verbalize her affectionate feelings. Perhaps I misunderstood because, in contrast to the other sessions, I wrote up the initial event some time after it came up. Our memories are obviously very fallible! But my error did not prove to be of great significance in these sessions where the emphasis was on *having a child* as the most emotionally laden aspect of that original event.

In another session, the patient spontaneously brought up his sexual fears related to the original event. He felt that many sexual anxieties were stirred up when Helen spoke of having a child. He is very often afraid of losing his erection, afraid that he may lose interest in women, and may even become attracted to men. "I am the type that if I saw a spring freely running from the rocks I would wonder if it might stop at the next moment."

In yet another session, he spoke of how severe his anxieties can be and of how he is learning to handle them. In many situations, he can now recognize how anxious he is, and he can calm himself down and tell himself, "Look, I am anxious; let's investigate," and then take some distance from what is going on. He finds this to be a helpful process. At other times he cannot calm himself down for days, cannot take any distance, and can hardly think. Everything gets drowned out, and he almost feels a loss of contact with the situation and the people involved. When he thought he had impregnated Doris, his anxiety was indeed enormous. It was also very intense when Helen spoke of having a child. I now think I may not have fully recognized how upset the patient actually was at that time.

The patient said: "I am often under the influence of a lot of anxiety and don't know it. And when I get anxious I fear dissolution, going crazy by contracting inwards and then getting smaller and smaller and disappearing. In contrast, when I am angry, I am aware of myself; I have a sense of me; there is no threat of dissolution."

One of the most moving experiences of these 6 weeks took place in a 2-hour session (arranged because of scheduling difficulties) just before the vacation. The patient was upset because of some problems at work and because Helen had not called when she was supposed to. He went back to the initial session concerning Helen having his baby and said, "I am afraid of having children. I am afraid of doing something that will affect the rest of my life."

When I suggested that he feared the responsibility, he corrected me and said that it was much more than that. "I would not be able to escape, get away, be or do something else." Obviously, my intervention was inadequate; at the moment, I was hardly tuned into the clinical material before me and not even into what I had already learned about the patient. When I recovered from my error, I said, "You would be trapped." "Yes, exactly," was his reply. "Marriage itself stirs up some of these feelings, but one can get a divorce. Not so with a kid. You know how I feel about women who fall all over me. It scares me. I am concerned when they call, and I want them to let me alone; I want my autonomy; I want to be able to be left alone."

When I then reminded the patient that his fear of impregnating Doris was because he feared being hounded for life, he replied, "Absolutely," and continued:

I think there is a basic mistrust of other people. I am less mistrustful of Helen. I used to think that my arguments with Helen were the essence of my relationship with her; then I realized no, not so, and I hang around not for arguments but because we have a nice time.

With Doris, I didn't see her as being with us at camp to enjoy it. Typical of me, this person was to be feared. Maybe some orgastic pleasure will be there, but be prepared for her to turn on me. The same with Helen; I still feel she can't be trusted.

Somewhere I know and feel that things come and go; things may not work out with Helen. Parents die; that is life. Maybe her not calling shows something, and so be it. If she goes away, that is okay, but it would be sad. I would miss her a lot if she were not to be close and yet I know this may have to happen. And this makes me feel like breaking apart. I am peaceful about what is happening, yet at the same time I can't stand it. I can't stand things being confused and not resolved. I cannot understand why she couldn't say "I love you" then, when clearly that is what she was feeling.

I may say something nice to my father or give him a kiss, but I don't participate fully, so that if he takes advantage I wouldn't get killed. Don't forget they read my letters when I was young [referring to letters to a girlfriend the parents disliked]. If I had trusted them, they would have destroyed me. I have to avoid forming an alliance with them. They are trying to make me be like them. I thought just now: They would make me have kids like they had kids.

I don't want a kid who would be like me. I felt so alone all of my life, and I feel that if I had a kid I would do that to him or her. I would love to have a kid and love to love a child of mine, but I don't know or feel if I can keep it from happening, keep what happened to me from happening to my kid.

I feel alone; I don't know if I can have something forever. Like having an erection; I feel I have to prove I can have one before having one. I don't know if I can be a parent before being one. I spent years depressed, alone, in bed, crying. Being a kid was never happy. I am happier now than ever before.

In a quiet, controlled, but deeply felt way, he then added:

I couldn't go through my life again. If there is one thing I can do for the world, for the world of souls, it is not to have one of those souls be me growing up.

I remember how my parents would fight and I would lie in bed and wish that I was dead and feel that it was all my fault. It was confusing to see how they could act very differently when I was ill. When I had croup, both my parents would take me to the bathroom. Father would come in every 10 minutes to get me to give me a steaming, and Ma would make tea. A little later they were both yelling at each other. Maybe I felt that if I died they would be better off. I hated to be sick, but at least when I was sick, we were a family. When I was sick, my parents got along; they did things; they would be up all night with me; and we were a family and I felt cared for. All my other memories of my early life are of my parents yelling and of doors slamming. I'm not sure what made them yell; I think I wondered if it was because of me or not. I wanted to be dead when they yelled: I felt that no one loved me. That's how I felt today when Helen didn't call.

It became clear in this hour that the patient felt that he was destined to be a "horrible" parent, as both his grandparents and his parents were. He could see no way to escape this destiny.

In this extended extract from 6 weeks of an analytic case, I have tried to indicate how the analytic data unfolded and widened in scope. I did not want to distract the reader by calling attention to some of the strategies used (e.g., how the patient was allowed to elaborate and correct my comments and understanding). I think the report indicates the kind of dialogue that characterizes the heuristic therapeutic process. Certainly, much was happening during these weeks that was not talked about. For example, I was listening to the patient, not belittling him, not getting angry, and not confusing the issues and intellectualizing, as he complained his parents did. I have no doubt that these corrective emotional experiences[2] were crucial during these weeks, as they were during all of his treatment.

Can I say that I learned the answer to the original event under scrutiny: Why did his feelings toward Helen inexplicably change so drastically when she spoke of having children? No, I cannot. And there may be no simple answer. But I learned a great many things related to that event, and so did the patient. Many new, unpredictable, potentially productive lines were opened, which could be followed up in the future. The process led to many discoveries. My working model of the patient had been markedly enriched in the few weeks of work, and I believe that the patient's model of himself was equally enriched.

As I view analytic therapy, I do not see it as a situation where the therapist has automatic answers, and certainly not simplistic ones derived from some clinical theory that is imposed on the supposedly ever resistant patient. I view analytic therapy as a unique method of inquiry and investigation, as a special probe (D. Kirsner, personal communication, February, 1983), which enables more to be learned about a patient's inner life and which simultaneously widens and enriches a patient's experiences. Analytic therapy is a process which, at best, allows us to struggle productively with the very complex phenomena of a patient's personal life. And its path is not simple, direct, or predictable. I agree with Freud's (1913) remarks:

> The analyst is certainly able to do a great deal, but he cannot determine beforehand exactly what results he will effect. He sets in motion a process, that of resolving existing repressions. He can supervise this process, further it, remove obstacles in its way, and he can undoubtedly vitiate much of it. But on the whole, once begun, it goes its own way and does not allow either the direction it takes or the order in which it picks up its points to be prescribed for it. (p. 130).

One may ask about my basic clinical model or theory, which guides the process I conduct. To this I can say that the clinical model or "theory" consists of all the working models or schemata that I can possibly activate. For convenience, I (Peterfreund, 1976, 1983) have divided them into several models: of myself; of the world; of infant and childhood development; of the therapeutic process; of general clinical experience and clinical theory; and of the patient, built up over time. Briefly, my overall clinical model is based on all of the experiences – cognitive and affective – that I as a human being can possibly be aware of, experiences

---

[2]When I speak of "corrective emotional experiences," I do not refer to artificially created experiences in Alexander's sense (Alexander & French, 1946).

that all human beings share, plus the enhanced experiences that come from one's personal analysis, learning, and clinical work. The working models form my stable reference points—my points of departure—for any understanding of the clinical material presented by a patient. I know of no broader, more encompassing, overall clinical model than this. How we use these models is governed by a host of strategies of the kind I have described elsewhere (Peterfreund, 1976, 1983). In a heuristic approach, phenomena variously referred to as infantile sexuality, penis envy, Oedipus complex, and the like can emerge in terms of experiences meaningful to the patient; they emerge not in an intellectualized way, but as though newly discovered as a result of the process.

Fundamentally, I see psychoanalytic therapy as a special extension of normal human interaction and communication, in many ways as an extension of ordinary common sense and knowledge of the world. It shares many of the attributes of ordinary communication, for example, the constant error correction that takes place which allows communicators to understand each other. But it also has very unique aspects not found in ordinary communication, for example, the careful introspection, the attempt to delineate one's inner life, and the verbalization of experiences, thoughts, and fantasies that one would never allow in ordinary communication. It uses strategies common to everyday human interaction and communication, for example, the constant matching of any input against expectable norms. But it also uses strategies not usually found in such everyday situations, for example, the interpretation of any given input in terms of models of early development.

Psychoanalytic therapy, as I view it, is a process that can lead to discoveries that refer to and are meaningful to a specific patient with a unique life history. The extensive models mentioned can provide sufficient broadly based reference points from which to make such discoveries.

REFERENCES

Alexander, F., & French, T. (1946). *Psychoanalytic therapy*. New York: Ronald Press.

Arlow, J. (1955). Notes on oral symbolism. *The Psychoanalytic Quarterly, 24*, 63–74.

Bowlby, J. (1969). *Attachment and loss: Vol. 1. Attachment*. New York: Basic Books.

Freud, S. (1913). On beginning the treatment (further recommendations on the technique of psycho-analysis, 1). *S.E., 12*, 121–144.

Peterfreund, E. (1976). How does the analyst listen? On models and strategies in the psychoanalytic process. In D. P. Spence (Ed.), *Psychoanalysis and contemporary science* (pp. 59–101). New York: International Universities Press.

Peterfreund, E. (1983). *The process of psychoanalytic therapy*. Hillsdale, NJ: The Analytic Press.

8 At Work

Warren S. Poland, M.D.

To help someone know himself, to know his own mind and how it works, and through that to help one increase his peace with himself and widen his range of actions in the world–the goals of analysis are not modest. The task of achieving these goals is pervaded with subtle conflictual pulls.

A central conflict results from the differing directions and opposing feelings these paradoxical aims stir within the analyst himself. Helping leads to lending a hand, whereas for someone to know himself leads to avoiding intrusiveness. The helpful attitude is often associated with psychotherapy; the exposure and exploration of unconscious fantasies are commonly recognized as requiring a more manifestly abstinent attitude. However, this paradox, the need to restrict helpful activity in the short term in order to provide substantial long-term help, exists within me, the analyst at work.

When I look back over how I have practiced in my office over the past decades, I realize that even when I conduct insight psychotherapy, psychoanalytic psychology serves as my organizing basic science. As a result, my ultimate orientation is always psychoanalytic.

Does the work aim toward making the unconscious conscious? Is that done by facilitating the crystallization of the transference? Are the clues that are inherent in that transference process, in dreams, in free associations, plus in the resistance all utilized to bring into the open the underground currents within the patient? Is the effort to achieve mastery through insight? These traditional defining characteristics of psychoanalysis are the ones most vital for my view and, I hope, to my work.

There are solid reasons for the conventions of psychoanalytic technique, reasons born out of what are by now generations of clinical experience. These conventions are all in the service of the ultimate analytic goal; they are not the ends in themselves. Whether one maintains a base-line stance that seems warm or cool, close or distant, will definitely influence the nature of the unfolding process. What determines the psychoanalytic work is the issue of what is then done with those factors, whether their effects are exposed and explored for the patient's meanings, or whether they are allowed to stand as if in a background "reality" beyond exploration.

This does not suggest, to me, that any intervention is acceptable or useful if only it is examined subsequently. There is, rather, the implication that the fundamental task is to expose, explore, and identify the forces and workings of the patient's inner world.

There are major differences between psychotherapy and psychoanalysis; there are significant effects from the differing range of techniques. In my practice, I always try to work toward an analytic goal of exploration and insight. My techniques, to the extent I can be aware, are always in the service of that goal.

As a result, my work experience is best described as psychoanalysis and preanalytic insight therapy. I do not conduct other forms of psychotherapy, limiting myself and my interests to those efforts where help is determined by the effort to understand. My patients, therefore, are not "in psychiatric hands" or "under psychiatric care"; they are all in analytic self-investigation, with a psychoanalyst in attending assistance.

For the rest of this paper, I limit myself to psychoanalysis, the vast majority of my practice. Nonetheless, reviewing what has gone on in my office through the years, rather than what I thought would go on or theorized should go on, reveals to me that some individuals with whom I worked on a twice weekly basis developed intense and relatively clearly crystallized transference neuroses. These few people were unsophisticated about analytic matters. Yet from their own fresh psychologic-mindedness, they developed complex transference processes which, with increasingly free associations and dream analyses, they were able to understand in a manner that connected their past and current lives.

These people have been exceptions and exceptional, but they have been there. For the most part, my experience has been that full transference regression and utilization require the continuity of daily sessions and the ambiguity that comes from greater levels of analytic abstinence and the use of the couch.

A law student consulted me because of problems he had making decisions. He felt he could never make a full commitment to a career because mixed feelings destroyed "total" certainty. Socially, too, he doubted the possibility of his finding "total" true love. He had "given up the idealistic ideas of things going well in marriage" and did not "want to impose" himself on anyone. He had few friends and got along poorly with his parents, though he was said to be just like his father.

The most striking qualities at the beginning of our work were his humorlessness (which when analyzed later revealed an uncommon dry appreciation of irony), verbal caution, and intense shame. He appeared markedly anxious, felt fragmented, was clearly perfectionistic, and was afraid of being dependent. The shame and obsessional effort to protect against loss of control was striking even in setting the original arrangements for an analysis. When I described these, he tried to negotiate on each point (e.g., he wanted three sessions per week rather than four), reinforcing his demand by the pressure of external forces. My response was to interpret the sense of danger rather than to negotiate.

During the series of consultative sessions, the patient reported a dream of selecting neckties and wanting to steal an ashtray. He then began to smoke and recalled an earlier dream that his grandfather died of cancer caused by the patient's smoking.

Much of his early position in the analysis seemed a passive masochistic presentation to me, the analyst, in what later came to be understood as paternal transference. He repeatedly attempted to mold the relationship in "seduction of the aggressor," that is, that I was to feel guilty and to react with retaliatory punishment. An example was the suffering I was implicitly causing by my fee and office location. Though he had no external financial problems, he walked daily the several miles to and from his appointment in order to save carfare, presumably to minimize his father's financial suffering.

Exploring the implications of this was like picking up a point on a net and discovering unexpected complex threads leading in many directions. What is central at the moment is not the story of the patient's psychodynamics and genetics, but the technique that aided their discovery.

Though I may have noticed incipient feelings of guilt in response to the patient's maneuvers, I took those noticings as significant data for understanding the unfolding associations, not as stimuli requiring me to alter the way I work.

For me, flexibility does not mean that anything goes, but it does imply that my primary concern is the understanding of the patient's expectations and fantasies. As a psychoanalytic technician, I have on the whole clear ideas of what works and what does not. I am comfortable being silent or saying, "No." Yet that silence or that statement, like all others, is not made capriciously or simply as evidence of my power.

Rather, it is made when needed in order to protect and to promote the analytic work. The analytic goal of mastery through insight takes priority over quick comfort for either the patient or me, the analyst.

In one way or another, every patient who has ever consulted me did so because something hurt. And each wanted to feel better, whether simply to relieve pain or to achieve power felt to be missing. Each came to a doctor for help. No matter what the appreciation of analysis as a technique in the service of insight, no patient was simply involved in an academic research project.

The word "doctor" requires clarification. I do not use it to imply anything at all about the question of lay analysis. I do use it to suggest that the analyst has a professional therapeutic responsibility to the patient, that a clinical analysis can never be an applied analysis addressed to a living human being as if he were nothing more than a text or art form. The destructive consequences of therapeutic zeal demand that the analyst has mastered his own rescue fantasies, his own sadism, his own urge to have power over another person. Although an analyst need not be a physician, I believe he must have worked through the crucial implications of responsibility in another person's putting himself at risk.

When I commit myself to analytic work with someone and explain that the way the work proceeds is for that person to try to follow the basic rule of free association, I am implicitly advising that many important executive ego functions be set aside during the analytic work. It is then my responsibility to watch them for the patient while the patient is vulnerable. In such a situation, matters that would otherwise be simple become complicated. My changing the schedule or my raising a fee, for instance, must of course be explored analytically for the meaning to the patient. No matter what the roots of the patient's attitudes – be they compliant, defiant, or whatever – I must, in addition to analytic exploration, watch out for the patient's interest. When someone is analytically exposed, I am not only trying to listen in order to interpret, I am also a temporary guardian of those ego functions that are set aside along with the censoring functions.

Privately, I feel a personal pride at being a part of the psychoanalytic movement, a movement that combines what I think are the best of liberating and civilizing effects. Yet I feel very strongly that I, the analyst, am there at work for the sake of the analysis, which exists for the sake of the patient. In some small manner, each analysis results in greater psychoanalytic knowledge. Still, in my view, it is primary that the analysis is there for the patient; the patient is not there primarily for the sake of psychoanalysis.

The most I have to offer to help someone in my office is that unique psychoanalytic tool that assists that person to be ever more open to himself and to broaden the range of his knowledge of his urges, his feelings, his experiences, his fantasies. Thus, the practice of abstinence, my with-holding of sought after help or other response, is not arbitrary. I do not define myself as an analyst either on the basis of the level of abstinence I achieve or the level of deep infantile sexual interpretations I offer. I am an analyst at work to the extent that I use the analytic tool, which I sub-sequently speak of at much greater length, to help the patient come to know himself, come to approach himself with an attitude of ruthlessly open-minded introspection.

It is here that I find the second of the major sets of responsibilities I feel in my practice. I am a guardian of the analysis. A friendly ear, an op-portunity for ventilation and catharsis, helpful advice, simple or not so simple compassion – all of these can be obtained many places in the world outside an analyst's office. Nowhere else, however, can someone obtain a psychoanalysis. For me, the early voice of authority was that of my father calling out, "Who's watching the store?" By now that voice of my own superego has been tamed to a softer tone of an ego-ideal. The message that voice speaks is now more of values than of threat, but it re-mains the message of the commitment to "watch the store." Despite the temptations to the contrary, and especially those presented by the pa-tient himself in the form of seductions and narcissistic bribes, it is I, the analyst, who must continuously watch the analytic store.

Analytic practice carries with it a frighteningly broad series of occu-pational hazards, to which neither I nor anyone else is immune. At this point, a specific matched pair is relevant: the analyst's belief that he could live the patient's life better than the patient can and the analyst's belief that he is engaged in an academic research project that is unrelated to how the patient's life proceeds. Both excessive helpfulness and disowning of analytic responsibility subvert the analytic task.

For me, the analytic technique is one in which I try to structure a fairly comfortable and standard basic relationship, the psychoanalytic situation, in which the patient is permitted and at times encouraged to let loose and to allow increasingly open experience and verbal expres-sion of all impulses, feelings, and fantasies. The couch, the daily ses-sions, and the minimization of external stimuli and unpredictable changes are all means, not ends in themselves. They are means designed to facilitate that regression by which the patient can best see and de-scribe the varied forces acting within.

I try to speak as little or as much as seems necessary to permit and aid the furthering of that opening up. I am essentially always behind the patient.

A bright but very frightened woman stated soon after the initial consulta-tions that she would never be able to use the couch. She said she would do what she could sitting up but would accept as just another in the long line of personally disappointing limitations in her life whatever it was she would lose by having an analysis that did not include the use of the couch. In fact, for close to a year, she worked hard and well while sitting face to face. Her fears of loss of control, the history behind those fears, and the revival of those fears in relationship to me all came before us. That did not make it easy for her to use the couch. However, she was a woman of genuine courage (as I find anyone courageous who presents for psychoanalytic investigation), and the time eventually came when she realized that she had to move over to the couch. She saw it as necessary not because she now understood why she had been afraid, but because she came to recognize she would never see through the fear without confronting it.

One day, long after further work had been accomplished, she reflected on all that had gone before. She found humor in the irony. She was afraid, she said, to allow me to be out of her view, behind her, because she never realized nor believed that I *was* in fact behind her. Raised by a mother who always knew what was best, who had eyes in the back of her head for seeing and knowing what the young girl was thinking and doing, she felt the couch manifested what was for her a major danger of analysis, the dreadful experience of having another person know more of what she was thinking than she did herself.

It is true that I often hear from the patient a hidden message before the patient recognizes that message himself. But I cannot hear it before the patient says it. No matter how much it may seem otherwise to the patient at first, I am always behind the patient.

Before going on to follow issues as they arise in the course of an analysis, there is more to say of what I have in mind from the beginning. The need to say this first is, itself, a statement of my understanding of analytic work. I am not only an outside assistant to the patient, but I am one who does the work by utilizing my own psychology as a cooperating medium onto which the patient can draw his own inner world. My ultimate responsibility is to protect and aid the analysis, my purpose deriving from my awareness that it is the capacity for mastery through insight that analysis has to offer the patient.

My overview of analysis, my own psychology of who and how I am, all inform my actual practice. I believe that each person – whether psychotic, Republican, Jewish, poetic, or whatever – does what he does and lives his life as he does because it is the best way of getting along in the world as he sees it. I believe that what analysis uniquely offers each person is the specially developed occasion to learn how it happens that he sees the world as he does and to come thereby to widen his range of vision and action both internally and, as a consequence, in the world he helps to create around him.

I try to structure a neutral setting that will allow the patient to expose his patterns of relating and experiencing. My use of my own psychology is not to suggest or to inspire, but to hear the patient's words, learn from the patient's music, and then interpret back that which I hear for the patient's observation and consideration.

Thus, the broad goals of analysis and the general responsibilities of the analyst that I have described are neither abstractions demanding perfectionism nor moralistic imperatives. They are the conscious aspects of the structure that determines the specifics of my daily work. Let us now turn to how I put these into practice.

I am reminded of the time the International Psychoanalytic Congress met in Jerusalem during a mind-searing heat wave. Retreating to my air-conditioned hotel room one afternoon, I happened to hear the English-language news broadcast. "Was this the hottest it has ever been here?" the newsman asked. The weatherman's answer was precise: "It was the hottest we have records for, but how can I say it was never hotter before?"

My concern here is with how I work, but like the weatherman, all I can knowingly tell is what I have in my field of vision, how I think I work. This is not an obsessional point but an essential psychoanalytic view. Unconscious forces may be mastered, but they are always alive and potentially active. Having stated my sense of what I am about, it would perhaps now be best to approach some of the specifics of my analytic practice, touching on several of the major clinical questions as they arise.

When someone calls me, even if for an analysis, I start with a consultation that lasts anywhere from 1 to several sessions. I consider the interruptions of the sessions to be the arbitrary effect of the rate at which the hands of the clock move, a rate totally unconcerned with the speed at which the patient opens up. I start by hearing as much as I can about whatever the patient cares to bring up. In this, I am determined not only not to prejudice the unfolding of the patient's ideas and pattern of relating in order to observe them better, but also to demonstrate my wares, namely, the practice of helping someone come to observe his own mind as seen both in content and in interactional patterns.

After I have a sense of the sorts of matters with which the patient is struggling, I state that it would be helpful if I could briefly interrupt in order to hear an overview of the person's life. I am interested in a general though short biographical survey in order to get the broadest sense of the context in which the patient lives, in which the troubles have arisen. Though I do not take a finely detailed history, I do want to know whom the patient considers to be the major characters in his life and how he initially portrays them. Also, it is helpful to hear of any earlier life incidents felt by the patient to be of relevance. All of this, naturally, not only informs me but also informs the patient, particularly that I think the past and present are connected and that past experiences may continue to live in the present.

My preference is to have the consultation extend over a brief period of time. I especially want to note how this other person responds to his consultative experience with me, to what extent he seems inclined to chew something over or to allow my presence or my comments to reflect themselves in an active inner reworking.

Having come to personal conclusions, I then feel it my turn to tell the person consulting me what I think. I state the major themes I have heard him working on. I comment on whether I feel there is value in his doing formal self-investigative work at this time, whether or not (and sometimes not) I think that he and I can work together, and what I consider the various options in terms of the differences between psychotherapy and psychoanalysis.

A word seems in order here about analyzability. I have read many studies, each of which labors to define the specific cues that are broadly and covertly subsumed in the analyst's intuition, the sense of whether someone is likely to make use of a psychoanalytic venture. Gross matters are, of course, easy. The problem is to move beyond such seemingly bold indications.

On reflection, I notice how often the question of analyzability turned out to be the question of the analysis itself. What would have seemed to be unanalyzable was precisely what required analyzing. I do not have an inordinately high opinion of the ability to predict what will be around the corner. Patients who seemed to be choice candidates for analysis have, at times, turned out to be the most stickily intractable, with dreadfully difficult negative therapeutic reactions. And I can think of those about whom one would not have started too optimistically, but who have subsequently developed and analyzed fairly classical transference neuroses. In contrast to some severe criteria for analyzability, I do not consider the presence of psychopathology a contraindication to psychoanalysis.

I believe I should tell the patient whatever I learn from him that he can make use of for himself. I also feel it is my task to tell what needs to be said about how to proceed. I have heard it said that the basic rule is best communicated by action rather than words, by attention. Generally, this is an attitude of wishing to avoid "rules," as if the basic rule were an evidence of power orientation rather than analytic neutrality.

My own view is that the analyst's neutrality does do away with enactments of domination, but that such true neutrality does not involve the analyst's going underground. For me, the analyst who orchestrates an analysand's direction, no matter how subtly, is manipulating. I see no room in analysis for tricks hidden up the analyst's sleeve.

My model is Freud's of the blind archaeologist. The analysand and I are engaged in a collaborative endeavor in which I am the expert hired hand. Thus, it is inconceivable to me that the analyst would not instruct the patient in what the patient needs to know of how an analysis works. With words that vary from patient to patient, I generally say that the way it works best is to try to put into words all thoughts, feelings, body feelings, dreams, ideas, or whatever as they come up. And all of this should be said aloud, whether it seems relevant or irrelevant, important or unimportant, polite, rude, or whatever imaginable. Occasionally, I add that if the answers to the questions the person is asking himself could be provided by simple logic or logical reasoning, he would long since have known them. I have never seen anyone in consultation who had not been trying to do hard psychological work long before I was called on.

This view of the basic rule leads naturally to one facet of the issue of resistance. If a rule is something imposed, then failure to follow the rule is a form of defiance or subversion of the residing authority. Resistance has long been recognized as the clinical manifestation within the analytic dyad of conflict and defense on the intrapsychic level. Resistance is of the essence of the analytic process; it is not insubordination.

Two additional points seem significant in terms of the basic rule. One is a matter of current vogues in analytic thinking. The analyst's empathy is a vital part of his work. The wish both to correct a mistakenly rigid and intellectualized picture of the analytic model and, more fairly, to notice the humanly dyadic nature of the analytic process has clarified the importance of empathy. However, the current preoccupation with empathy has at times seemed to obscure the importance of free association and cognitive understanding. I consider this an error, a misuse of the concept of empathy. To be analytically informed and accurate, empathic perceptions must be combined with what is learned by attention to the content of free associations. Both are essential for validity in determining unconscious fantasies.

Second, there is also a fundamental rule for the analyst. Just as the patient has no exceptions to his basic rule, the analyst must consider all experiences within the analysis for their informational value. Observations of what passes within me are vital data that I examine to sort out what they tell me of myself from what they tell me of the patient. Nothing that goes through my own mind or feelings can be dismissed out of hand.

As analyst, I both effect and affect the analytic work. My attention to myself results not simply from a wish to express how *I* work, but rather my sense that I as analyst am a vital tool in effecting the analysis. My personality and technique effect, that is, make possible the basic work; my personality and style affect the tone of the unfolding work.

It is as a collaborator that I can invite the patient to tolerate regression and exposure for the sake of our common goal. It is as someone with technical expertise and at times greater experience in analytic introspection that I can often hear the hidden messages from the patient, sort out my own contributions to them, and report back to the patient that which I hear.

These points emphasize a concept I feel essential to analytic work as I see it: If analysis is a journey, the transference is the train, not the destination!

I believe that the spontaneously unfolding transference provides the primary and crucial set of data about the patient's inner life. The consciously and unconsciously experienced fantasies, feelings, urges, and inhibitions provide the heart of the difficult analytic work; hearing about displaced relationships is peripheral.

Early in the analytic work, I find such "talking about" informative for bringing to open life the transference neurosis. Late in the analytic work, I find myself sitting considerably more on the sidelines while I listen to the patient's growing self-analytic functions in action. But the central part of the analytic work takes place in the area of the transference, which is what I think Freud meant when he observed that one cannot execute a man by hanging him in effigy. That transference is not the end point for cure simply by the dynamics of a corrective interpersonal experience. It is rather the means by which underlying genetic roots can be known emotionally and intellectually and be mastered.

A young accountant opened his analytic work in an unusually dramatic fashion. Its very exaggeration shows how the transference at times takes shape, how I at times observe it, and how at those times when I work well I utilize my experience of the transference in the service of insight rather than primarily in the service of my own comfort.

This man had been sent for analysis by his wife, whose own analysis had gone to the point when she realized she could not continue living with him unless he changed.

When he consulted me he presented himself as an incredibly controlled, detached, rigid, obsessional professional man. He was ruled by such totalistic perfectionism as almost never to be able to effect any simple action. The purchase of an unfinished bookcase involved more than a 6-month city-wide search and accumulation of files to determine which was the best bookcase to buy in the entire metropolitan area. He was bright and talented enough to have a modicum of success professionally, though completion of any project always required another person to do the final write-up.

At the outset, the patient appeared formal, precise, cooperative, and proper, a person greatly concerned with "bookkeeping" even balances in his contacts with others. He was not on a first name basis with any of his colleagues; his obsessive control and perfectionism were robbing him of apparent satisfaction in any area of his life.

In his first session, he spoke of his background, an incredibly barren one as an isolated only child on an isolated southern rural farm. During that first hour, I had a momentary sense of complete freedom and power, a sense that I could schedule his appointments with any frequency, any timing I chose, that I could shift his hours as I wished, all with no concern for his reactions. In a clearly crazy way, it was a fantasy that he would be an "ideal patient" (reflecting what was later understood as his concept of his parents' image of an "ideal child"), that is, one who was no threat, no challenge, no problem, no burden. It was a feeling there need be no dream of future demands or complications, that the analysis would be easy and effortless, even if inconsequential. There was even a sense that the patient would allow me absolute importance without my ever having to be confronted by his being accommodating or compliant, simply with a sense that he did not matter. This brief flight of fantasy during our interchange was followed by a second shift in my mood, a strong wave of sleepiness.

During the course of the analysis that followed, all of my reactions became comprehensible in terms of his infantile and childhood development. It is that such subsequent understanding took place, not the details of his life, that is cogent here.

For several months, he came daily, got on the couch, and filled the hours with what he thought was expected of him. After he had been in analysis a few months, his wife asked how it was going. "Very well," he assured her. "Why shouldn't it? It's nothing personal."

The first half year or so continued as if not "personal" in the analysis. A minor automobile accident provided an opportunity to explore his self-destructiveness, but almost everything, including dreams he reported, was offered as detached content. My questions, comments, or preliminary interpretations addressing what he was feeling or doing or what was going on between us were all ground into meaninglessness.

Much time was spent by the patient's making mountains out of molehills, speaking of trivial details with exquisite precision. Minutiae of daily life and of professional projects were offered endlessly. I found it harder and harder to follow him, feeling increasingly impotent, in striking contrast to my feelings in the first session. I felt the patient and his analysis more and more remote. At times, I thought he came for the sole purpose of driving me crazy, but it was difficult to hold onto even that fantasy version of attachment. I fought to stay awake during the hours, feeling as if I were simply filling time and were now totally irrelevant in the analysis. Yet he appeared neither satisfied nor dissatisfied as he dragged on.

Once again, my private theoretical speculations at the time, including those regarding issues of aggression, are not cogent here. These, too, later came to be understood, but for about a half year the situation I have described continued.

The patient droned on. I began to feel I could take it no longer. One day outside the hour, I had the fantasy of his getting away from me altogether, of my reaching out and grabbing him by his foot to pull him back into the world.

I mentioned, as a complaint to a colleague about the patient I was to see the next hour, my thought of pulling the patient back by his foot. The patient then came in and reported a dream in which his mother was arranging his father's body in a coffin. (Actually, both parents were then living.) In the long and complex dream, the patient found one minor detail confusing. In the coffin, one of the father's feet was broken at the ankle and bent back, "as if someone had grabbed hold of his foot and pulled him back."

The taste of the earlier detachment returned from time to time, but it was never again the same, never again so total. That dream became the text for the dreams of the next few years of analytic work, with new dreams generally connecting by some detail to that crucial dream. About a year and a half later, there was another person looking through the door of the room, an aunt never before mentioned. In most instances, the patient stated that such an element had been present in the earlier dream but that he had neglected to mention it.

The patient's analysis and life story unfolded in broad reference to that dream. The only element that was never understood, even to the time of termination, and which continued to puzzle the patient, was *why* the foot was bent back. Phallic and castration issues were explored, but that specific symbol never lost its mystery.

Anecdotal vignettes can demonstrate, but they bear their own hazards. This uncanny transference–countertransference phenomenon was attached to a dream that turned out to be the skeleton on which subsequent analytic work was fleshed out. In this analysis, it was precisely such an uncanny experience that announced a crucial shift in the transference. I believe it reasonable that the patient's move evidenced some subterranean, essential work already done. This "turning point" (the "twisted foot" comment I made to a colleague and the simultaneous parallel image in the patient's dream) may well have represented a shared preconscious and unconscious understanding in which the patient and I were about to become attuned to the meaning of his massive affective resistance.

The vignette demonstrates an extreme. Most analyses progress within a narrower compass of experiencing and understanding, yet all include unconscious and preconscious components. Conscious mastery is essential and is certainly the desired end point, but it does not exist in detached cognitive isolation. Before I can interpret to someone, I must know what it is to be interpreted. Despite current tendencies in some analytic circles to establish allegiances toward primarily cognitive or primarily empathic modes of knowing about the patient, I think there can be no doubt that the two are different aspects of an essentially unitary process. My efforts to exemplify should not mislead. The ability to interpret requires attention to pattern, content, and details of associations and also to the emotional forces evoked and elicited in the analyst.

When I was a beginning psychiatric resident, I heard an admired professor comment that the longer he worked in the field, the more he came to realize how much all people are alike. It was not much later that I heard another reflect on how the longer he continued in the work, the more he came to appreciate how very different each person is from the other. At the time, I was amused by the contrast.

Now, particularly as I reflect on my past years of analytic practice, I come to see how much I fundamentally agree with both. Thinking back over the people with whom I have worked analytically and whom I have come to know through their analyses, I am struck both by the universality of human emotions and limitations, my own included, and by the uniqueness of each individual's analysis.

I sense that my personality, my style, and also my understanding of proper analytic technique all limit my functioning at work to a fairly narrow range. Yet there are some patients who know me as cold and remote, and others who feel I am warm and personal. To some, I have seemed hopelessly detached, even emotionally absent; to others, I have seemed ever present. In some important way, each was right.

I participate with each patient in structuring an analytic situation and in trying to do the analytic work. But unless I interfere with some grievous personal intrusion, which is fatal to a significant segment of the analytic work, then neither my proper technique nor my errors determine the basic course of the analysis. The nature of each unfolding analysis is overwhelmingly determined by the power of the patient's transference processes.

Life in the middle phase of an analysis has very little of the clarity retrospectively imposed by case reports. Ambiguity, paradox, and even seeming amorphousness abound. Never able to grasp consciously more than a fragment of the forces at work, I find that I have to pressure myself against the tendency to premature closure, to false understanding. I do not feel I owe it to some inner perfectionistic pressure to be instantly understanding, but I do feel I must try to understand.

Tolerance for feeling lost at sea is essential, particularly in the middle phase of an analysis. Here my conscience has been a difficult adversary. Repeatedly, I find myself in the position of stupidly not understanding, of trying to understand but missing the point. The great ally of that enemy is the professional community's perfectionistic proclamation of standards of excellence, standards at times that seem to suggest that somewhere someone knows exactly the right word to say in each situation, that my own confusion is evidence of inexcusably sloppy inadequacies on my part. (Knowing that such a professional perfectionism somewhere "out there" is *both* a projection of a part of my own superego and a partial external fact, I am painfully aware how much I have played the game, have participated in competitively doing the same unto others.) My own great ally in the face of such perfectionism is honesty. Honesty here is not simply a personal value but also a benefit of the reality principle. It makes life incredibly easier. I am quite content to have patients conclude in the course of their work with me that "dumb but honest" is often a fitting motto.

I tried to work analytically one time with a woman who was simply too much for me. Believing that I could hang in with her to get the work done, I tried to continue despite the presence of a flood of primitive forces that was more than I could handle. Finally, I told the patient so. She said, with some indignation, that she thought the analyst was supposed to be able to take anything. I answered that at the moment I was not too clear about that, but that I knew what was going on was more than *I* could take. If that was what had to be dealt with, then there could be no question she was entitled to have it dealt with. I could not be of analytic use to her and so suggested she consult a colleague I felt could be of benefit.

I am not pleased by this vignette, but the postscript strikes me as being to the point. A year or two later, I received a telephone call from a woman requesting a consultation. I was so startled when she identified herself on the phone that I blurted out the question of where she received my name. I recognized this person as my prior patient's best friend. The lady on the phone laughed. She said that her friend had made the referral, that her friend had told her all about how the work had gone, but had added that I could be trusted as honest.

In general, I find I make several sorts of mistakes. The type that often troubles the patient the most is that for which I feel the least responsibility. What I have to say is both slower and more imprecise than either the patient or I would prefer.

The other categories of my mistakes are those arising from ignorance or from intrusions of unmastered personal conflicts and needs. Ignorance is a troublesome enemy. I am distressed at the frequency with which I hear people speak of how little is known by and about psychoanalysis. There is already more known than any one person can learn in a lifetime. That is a fact, not an excuse. It certainly offers no help to the patient tangled in a subtlety of psychopathology which I do not yet understand and which someone else would. The other category, that of eccentric countertransferential distortions on my part, is like a plague: repeatedly fought, yet never eradicated.

Whatever the source of error, the primary cure is candid clarification. Once seen, it must be acknowledged. That is not, however, necessarily immediately. The aim of analytic technique is always analytic understanding, not simply making me, the analyst, feel good. If an acknowledgment would interfere with an unfolding understanding of the patient's significances, then it must be deferred. The effort is to analyze anxiety, not to obscure it. Acknowledgment does not mean confession, exhibitionism, or revelation of my personal fantasies. The formal work in the office is the patient's analysis.

These issues of ambiguity and error are to the point of my activity particularly during the middle phase. I try to follow the patient, but I also try to interpret what I hear and what I think is going on. What I think the patient will make of my interpretations is for me unimportant, but what the patient makes of them is important. The possibility of a patient's finding what I say as implying something idosyncratic does not inhibit me. Tact involves respecting the patient's underlying equal validity, equal to mine. It does not mean demonstrating what a sensitive, nice chap I am, who would never risk hurting anyone.

Knowing that whatever I hear has been processed within me, and therefore knowing that whatever I interpret cannot be totally precise to the patient's meanings, I try not to offer interpretations ex cathedra. Most interpretations are trial interpretations aimed at getting ever closer to whatever forces are unfolding from the patient.

Yet there are frequently times, often when issues of domination and submission are being dealt with, when the patient acts and feels as if I, unlike the imago of the parent, must not be too definitive. There are times when someone tries to slip around issues without ever experiencing the feelings that would accompany the forbidden confrontation. There are times when for many varied reasons the patient works subtly to keep me from speaking clearly. When something seems clear to me, I try to say it clearly, not with, "I wonder whether . . ." or "What about . . . ?" or "Do you think, maybe . . . ?" but in simple declarative sentences. There is, of course, the danger of my engaging in a power struggle. I do not have the right or analytic reason to start such an issue, but if that is what the patient is engaged in, I neither have the right nor the inclination to avoid it.

Also, despite the need for prolonged silence on my part in the service of the abstinence principle, there are times I speak up to avoid misunderstandings. After a while, all patients catch on to my frequent lack of response to questions, to my silence, as appropriate and useful analytic technique, not as evidence of my capricious and arbitrary whims. However, especially in the earlier parts of an analysis, silence generally is taken as communicating assent.

No rule holds up across the board in the face of individual unconscious meanings. For several years into an analysis, my silence was felt by one young person as my unspeakable contempt and criticism. Indeed, that has proved analytically to be at least as common a meaning of silence as communicating assent. My preference is to make statements as called for to clarify. I do not wish to make statements to avoid having disagreeable motives or feelings ascribed to me.

The question inevitably is one of what to interpret. I find the old saw of interpreting what is on the surface to be generally useless for me and at times wrong. Its uselessness arises from the frequency with which one finds very much on the surface; the saying offers me no help in choosing. Its wrongness comes from its implicit bias toward the conscious and away from the unconscious. If I as the analyst will not aim toward the deep water of the unconscious, who will?

The two major guidelines I have for choice are those of affect and transference. Every statement I, the analyst, make involves a choice. Free association is the technique for the patient to attempt. If I randomly accept all messages as being of equal importance, I trivialize all significance. I prefer to comment on messages that include affective experience or defense against the experience of that feeling by the patient. My theme is to go into the direction of anxiety. Interpretation of symbols as such seems to me sterile and intellectual, usually without power for the patient.

The other guideline for interpretation is that of the transference. This does not mean that I pounce on the transference implications of everything the patient says. That strikes me as an effective way to interfere with the crystallization of an intense transference neurosis. I do try to conceive of what patterns I notice outside the analysis in terms of how they relate to what occurs within the transference–countertransference relationship. For me, that relationship is the living specimen of the patient's life and patterns.

The question of interpretation also demands attention to the relationship of resistance and drive. I am not entirely comfortable with the word "resistance." It seems a fine word when used to name a clear process, such as in the phrase "inner resistance." But for that we have the word "defense." Resistance is traditionally and properly used to refer to the manifestation of that inner defense in the analytic context. As such, it is a useful, indeed vital, signal of the presence of a not yet fully exposed conflict. And as such a signal, it is to be welcomed as a harbinger that something is working its way into the open.

But the word readily lends itself to part of its meaning, to that of a signal that goes unrecognized. Then I, the analyst, sense frustration. There is the sense that the patient is frustrating the analysis and is frustrating me. Reaction to such felt frustration without analytic processing is a countertransferential intrusion. Unrecognized, resistance becomes a hook that captures the analyst on his own ambition, his own urge for power or control. Recognized, resistance is a valued friend. Without resistance there is no analytic work, but recognized, resistance is the cutting edge of progress, the primary road to clinical analysis. Resistance brings forth the analytic questions, "How come this?" and "Why now?"

Consistently, the theme is that of attending to the meanings revealed by the process of the unfolding transference forces. It is in that sense that I attend to process over content, or at least to content in the context of process.

It is in that context that I consider the question of the central importance of dreams in analysis. There can be no doubt that dreams are the royal road to the unconscious, but a clinical analysis is not a royal journey. In a clinical analysis, one leaves the royal road for the mud and the underbrush, returning at times to the high ground to extend the view. Brilliant views, like that of Moses looking over the Promised Land, are wondrously impressive, but they are no substitute for the struggle to capture new territory. Working to expose a clearing, getting lost and then finding new paths, revealing the intensities of one's struggles in the actuality of the analytic experience – it is the transference neurosis and its resolution that provide the crucial road in clinical psychoanalysis.

From time to time, I do get a glimpse of an unfolding pattern before the patient has come to recognize it. If I feel it to be clear, I interpret what I see to the patient. Interpretation of resistance may come first, but I do not believe the discoveries of ego psychology are properly used if they are put in the service of avoiding deep meanings. An analysis, I believe, should expose and examine hidden horrors and ghosts, not sidestep them. The depth to aim for is always the most the patient can take, a depth most often underestimated by both analyst and patient.

The unfolding dialectic of the analysis in the context of the analytic dyad gives each interpretation a double quality. Work had to proceed before an interpretation could be offered. In that sense, interpretations are, as they have been called, commemorative events. Yet they open new ground at the same time that they consolidate the old. I am not in accord with those current theories that would seem to minimize the importance of interpretation. It is not enough that I understand something going on within the patient; I have to share that knowledge with the patient. Although they are commemorative events, interpretations are essential parts of the ongoing war, not dispensable subsequent memorial ceremonies. Working out and working through take place in stepwise fashion, even if small step by small step.

I have addressed the major themes of analytic work: active unconscious forces and fantasies, their exposure within the transference neurosis in an analytic situation, interpretation of resistances and unconscious forces so as to expose the unconscious to conscious mastery. The daily work proceeds in the presence of routine problems of everyday analytic life, which I have not presented.

Fees, schedule changes, missed sessions, acting out, and so on are the stuff of daily work. I make errors, but in terms of what I try to do, my routine handling of such issues is determined by how I understand each of them in the context of the broad themes I have described. An example is that of the patient's actions outside the analysis. Early on in the work, especially as I try to help the development of the transference neurosis, I am alert to outside action for its possible implications of the patient's defending himself against emotional intensity by diluting our relationship, carrying out part of the feelings and urges "out there" rather than "in here." When I see it, I tell the patient. Enacting can be a powerful defense against experiencing and remembering.

It is not always so, however. As the work is proceeding, what might seem to be acting out may turn instead into enacting in the service of extending insight and actualizing growth. An analysis is not a verbal chess game. Insight that does not extend the range of a person's potential in his life in the world is not true insight. Therefore, I value action not only with the phobic patient who must be assisted to confront anxiety. With anyone who seems to be exploring, who is working in the service of insight and growth, I value action and avoid interpreting all as acting out.

As with passing years I find myself ever more at ease, I find it less often necessary or appropriate to vary my basic routines. On reflection, I think this arises from increasing respect for the analytic process, not simply from personal aging. For instance, though there might be a minor convenience for me, I do not lightly or frequently change a patient's hours or cancel an appointment.

When it comes to money, which is always an area of important private meaning to each patient, I try to maintain a predictable consistency. I earn my living by selling my analytic services. I charge by units of time, though it is my service that I sell, not my time. Once time is committed to a patient, he is responsible to pay for it whether he uses it or not. I do not see myself as having either the right or even the inclination to decide when a session should be "excused" or not. Within the context of the analytic regression, the patient exposes childlike aspects of himself. But he is an adult exposing that portion of his personality; he is not a child. As a person, his validity is equal to mine, and he has equal responsibility for his life, as do I for mine.

The list of such routine issues of analytic practice is far from exhausted. My wish, without trying to touch every imaginable base, is to demonstrate that for me the criteria of how to handle such matters as they arise are those determinants that are realistic, honest, and will protect the continued course of the analytic work.

Just as no two analyses are alike, no two terminations are the same. Some analyses have a classical shape, an intense clear transference neurosis, and a well-defined clear termination phase, heralded by termination dreams and marked by intense recapitulation of previously worked-through conflicts. Many are less clearly demarcated, though in each the heart of the transference neurosis has been exposed and explicitly explored before an authentic termination arises. I prefer to call things by clear names: termination, stopping, and quitting are each called what they are, with an effort to avoid any glossing over.

Throughout my description of my work, I have been ever aware of my not mentioning my teachers, my models, or those before me and with me who have taught me, influenced me, and sharpened my skills and my ideals. It is not my undervaluing them that has kept their names out. Instead, it is my recognition of how broad and deep the contributions of others are to my thinking and my work. I take responsibility for myself, but I have no illusion or pretense of taking credit for a field in which I am a technician. My debt to my patients is not only for teaching me what it is like to be someone else but also for teaching me how to analyze. Some have borne with me as if I were a retarded child, slow to learn; I have benefited from their patience.

My focus in this paper has been on myself at work. That focus has distorted attention, turning it away from the patient and the analysis proper to that segment in which I am most apparent. In the whole picture of a clinical analysis, my own contribution is less noticeable, more a part of the background canvas on which the patient paints the tableau of his inner life.

I return to those other than patients who have taught and influenced me. In this paper, I have consciously restrained myself and mentioned only Freud, whose combined genius and humanity have created the language in which the rest write sentences. When I start to refer to others, I am flooded by a list, such a fond list—that I fear to forget one—that I worry who should go first, who could go second. I am a product of my teachers, my times, and my patients, as well as myself. Those whom I know only by reading are as intimate a part of my life as if I had spent hours with them personally.

Yet at this last moment, at the bottom line, I, like all analysts, am in my office daily, alone with one other person with whom and for whom I work and to whose psychoanalysis I am responsible.

9 Psychoanalytic Technique: Some Personal Reflections

Sydney E. Pulver, M.D.

I value writing highly, and although I do it with some difficulty, the opportunity to write this chapter was welcome. I suspect that most of what is written in the psychoanalytic literature sinks into oblivion, but as a glimpse into the way analysts actually practice, I had a hope that these chapters might not, or at least that they might only sink to the 40-fathom mark, where they could be periodically explored by adventurous young psychoanalysts. I say young because I am a teacher at heart, and I see this chapter as an opportunity to reach the young. I suppose this book will be read by experts as well as novices, but as the reader will see, my orientation is toward the latter. I go into a great deal of detail about certain routine and elementary things because it is precisely those things which are so often confusing to the beginner. It should be obvious that I focus on controversy, partly because I love dialectic but even more to warn the tyro away from the blind acceptance of tradition. The expert may test his views against mine and do what he will with the comparison.

A chapter of this nature poses a particular problem in the area of self-disclosure. A man's clinical work is intimately connected with his personality, and an understanding of what a therapist does is greatly enhanced if one knows what kind of a person he is. Considerations of this kind tempt me to give a good deal of personal detail about myself. However, I intend to go on practicing psychoanalysis, and issues of personal privacy aside, some degree of professional privacy is crucial to that practice, particularly because as a training analyst, there is a greater likelihood that my patients will read what I am writing. So, aside from saying that I have been practicing analysis for 24 years, I let the reader glean what he can about me from my productions. After all, both style and content are revealing, and by the end of the chapter readers may feel that they know me pretty well. Let us start, then, at the beginning. In a certain sense, analysis begins with the patient's initial contact. Consistency is a hallmark of analytic behavior, and if one values courtesy and understanding, one must value them all of the time and not just in the analytic situation. It simply will not do, regardless of the pressure of affairs, to permit a patient to be treated discourteously either by oneself or by one's secretary.

Within that framework, it is nevertheless important to do a certain amount of screening over the telephone. My first session with a patient is an evaluation, and there are some patients, such as those clearly requiring hospitalization or those requesting specific therapies which I do not do, for whom such an evaluation would be a disservice. To avoid this, either my secretary or I (whoever happens to answer the phone when the patient first calls) will ask, "Are you able to give me quick idea of what the problem is?" This is obviously a delicate question, because some people are understandably reluctant to talk about personal matters with a disembodied voice, particularly if it is not the voice of the doctor whom they wish to see. It is delicate, but it can be asked, and it helps me steer grossly inappropriate patients in the right direction. I see all patients who are not grossly inappropriate, whether or not they are requesting analysis. I always see them initially for purposes of evaluation, and that is made clear to everyone before scheduling the appointment. If I have no time in my schedule at the moment, I tell them so but offer the evaluation in any case, because it is a procedure that serves both the patient and me. For patients who do not wish analysis or are not suitable for it, an initial evaluation permits me to select those with whom I want to work psychotherapeutically. At the same time, I try to make the best referral that I can, and this enhances the patient's chances of ending up in the right therapy with the right therapist.

For those who do come specifically for analysis, the initial evaluation is brief, often no longer than a single session. I indicate at the beginning that its purpose is to give me a chance to see whether analysis is the treatment of choice and to give both of us a chance to at least get an impression of whether we can work with each other. The concept of our working together is both real and important. I do not feel that patients should go into therapy with a therapist whom they immediately dislike, and I emphasize this to those whom I am evaluating for therapy with me as well as to those whom I am referring to others. Usually, this initial evaluation is useful and appreciated. At times, however, it is clear that an evaluation was not really necessary and that an appropriate referral could have been made over the telephone. In such a case, I do not charge for the evaluative session. I am not claiming that not charging in this situation is necessarily a reasonable procedure, but it does make it easier for me to live with myself.

From the voluminous work on the topic of analyzability in the literature and from the scholarly contributions on the part of several close friends, I suspect that the determination of analyzability should be of major clinical concern to me. In fact, it is not. Although I do try to form an opinion as to the likelihood of a good therapeutic result, I do so more to be able to give some sort of estimate to the patient than for any practical utility such a determination has in selecting patients for analysis. My clinical experience has convinced me that deeper and more important changes are achieved with analysis than with other kinds of therapy, and that patients who are able to participate in the analytic process will benefit more from it than from other therapeutic approaches. Whether they will be able to undergo an analytic process is frequently quite clear on the basis of criteria much less subtle than those usually found in the analyzability papers. If it is not clear, I have found that for me it is largely undeterminable, at least with enough sureness on my part to lead me to recommend some other therapy. My practice, in other words, is to recommend analysis in all cases where some simpler and more convenient therapy will not do and where I think that there is at least some small chance that the patient will be analyzable. This is the approach of the trial analysis, which I subscribe to, without labeling it as such to the patient. I have occasionally had to change an analytic approach to a less intense form of therapy, but this has always seemed to work out better than in the early days when, inspired by a novice's confidence, I recommended some briefer therapy and lived to regret it. A similar mistake, I have found, is attempting to base my recommendation on my estimate of the patient's finances or motivation. One simply cannot make those kinds of determinations. Patients come to physicians to get an expert's opinion about the treatment most likely to help them, and I always try to give my best advice. I also always give options. Analysis may sometimes definitely appear to be the best therapy, but it is never the only therapy. I tell patients what the other possibilities are and, when I have a sense of it, what the likelihood of success is with each.

The rules that govern the actual analytic situation, the "frame" as some people call it, have been discussed at some length, particularly from the standpoint of the importance of consistency and the effects of altering them. Higher level theory has played little role in their construction. Instead, their broad outline has been determined by the accumulated clinical wisdom of several generations of analysts, and their specifics are determined by each individual on the basis of his own clinical experience. In psychoanalysis, particularly when we are dealing with details about the arrangement, there is no single correct way. All rules create new problems at the same time that they remedy old ones, and the best ground rules are those applied consistently, fairly, and in consonance with the analyst's personality, regardless of their specific content.

I set the ground rules in my own practice with a certain crude philosophy in mind, a philosophy which says that: (a) much as I would like complete flexibility, some kind of rules are necessary; (b) an intellectual understanding of the rules by the patient, an explicit clarification, is important early in analysis (hence I always discuss them after the evaluation, when the patient and I have agreed on analysis but before the analysis has formally begun); (c) these rules are for my good as well as the patient's, and when our interests conflict, my good usually takes precedence. I convey this implicitly, but if a patient protests a rule early on, I will make it explicit. This may seem unnecessarily offensive, but as in all aspects of analysis, it is not precisely what you do that makes the crucial difference but your attitude and intent in doing it, and this particular principle can be conveyed tactfully. In any case, it is worth taking the risk of giving offense, because it is above all crucial to avoid the pretense that everything one does is only for the patient's own good, a common parental hypocrisy which beginners sometimes feel forced into. Hopefully, the analyst's values and understanding of the consequences are such that he will not impose a grossly exploitative arrangement on a patient too vulnerable to defend himself.

And now for the ground rules themselves. Glover (1955) discusses them in what I consider to be the most outstanding textbook of psychoanalytic technique ever written, and I follow his list of topics.

1. *Number of sessions per week.* Four are workable, but five are infinitely better. I imagine that six or seven would be even better, if we could find analysts and patients willing to work that way. In practice, I always recommend five, and settle for four only when five are completely impractical. A rare patient can go through an analytic process in three or even fewer sessions per week, but I have never been able to predict this and thus do not recommend it when I feel that analysis is the treatment of choice.

2. *Length of the session.* The optimal time for a psychoanalytic session is not absolutely clear. Freud began with 60-minute sessions, but the exigencies of practice (including, probably, the advent of the telephone) eroded this to the present 45- or 50-minute hour. I have settled on 45 minutes, a fairly standard time in the Philadelphia area, plus or minus a minute or two as the flow of events dictates. I schedule patients

back to back, with a 15-minute break after every third patient, and find this approach quite workable, Greenson (1974) notwithstanding. I do not think it technically wise to go much over the allotted time, nor do I like my schedule disrupted, so I do not do so unless there is a genuine clinical indication. Going under the allotted time is obviously unconscionable if done on a regular basis. When I must do so, on rare occasions, I make the time up in a subsequent session. I seriously doubt whether analysis can be carried on in shorter sessions, based on my experience with two patients with whom, for financial reasons, I agreed to try analysis using 25-minute sessions four times a week. In neither patient was the attempt successful; we switched to twice a week psychotherapy after only a few months. This confirmed my impression, in dealing with patients who come consistently late, that the shorter time is a real handicap, although the added factor of acting out complicates the judgment.

3. *Fees.* Occasionally, I am willing for one reason or another to see an analytic patient at less than my usual fee (which, at this writing, is $85 per session). More often, I am not willing, and I do not do so unless I am relatively unambivalent about it. My firmness about this has been reinforced by several experiences in which I took a low-fee patient against my better judgment or, I should say, with a sense of deep unwillingness, and my ambivalence created major countertransference problems. I bill patients at the end of each month and expect payment during the succeeding month. I have learned (and continue to learn, I am afraid to say; I have some difficulty in practicing what I preach in this area) that failure to insist on the bill being paid is disastrous. One must attempt to understand analytically a patient's failure to pay, but analyzing at the expense of a firm policy is not workable.

4. *Charging for missed sessions.* Cancellation, like any consistent deviation from the ground rules, is likely to be loaded with signficance and is grist for the mill. Analysis of this behavior is facilitated by a firm and clear policy about charging for missed sessions, and it is probably not too important what that policy is. My own practice in this regard has shifted. For many years, I did not charge patients who canceled 24 hours in advance, and this system worked well. Recently, my time became much more tightly scheduled, and I found myself significantly more irritated at patients who canceled frequently in the service of acting out. I shifted at that time to a charge for my time regardless of notification, as recommended by Freud. This seems to work better, although I strongly suspect that this is due to its greater congeniality to me personally rather than to any inherent value as a procedure.

5. *Vacations.* I inform patients as far in advance as possible of the dates of my coming vacations and ask them to arrange their vacations at

that time if possible, both for the sake of my schedule and for the continuity of the analysis. If they cannot, I do not charge. I realize that this is logically inconsistent with my position on missed appointments, but I would feel uncomfortable charging for large blocks of time in which I was not seeing the patient.

Because my analytic technique depends to a large extent on my view of how analysis works, a discussion of my ideas on the mode of therapeutic action is in order. That topic, of course, has been a subject of speculation since the beginning of analysis, and from that speculation, insight has emerged as the mechanism par excellence of analytic effectiveness. Through insight, the patient is able to use rational judgment, to recognize fantasies as truly fantastic, and to make decisions on the basis of all the facts, intrapsychic facts included. One cannot change if one does not know how one is trying to change and what one is trying to change.

Insight, however, has not held the field uncontested. Many other mechanisms of change have been described, among which one of the most important is identification with the analyst. The identification resulting in the amelioration of a harsh superego and that resulting in greater introspection, for example, are two phenomena familiar to every analyst. Unlike most identifications, these are identifications that we do not try to "analyze away." This particular mechanism has been claimed by some to be the most important, and to some extent an insight versus identification controversy has crept into the literature. My own feeling is that both insight and identification are important, but insight is crucial. One of the reasons for this tends to be neglected, and I wish to call attention to it.

Insight is crucially necessary for mourning to take place. Mourning, of course, has been discussed by those describing psychoanalytic change, but its importance tends to be underemphasized. Rangell (1981), for example, in a good article on the movement from insight to change, only alludes briefly to mourning. The process from insight to change does not, however, simply involve an act of will, as Rangell implies. It always involves giving up either a self-representation or an object relationship, and both of these involve loss and mourning. Becoming less enraged at an absent father, for example, involves giving up one's relationship with that father, giving up all of the hopes, expectations, and passions that went with it, and mourning them. Freeing oneself from a passivity that results from an identification with a passive mother does not automatically occur after insight into the existence of that identification. In addition, one must deeply recognize the motivations for that identification, and these always include the preservation of some aspect of an object relationship with mother. Giving up the identification means giving up the relationship, and that requires mourning. Change takes place for many reasons, but I hold that change in the absence of this process of giving up a relationship and its accompanying mourning is usually not the deep kind of change that we call structural. And mourning, as we well know, is a genuine relinquishment which cannot take place without awareness of the loss, without insight. To be sure, a sense of loss can occur unconsciously, but the reparative mourning process, the actual affective giving up, requires conscious awareness for its successful completion. The need for mourning, incidentally, is probably one of the main reasons for the importance of working through.

These considerations are intended to demonstrate why I feel insight is central in change. However, they also throw light on another minor controversy in the psychological arena. Few experts in the field of psychotherapy research hold that the changes which take place in psychoanalysis are based on behavioral, conditioning mechanisms. I suspect that this claim is at least partially correct for some of the changes we see. If, for example, a patient feels terrible shame over a fellatio fantasy, the amelioration of that shame will involve psychological processes such as identification with the analyst's noncondemnatory attitude, but it will also involve something like desensitization or extinction during the course of repeated talking about the fantasies, a process which probably needs to be talked about in behavioral as well as psychological terms. Nevertheless, the primary mode of therapeutic action is distinctly and crucially different in psychoanalysis than in behavioral approaches, and that difference depends precisely on insight. The mourning process that I just described is at least one reason for this; it does not go on in the noninsight psychotherapies.

In addition to insight and identification, another factor that must be considered in thinking about how analysis works is abreaction, a process that is necessary because of the importance of early trauma in the etiology of psychopathology, an importance which I feel is currently underemphasized. Freud's peregrinations around the question of actual seduction in the etiology of hysteria are well known, and his dramatic reversal of opinion in favor of fantasy rather than reality has, I believe, had too great an effect on analytic thinking.

We currently tend to think of motivation primarily in terms of drive-determined fantasies, when in fact, early repressed traumatic episodes serve as just as important a locus of motivational fantasy production. Some very tentative speculations about the repetition compulsion may serve to illustrate the way I think about this. The repetition compulsion is one of our more obscure concepts, and the tendency to repeat that I am describing is only one of the things subsumed under that term. I see this tendency as ubiquitous. In our daily struggle for survival, we constantly encounter challenging situations that we handle more or less successfully. Successful handling results in a euphoric affect such as pride and a sense of accomplishment. Unsuccessful handling results in dysphoria, and this kind of dysphoria activates an innate tendency to repetitively think about the situation and try to figure out a better way of handling it. When we achieve a successful solution, the tendency subsides. This is something we all experience daily. The French, indeed, have a term for it, *esprit d'escalier*, describing the all too familiar phenomenon of being insulted at the bottom of a staircase and being unable to think of a suitable retort until reaching the top.

The adaptive value of such a tendency is clear. With it, we continually mull over our failures and figure out ways to prevent them the next time. Without it, we would enter every situation with very much the same inadequate repertoire. Unfortunately, from time to time we undergo failures that no amount of thinking about will help us handle better next time. The tendency to repeat is not deactivated, and unable to do anything more than undergo repeated dysphoria, we resort to a psychological defense: We cast the memory of the failure out of our awareness. But because the only true deactivator of the repetition compulsion is successful mastery, these repressed traumatic experiences remain active, and their activity is in direct proportion to the intensity of the dysphoric affect they have aroused. These repressed traumatic events, referred to earlier as motivators and just as important as drives, stir up fantasy systems just as elaborate as drives and are just as important to analyze. The mechanism by which such analysis is therapeutic is different than it is with drives in that it involves abreaction. There is, of course, an elaborate interplay between the two motivational systems, but that is not for discussion here. I realize that all of this is somewhat speculative, and perhaps not entirely clear, and I try to elaborate on it in my discussion of reconstruction and the transference.

I wish to emphasize the need to give traumatic events their true place in neurosogenesis, but I hasten to add that our attempts to analyze them are more often than not unsuccessful. The reconstruction of a specific traumatic event is of a different order than the clarification of more general patterns of sexual and aggressive feelings. In my less disciplined moments, I have wondered whether, as part of the analytic process, a very vigorous effort might be made to uncover these early traumas, vigorous to the extent of using LSD, hypnosis, and like approaches. Doing these things outside of analysis turns up traumatic events, but neglects the interplay of motivations, defenses, and character structures which surround them, and produces only transference cures. Using these approaches in analysis, even by someone other than the analyst, introduces such complicating factors that I have never had the nerve to try them. But I wonder.

A final word about therapeutic process. People are different, and so is the process of each analysis. In some, identification with the analyst's benign superego is the predominant therapeutic mechanism. In others, relinguishing the lost object and mourning are more important. In some, the interaction between the patient and the therapist is the main battleground. In others, it is the outside world. And in still others, it is the self and its vicissitudes. The idea of a unitary analytic process is an idealization, and although it is useful to have some generalizable ideas about what happens, expecting every patient to conform to these ideas is simply too Procrustean.

Three aspects of the analyst's attitude deserve special comment: his spirit of inquiry, his activity, and his flexibility. The spirit of inquiry, of course, is what analysis is all about, but it took me some years to recognize the extent to which this spirit guides and informs all of psychoanalytic technique. Freud's "Recommendations to Physicians Practicing Psychoanalysis" (1912), particularly his injunction against excessive therapeutic zeal–his famous surgeon metaphor–always struck me as terribly cold. Nevertheless, it was quite helpful early in my career in controlling my tendency toward therapeutic ambition and overinvolvement.

But I considered this to be only one of a number of guidelines until, as time went on, I realized that Freud was implying much more than I had appreciated. He was, in fact, setting forth what I consider to be *the* guiding principle in psychoanalytic technique: the search for understanding. Expressed as one might say it to a patient, the principle would assert, "My aim is to do everything I can to help you understand what is going on in your feelings. In working with you, I am going to try to do *only* that which leads to greater understanding. I could probably be helpful in many other ways, but unfortunately, they would interfere with the most basic, the most important part of what we are doing, namely, understanding." I do indeed occasionally say that, but whether I say it or not, it is always my guiding attitude. It does, in fact, take precedence over all other rules, procedures, and techniques, and I do not feel it is going too far to say that if one's attitude is as I have described, exactly what one actually does in any specific situation probably is not crucial.

Deriving from this quest for understanding is a second facet of the analyst's attitude: the need for activity. This is not news to any experienced analyst, but it may be news to analytic candidates, who have a tendency to view the role of the analyst as a passive one and at times literally to abhor activity. Many pressures toward passivity act upon the neophyte: the need for even-hovering attention, a listening stance which seems passive; our emphasis on interpretation, an emphasis which seems to illegitimize other analytic behaviors; the undesirability of active acting out, a relatively visible technical mistake, as contrasted to acting out by passive withdrawal, which is less apparent but equally destructive; and the student's tendency to misinterpret his own analyst's silence as passivity and identify that as desirable technique. All of these incline our students emotionally toward passivity, even if intellectually they know better. But the practice of analysis does not call for passivity. The fact is, one must not only want to understand, one must work to understand. Part of this work is active listening, a major mode of which is even-hovering attention. That ego state is a relatively passive one, but it is a passivity that is actively arrived at, a passive regression in the service of activity. And even-hovering attention is not descriptive of our state of mind all of the time, even as an ideal. In addition, we move back and forth, always actively, between many ego states: even-hovering attention, remembering, identifying, testing theoretical notions, conjecturing, and so on.

All of the foregoing is listening, an activity that takes up a good deal of our time. But we also engage in many other activities, and it is not always easy to know which is best at any particular time. Tensions exist between listening and these other activities, as exemplified by the following vignette, in which the question is: To listen or to inquire? A patient of mine in the latter part of the first year of his analysis mentioned that his mother had had a miscarriage when he was 1½ years old. Potentially important historical information of that nature always alerts me and makes me wonder: Do I inquire further or do I continue listening? Is elaboration of the current theme likely to be productive? How pressing is it, and is it likely to be more pressing and productive than information about the miscarriage? I try to answer these questions and decide whether to wait for further inquiry or to inquire on the spot. In this case, I asked the patient to tell me everything he knew or was told about the situation, and information emerged about his mother's ensuing depression, information which, although it seemed likely to be extremely useful later, did not seem to have any immediate pertinence. I stored it away and let the patient go on, which he did with apparently little deviation from the theme of his previous free associations.

In short, we listen most of the time, but we also do many other things. Moves away from the listening stance do not interfere with the analytic process if they are motivated by the desire to understand. They do interfere if they are systematically motivated unconsciously, but that is obvious. A lot of talking some of the time is not prima facie evidence of poor analysis. The truth is probably to the contrary. I realize that all of this amounts to a harangue against passivity, but I consider it a justified stroke against one of the more severe technical mistakes that analysts are prone to make.

Finally, there is flexibility. One would think it unnecessary to elevate such a common-sense good thing as flexibility to the status of a principle, but I have found that analysts, daredevils though they may be in everyday life, are more than ordinarily governed by rules when it comes to the practice of analysis. This quest for rules has a strong superego flavor, which I attribute to our nature, our organization, and our personal analyses. Our nature – at least the nature of those analysts I know most intimately – is obsessive-compulsive (probably because most of us are physicians). We share the usual obsessive desire to regulate our ambivalence and control our fate through clear definitions and procedures, and the effect of our nature is compounded by the effect of our organization. Our profession has become institutionalized. Psychoanalysis is now a body of theory, a mode of research, a therapy, and an organization. Organizations are notorious for structuring themselves by rules, and the impact of this institutional structure on psychoanalysis and psychoanalytic education is well known. Change can occur, but institutionalization tends to oppose it.

To add to all of this, we have all undergone training analyses, and for a variety of well-known reasons, they are on the average less successful than we would like, particularly from the standpoint of rule-following professional behavior. The unique situation of the analysand completing his analysis and moving into the direct personal and professional sphere of his analyst peculiarly favors the handling of unresolved transference hostility by identification with the aggressor. The aggressor in this case is seen as a powerful, depriving, and prohibiting analyst who always follows the rules, and our identification leads us to follow the rules just as strictly.

Whatever the reasons for it, any attempt to practice analysis by following rules must fail. Different clinical situations require different courses of behavior, and patients will quickly sense whether we are following an approach that is truly useful or are simply bound by rules and unable to interact meaningfully with them. Fortunately, if the analyst can maintain the search for understanding as a guiding attitude, he will automatically be flexible, as an example may illustrate. An obsessional patient in the third month of his analysis had been reading Freud and had come across his recommendation against reading about psychoanalysis. The patient posed the question: "Do I feel that he is creating a problem? Should he refrain from his reading?" The analyst who is more interested in understanding than in following rules will wonder whether the patient's reading is interfering at this time with the analytic process. The "rule against reading" grew out of Freud's recommendation that one must use caution and self-restraint in seeking the patient's intellectual cooperation in the treatment. As Freud warned it might, this recommendation became a rule, the purpose of which was to circumvent the intellectualization that reading may in some cases foster.[1]

In this analysis, it was already quite clear that reading was partly an identification with the analyst in a competitive way with some depreciatory implications ("I can get more from books than I can from you") and partly a manifestation of a genuine wish to understand. Its clinical effect had been minimal; if anything, it had stimulated the analytic process. With all that in mind, there was no reason to recommend against it. If the situation were otherwise, one might inform the patient that, in your opinion, the reading was interfering with the analysis, describing the manner in which it was doing so as clearly as possible. If that is taken as a prohibition—and always be alert for this kind of reaction—then it should be explored.

But the example raises a second issue, and perhaps a second rule. The issue is: Should the question be responded to at all? The rule, of course, is: Usually no. Surely it is being asked in the service of unconscious motivations (e.g., to get permission to carry out the depreciation referred to earlier). The principle of inquiry first would seem to dictate that it be explored rather than gratified. But now we must take another step away from rules and narrow-mindedness. The principle of inquiry and understanding refers to the entire psychoanalytic process. To advance ultimate understanding, one may have to forego immediate understanding. To preserve the observing ego and minimize unresolvable idealization and hostility, questions about treatment sometimes require reasonable answers. One might say that the earlier in treatment they are asked, the more likely they are to need an answer, but the determination should always depend on a clinical weighing of the vicissitudes of unconscious motivation versus the real need for information, rather than on adherence to a rule.

Although transference is the essence of psychoanalysis, I do not give a comprehensive description of my handling of it here because, by and large, I do not think I handle it very differently than most analysts. Instead, I discuss three topics that relate to transference, topics which in some way are controversial and about which I have rather strong feel-

---

[1]Interestingly, the "rule against reading" has its organizational counterpart in the rule in many psychoanalytic institutes that candidates must have 6 months of training analysis before they begin didactic classes, so as to minimize intellectualization. The notion that we can overcome resistance by a mandate from the education committee is quaint.

ings. These are: (a) analytic anonymity; (b) transference interpretation versus reconstruction; and (c) the use of the positive transference. To do this, I need to define transference, but first a word about me and definitions because I am a little peculiar about them.

One of the painful aspects of my psychoanalytic experience has been my repeated encounters with obscurity in our literature. If there is a note of bitterness in this statement, it is because I wasted many hours during my early psychoanalytic career trying to conceptualize – or trying to understand why I could not conceptualize – such arcane things as the manner in which the ego, a psychic structure, could take itself as a love object. Thank heaven, I have at last reached the point of being able to realize that when I cannot understand a concept it is probably the fault of the concept. But my early trauma has had an effect, and I now do my best to make myself as clear as possible. To that end, transference requires a definition because so frequently its usage in the literature is inconsistent with its widely accepted definition. The definition from "A Glossary of Psychoanalytic Terms and Concepts" illustrates this: "Transference: The displacement of patterns of feeling and behavior, originally experienced with significant figures of one's childhood, to individuals in one's current relationships..." In common analytic parlance, however, *any* distortion of the analyst is considered to be transference, and there are many such distortions that are not displacements from early objects. There are, for example, misconceptions about the analyst and his role that are based on myths and other sociocultural constructs. The New Yorker analyst who sits back and says little to nothing during the entire analysis is one example. The unsophisticated patient's early expectation that the analyst will behave in the same way as any other doctor is another. More important from a clinical standpoint, there are distortions that arise from the projection of unconscious self-representations, as in the patient who fears his own femininity and sees the analyst's African violets as an indication that it is the analyst, not he, who possesses this despicable trait. To inform the patient that he looks down on the analyst's penchant for horticulture because it reminds him of his mother is neither accurate nor effective if the truth is that it reminds him of himself. I emphasize this because it is a problem frequently encountered in beginning therapists and enhanced by the standard definition of transference. In this paper, I use the word transference most often in the standard sense, but it may also signify those aspects of the emotional relationship to the analyst that are not determined primarily by reality factors, whatever their origin.

The need for analytic anonymity arises directly from considerations of transference analysis. Anything that arouses unconscious fantasies promotes the development of transference. In the analytic situation, these things include the development of feelings for the other person, which are always part of an intense relationship; the potential for gratification promised by the removal of prohibitions against thinking whatever one wishes; the regression facilitated by the surround of the analysis (the couch, the recumbent position, etc.); and finally, the effect of knowledge, or lack of it, about the analyst. As a general rule, it seems to be true that lack of reality knowledge enhances the development of transference, and it is at least partially from this that the principle of analytic anonymity developed. However, it is by no means the case that absolute anonymity is always desirable, even if attainable. At times, some kind of reality contact with the analyst is positive and even invaluable in facilitating awareness of the transference and helping in its resolution.

This statement, I realize, is radical enough to require some support, so I call the reader's attention to the substantial literature on accidental encounters with the analyst outside of the analytic situation. There one will find ample evidence that such encounters have an effect, sometimes negative but often positive. In most cases, this is gratuitously positive in the sense that the transference neurosis is unfolding anyway and would have unfolded without the encounter. In my experience, however, such encounters have occasionally triggered a piece of transference analysis that advanced a process which under other conditions might have unfolded at a much slower pace. I am not maintaining that such encounters rectify stalemates or do anything that might not have been done anyway, but I am saying that in some cases the overall effect may be a positive one. Unfortunately, it is extremely difficult to predict the impact of such an encounter and thus extremely difficult to plan it. In other words, analytic anonymity should be maintained as a principle, and anonymity should be violated only when other considerations make it important to do so. I am against the horror that is felt when chance violations occur; some knowledge about the analyst does not automatically make for an impossible analysis.

A word here about the tendency of some to let the need for analytic anonymity and the need to preserve analytic neutrality move them into a stance of affective withdrawal from the patient. From the standpoint of resolving the transference, a sense of real affective contact with the analyst is sometimes essential. Analytic anonymity and neutrality alone will be sufficient to enable those patients with relatively intact reality testing to recognize that their transference fantasies are not based on any evidence and therefore are perhaps distortions. However, a significant number of patients have minute lacunae in their reality testing, and it is not uncommon for such patients to maintain a conviction that a transference distortion is not a distortion at all. In such cases, some affective expression by the analyst may be necessary for the patient to recognize that the analyst is not quite the way the patient pictures him. Again, this is difficult to plan and probably always happens as the enactment of the kind of countertransference scenario described by Tower (1956) and Bird (1972). My point, however, is that it does not happen if the analyst, in the search for perfect neutrality, phobically avoids an emotional participation in the relationship, an avoidance that our training tends to facilitate.

And now let us turn to that perennial and probably never to be solved controversy, "transference interpretation only?" The most recent flare-up of this controversy has been stimulated by Gill (Gill & Hoffman, 1982) in his persuasive publication *Analysis of Transference*. I use Gill as an example of those who advocate the exclusive (or almost exclusive) use of transference interpretations. This is perhaps an overstatement of his position, the spirit of which might better be captured as focusing upon the patient's experience of the analytic situation is the crucial mutative factor in the analytic process, and the crucial activity of the analyst. Of course he does other things, but these are all peripheral to what is important and should be done minimally.

I see two problems with this position, the first having to do with empathy. Making *only* transference interpretations must be intrinsically unempathic. Even in the midst of a florid transference neurosis, other things will happen to patients and other things will preoccupy them. Granted that everything in analysis is said in a dyadic context (i.e., that there are two people present, one of whom is speaking to the other) and that everything said must therefore be imbedded in a matrix of some kind of feeling about the therapist, those feelings are not necessarily primary at any one moment or during any one session. Interpreting the transference when it is not primary is at worst a sign of self-preoccupation by the analyst and at best a mildly irritating kind of nagging.

A second problem with the here-and-now approach is its neglect of genetic material. Gill's position, as he made very clear in a clinical seminar I recently attended, is that although genetic material does have psychoanalytic relevance, it is not of central technical importance. When it is pertinent, it will emerge by itself after a correct understanding of and interpretation of the here and now. Reconstruction, in other words, is an unproductive if not actually distracting procedure. In my opinion, this implies a theory of the psychoanalytic process that is off the mark. It is true that most patients will make substantial progress if the here and now is the sole focus. Some patients, however, will make substantially greater changes if the genetics of their illness is considered something more than a trivialty.

Here, my previous remarks on early psychic trauma are appropriate. I would suggest that the relative importance of reconstruction is directly proportionate to the amount of trauma the patient has undergone. By trauma, I am referring to acute psychic trauma of the stress rather than the strain variety. All children go through episodes and periods of stress trauma, but it is more important in some than in others. Traumatic episodes act in children exactly as they do in adults: They produce a syndrome of traumatic neurosis accompanied by typical symptoms such as anxiety, bad dreams, phobic behavior, and so on. As in adult traumatic neuroses, therapy requires an abreactive experience in which the patient can relive the trauma and reintegrate it, and this kind of experience is facilitated when the analyst makes attempts at reconstruction.

I can illustrate this point by describing a session with Mr. N, a 26-year-old lawyer who had been in analysis for almost a year for a severe obsessive neurosis. The theme of the last 2 months had been a negative paternal transference, characterized by an increasing sense of disappointment in the analyst. This began to develop in the sixth month of analysis as he began to realize that his wish for a magic cure (underneath, for a perfect relationship with father) was not going to be realized. Most of the work since then had been directed toward what Gill would call resistance to the awareness of the transference. He defended against awareness of his disappointment and the accompanying rage in several ways. He buckled down and worked harder, with the unconscious expectation that if he worked hard enough I would finally do something. He handled his fleeting conscious wishes for my help by telling himself that he was expecting too much, by reading books on analysis and comparing me favorably with the authors, and by telling himself that my failure to actively help him was basically good for him because he had always been too dependent on others. When, as happened periodically, he was unable to sustain this and became depressed, he attacked himself instead of me and berated himself for being an incapable idler.

In the session I wish to focus on, Mr. N began with vehement anger at his boss. He had been working there for 7 months, and it was clear that they had absolutely no interest in teaching him anything. They were merely using him and exploiting him. Sure, he had learned a little, but that had been mainly because he had been working so hard at it by himself. It was clear early on that he was referring to the analytic situation, and I wondered whether to interpret this solely as a displacement or also as a sign of progress, because he was much more in touch with his anger and his disappointment than he had been previously. In the event, he made the interpretation himself and began describing how much his job was like the analytic situation, but also how essentially different it was. It was realistic to expect more active interest from his boss, who really is a son of a bitch. I, in contrast, did seem to be interested and trying. Nevertheless, his sense of disappointment was acute.

He spent the remainder of the session (in response to my inquiry) looking at just what he was disappointed about. It became clear that his more conscious feelings had to do with disappointment about not being guided and taught anything. Less conscious, but something he was beginning to become aware of, was his desire for a teaching *relationship*, a father-son relationship in which his boss and I would respect him and care for him. His more unconscious fantasies of anal homosexual penetration, with its corresponding feminine identification, were defended against by his anger and were only hinted at in such comments as, "I've decided that I don't give a shit about the boss or his work. He's been screwing me, and I'm going to screw him. I'm only going to be there 3 more months, and I'll just do what I need to and then get out!" The early traumas surrounding seduction by enemas and primal scene episodes, which were an important part of the genetic roots of these fantasies, had been apparent from the history and a number of dreams early in analysis, but they did not manifest themselves at all in this session.

The course of the analysis from this point will, in my opinion, be markedly influenced by the analyst's stance vis-à-vis the transference versus reconstruction controversy. If he chooses to focus solely on the here and now, it is likely that the deeper unconscious fantasies will emerge and, with this patient, that a shift will take place in the direction of Oedipal competitiveness, from which this anal position is a regression. Mr. N will come to understand his current desires for help from father and for a relationship of mutual respect with him. He will be more familiar with the ways these desires express themselves in his fantasies, the ways by which he keeps himself from knowing about them, and the ways he prevents himself from actually gratifying them: his aloofness, his distance, his identification with father. Worked through in the transference, he will come to see that he imposes these things on situations where they need not be, and in the course of experiencing all of the aspects of his behavior in the therapeutic situation, he will be able to change it.

These changes will be major, the kind of change that we call structural. It is much less likely, however, that the specific genetic roots of his problem will become clear or that the major traumatic episodes which play an important part in determining the intensity of this constellation will be revealed and worked through. The repressed experiences will remain repressed and active, and as they continue to exert their motivational influence, Mr. N will constantly feel impelled into replicating the traumatic experiences and trying to master them. The only way to reduce the motivational impact of these events is by abreacting them, and this is much more likely to be accomplished by reconstructive efforts in the transference. I grant that this kind of abreaction takes place less frequently than we would like, but it does take place in some patients, and it is for this reason that, when it seems appropriate, I attempt to make reconstructive as well as transference interpretations. I do, of course, understand Gill's point, and in one sense, I agree with it. Failure to interpret the transference properly is a much more serious problem than interpreting it too much and is ubiquitous in the analytic community. But recommending "transference interpretation only" is not the way to improve things.

Finally, a few words on the concepts of *the working alliance* and *the real relationship*. A honeymoon period of several decades after the introduction of these concepts has been followed in the past several years by a spate of criticisms, the gist of which is that they provide excuses for analysts to depart from true neutrality by way of small gratifications, to act out rather than to analyze. This is countered by those who argue that all too often analytic neutrality is merely an excuse for a kind of schizoid withdrawal of the analyst from the necessary intimacy of the analytic situation. Both sides quote Freud on the unobjectionable positive transference, but I believe that Freud's actual use of the positive transference has not been sufficiently understood. Lipton (1977) notwithstanding, I would maintain that Freud's psychoanalytic technique is not representative of the best of current psychoanalytic technique, nor is it something to be desired. On the surface, Freud's observation sounds valid: The positive feelings in the analytic relationship, some of which are certainly transferential, are useful to keep the analytic process going and thus need not be interpreted. When, however, one examines Freud's actual behavior as it is described by his analysands, it is obvious that he used the positive transference in a way that is not at all consonant with our present ideas about the analytic process. Specifically, he used it to overcome resistance. Time after time, he admonished patients, told them that they are resisting, congratulated them on having a productive analytic hour, exhorted them to cooperate, and in general, browbeat them in the service of understanding. This is a holdover of the hypnotic technique, a holdover rooted in the sociocultural position of authority of the physician in fin de siècle Vienna, in Freud's early training, and perhaps in some aspect of Freud's character.

The way we use the positive transference today is entirely different. I believe it is true to say that we *do* use it, but only in the most mild and derivative form. We will, for example, occasionally urge a patient to say what is on his mind when he is reluctant to do so and things of that sort, but for the most part, we try to help patients understand their resistance rather than to overcome it forcibly. The point of all this is that we cannot call upon Freud's use of the unobjectionable positive transference as support for the concepts of real relationship and working alliance. Nevertheless, I believe these concepts are useful. There *is* an aspect of the analytic relationship that exists mainly, not exclusively, in a matrix of reality, and we need to pay attention to it. As for the working alliance, thinking in terms of that concept calls our attention to those aspects of the transference which impinge on the way we are working together and which need to be analyzed for the analytic work to proceed. We don't need a new concept in order to do this, but thinking of the working alliance can be helpful.

I would now like to emphasize the importance of making interpretations that are preconscious – close to the surface – and I intend to do this in the context of a discussion of the manner in which empathy has burst upon the psychoanalytic scene. Self psychology, of course, depends heavily on empathy. An important feature of Kohut's technique is the focus on making empathic interpretations and exploring the patient's reaction to empathic mistakes on the part of the analyst. But this has been an important part of psychoanalytic technique ever since Freud made his famous statement about interpreting on the surface, and the obvious question that comes to mind is, "Why does this have such an impact on us now?" For the answer, we must examine the concept of empathy a little more closely.

To many psychologists, empathy refers to an understanding of what the patient is consciously feeling. To psychoanalysts, empathy means something different. It denotes the ability to appreciate affectively and understand cognitively what someone else is feeling and thinking in all of its ramifications: conscious, preconscious, and unconscious. There is, of course, no such thing as complete understanding, but the closer we come to it, the more we may consider ourselves empathic in the psychoanalytic sense. An important part of psychoanalytic empathy from a technical standpoint is being able to tell at what level the patient is feeling these things, to tell what feelings are in his immediate conscious experience, what fantasies are preconscious, and which are more deeply defended against. This is the point that Kohut and his followers are making. An important emphasis in Kohutian work on empathy is the interpretation of what the patient is consciously or, at the deepest, preconsciously feeling. It is very near to, if not exactly the same as, interpreting close to the surface à la Freud or interpreting what is preconscious à la Kris (1975) and many others. Why, then, did we need to be told this again? I suspect it is because, although surface interpretations are a sine qua non of our technique, we have major difficulty in making them. I detect the tendency to interpret too deeply, even among experienced analysts, and I believe we do this on all levels and in all areas. When, for example, I tell a patient who is furious at himself for his failure to respond to analysis that he is furious at me for not helping him, I am probably too deep. When I tell him that he seems to be taking all of the responsibility himself and is having trouble seeing me as having a role in what he and I are doing, I am probably closer to the mark.

To some degree, we have this kind of trouble because of our normal human difficulties with being empathic. To a much larger degree, it is due to our knowledge of and fascination by the unconscious. In a way, this is as it should be. Our clinical theories abound in unconscious psychodynamics, and a good part of our training *is* devoted to understanding unconscious processes. When an obsessive patient speaks of contamination, anal smearing leaps to our mind. When an actor complains of stage fright, exhibitionistic or primal scene anxiety immediately occurs to us. Such insight has been a source of personal and professional help to all of us, and it is understandable that we should want to impart it to others. Understandable, but not desirable. Our training should correct for this tendency, but I fear that it very often does not. At any rate, I personally feel strongly about it, and it is an issue that I focus on in all of my supervision and in my didactic teaching on technique. To this end, incidentally, Paul's *The Form and Technique of Psychotherapy* (1978) is superb. Paul's examples tend to be intellectual and obsessive, but once one makes allowances for that, his exercises on psychotherapeutic intervention are very often applicable to analysis and, in my course on technique, have proven to be a useful way to highlight preconscious interpretation.

The term "countertransference" has been used in the analytic literature in a variety of ways, ranging from such narrow meanings as the analyst's transference to the patient's transference to the very broad meaning of any and all of the analyst's affective reactions to his patient. My own use of the term has progressed from narrow to broad, a definitional change that was accompanied by an attitudinal one. This change on my part has followed a pathway similar to the evolving shift in attitude toward countertransference on the part of analysis as a whole. It has played a large part in shaping my psychoanalytic technique, and I would like to try to trace it here.

When I started doing analysis in the late 1950s, I viewed countertransference much according to the fashion of the day as an undesirable manifestation of psychopathology on my part, one which had to be ruthlessly searched out and eliminated, if possible in status nascendi. Tower's (1956) excellent article on countertransference had appeared by this time, and I had gained hints from my reading and my experience that my emotional reactions to my patients were perhaps somewhat more useful than I was permitting myself to believe and that analytic neutrality did not inexorably require emotional impassivity. However, the effects of my training and the attitude of my supervisors were powerful, and it took me almost 10 years of struggle before I was able to shift my position. The catalyst for this shift was Joseph Sandler, who visited our study group and expressed the opinion that countertransference could not be avoided and that the analyst typically and routinely gets drawn into a countertransference situation, notices it, and then analyzes it, as a result of which the countertransference reaction subsides until the next episode. This, you should notice, is a much more tolerant attitude toward countertransference, but one which still implies that countertransference ultimately has to be avoided or eliminated.

At about this time, I began recognizing that it was useful to divide my emotional responses to my patients into two kinds. The first were reactions having important conflictual elements. Aspects of these reactions were unconscious, and I not infrequently detected them through some symptomatic act. These corresponded to my old picture of countertransference, and I felt and continue to feel that this type of reaction, inasmuch as it remains unconscious, interferes with the analysis and must be detected and understood (not, of course, eliminated). There was, however, another class of emotional reactions that occurred far more frequently and, indeed, ubiquitously. These were my everyday emotional responses to the patient, relatively appropriate to the patient's behavior and relatively unentwined with my own conflicts. These feelings, once I truly came to accept them, became invaluable aids in understanding what was going on in my patients. I shifted, in other words, from what Schwaber (1982) calls the objective to the subjective listening perspective. Instead of being a somewhat detached observer, I have become an involved participant in a relationship with another person.

Granted, these are relative terms. When I say I was a detached observer, I do not mean that I was the aloof, distant, unfeeling analyst who delights the caricaturists. I always empathized, identified with, and reacted to my patients, but my attitude toward these reactions was different. I tried to keep them under control, rather than permitting them to flourish internally and be useful. And when I say that I am an involved participant, I do not mean that my involvement goes beyond the bounds of analytic neutrality. That is, I do not act out, or at least, I attempt not to. But I *feel* involved and have come to regard that involvement as an essential part of the analytic process and, to my great good fortune, an essential part of what makes analysis a deep pleasure. And this, I think, is a good note on which to end.

REFERENCES

Bird, B. (1972). Notes on transference: Universal phenomenon and hardest part of analysis. *Journal of the American Psychoanalytic Association, 20,* 267–301.

Freud, S. (1912). Recommendations to physicians practicing psychoanalysis. *S.E.,* 12, 111.

Gill, M. M., & Hoffman, I. Z. (1982). *Analysis of transference.* New York: International Universities Press.

Glover, E. (1955). *The technique of psychoanalysis.* New York: International Universities Press.

Greenson, R. (1974). The decline and fall of the 50-minute hour. *Journal of the American Psychoanalytic Association, 22,* 785–791.

Kris, E. (1975). On preconscious mental processes. In *Selected papers of Ernst Kris* (pp. 217–236). New Haven, CT: Yale University Press.

Lipton, S. D. (1977). The advantages of Freud's technique as shown in his analysis of the Rat Man. *International Journal of Psycho-Analysis, 58,* 255–273.

Moore, Burness, E., & Fine, Bernard, D. (1968). *A glossary of Psychoanalytic terms and concepts* (2nd ed.). American Psychoanalytic Association.

Paul, I. H. (1978). The form and technique of psychotherapy. Chicago: University of Chicago Press.

Rangell, L. (1981). *Journal of the American Psychoanalytic Association, 29,* 119–141.

Schwaber, E. (1982). Narcissism, self psychology, and the listening perspective. *The Annual of Psychoanalysis, 9,* 115–132.

Tower, L. E. (1956). Countertransference: I. Theoretical considerations. *Journal of the American Psychoanalytic Association, 4,* 224–255.

10 An Analyst at Play

James T. Thickstun, M.D.

When I first took a patient into analysis, 35 years ago, my attitude toward the work was much as portrayed in the surgical analogy – the analyst actively analyzing material presented by the relatively passive patient. Analysis was work, and I would say my work was heavily burdened by my superego. My supervisors, who were quite human, reasonable, and friendly, became superego surrogates. The relationship of patient to analyst was transference, and countertransference reactions were more to be avoided than understood. These simplifications exaggerate the situation, but nevertheless, they do represent a dominant aspect of my work at that time.

My first supervisor, Dr. Edith Buxbaum, who was also a friend, happened to be a child analyst. During my work with her, I came to understand that in doing adult analysis child analysts have the advantage of being in a better position to understand and reconstruct the childhood of their patients. In the back of my mind, I have always carried the idea that one day I would undertake to learn child analysis, but I never have; playing with kids may not be my idea of a serious adult pursuit, or more likely, such play might reveal forbidden instinctual impulses and behavior. Whether with conscious intent or not, Edith once put her finger on the heart of this matter when we had been discussing some anxiety of my Oedipal-age son. She suggested that it might be good if I would play childhood games with him. When I responded that playing such games was difficult for me, she quickly said in that case it might be good for me, too. She was probably right.

A significant aspect of myself involved in the choice of topic and in the development of this chapter has been conflict between a playful, childish, joyous part of myself and an authoritarian, severe, work-oriented aspect; or if you prefer, between id and superego, pleasure principle and reality principle, child and parent–play and work. This conflict must also include superego response to the sexual and aggressive impulses and the competitive and narcissistic strivings expressed in play. Issues such as these are reworked over and over by analysts in their analytic work and in other aspects of their lives. Such reworking can be followed in this chapter and may be conceptualized in the form of dialectic found so often in Freud's writings–thesis, antithesis, and synthesis. Here it is framed as play, work, and play-work. Over the years, my work has gradually been modified to play-work as the tension within me between work and play has relaxed–not vanished.

So many experiences within my analytic career have assisted in this modification that I would not be able to name them all–my own analysis, my patients, colleagues, analytic and other writings, seminars, family experiences, vacations, hobbies, and on and on. The influence of supervisors over these years has always been meaningful to me. In chronological order, Edith Buxbaum, Douglass Orr, David Brunswick, Ernst Lewy, Carel Van der Heide, and Ralph Greenson have occupied this role for me, Buxbaum and Orr during my formal training and the others for lengthy periods during the 1960s when I was revitalizing myself as analyst. That puts me in my mid- to late 40s. Call that midlife crisis if you like, but it now sounds awfully young. All these analysts were very helpful, each adding to my understanding of my patients, my work, and myself. In the general area to which this chapter is addressed, Greenson was most influential, not in the particular formulations relating play and its derivatives to psychoanalysis, but in the more general area of relationship of patient and analyst, from which I see this chapter as a variant. For someone who enjoyed center stage as much as Greenson, it amazed me to see the change when we entered his office. He was quite simply no longer the most important person in the room. The patient and the process occupied that position; he was sensitively insightful, empathic, and able to help me understand, and do, what was necessary to facilitate the therapeutic process.

One of the central lines of development of clinical psychoanalytic thought from the time of my training has been that of exploring the intricacies of the analytic situation, relationship, and process. There has been increasing interest in pre-Oedipal development and pathology, in issues such as "basic" transference, working alliance, therapeutic alliance, the uses of countertransference in understanding the analytic relationship, the influence of the analyst's character traits on the analytic process, the nature of the therapeutic action of psychoanalysis, and so on. Some of the authors prominent in this line of development are mentioned here, but only those whose work seemed most pertinent to the theme explored. Many others have contributed meaningfully to our analytic literature, and many have also contributed their understandings as teachers and colleagues, but have not written – because many analysts do not. The interactive nature of the analytic partnership has been increasingly understood through these significant contributions. During these years, my experiences have led to greater comfort and less defensive rigidity in my "work". As you can see, I believe looking at analysis as related to play (as well as work) is consistent with a developmental trend in psychoanalysis as a whole, a trend that has influenced all of us and is consistent with a developmental process within me moving toward a reconciliation of my own dichotomy between play and work. During these years, I believe my analytic relationships have deepened and are better understood, and that my patients have increasingly become partners in the enterprise, which is an actively interactive, mutually shared process benefiting both of us.

In addition to the nature of my conflict between play and work, the general evolutionary developments in psychoanalysis, and my own experiences as a psychoanalyst, there has been the important influence of immediate nonanalytic life experiences. My family experiences are first among these. During these years, five children have grown up, and our third grandchild is now of pretend-play age. A different but equally important influence has been my wife's becoming a psychological anthropologist, focusing primarily on child development. Her avid interest in infancy and early childhood has been somewhat contagious and has given rise to frequent discussions on such matters, as the house has filled with books on child development, mother-infant interaction, and – oh, yes – play.

Mix all of these together because that is how they occurred, none really isolated from the others within my experience. And don't forget our 4-year-old granddaughter.

In this chapter, I examine the process of psychoanalysis and its participants from the point of view of play and play-related phenomena. Important aspects of psychoanalysis in patient, analyst, and process are related to the role that play had in the childhood development of each participant, the characteristics and capacities that derive from play, and the phenomena in psychoanalysis that are related to play.

Play is among the earliest activities of the infant with the mother and is important to the most fundamental developments of infancy, childhood, and the entire life cycle. Although the proximate motivation for play is pleasure, the functions served by play are fundamental and wide-ranging. The capacities for object relations, learning, communication, creativity, and imagination are all dependent on play for their development. Derivatives of early behavior are not identical with their sources, however, and when Freud (1908) wrote that "the creative writer does the same thing as the child at play" (p. 144), he did not mean that the two behaviors were identical, but rather that they were similar, or identical in certain abstract respects having to do with fantasy and imagination. Both the creative writer and the analyst have highly developed skills characteristic of each craft; however, these are not the focus of this chapter. A psychoanalysis is not two children playing together, but it is similar. Capacities developed from, or in conjunction with, childhood play (particularly symbolic play) make psychoanalysis possible, both in patient and analyst, and the psychoanalytic situation itself demonstrates many of the elements of childhood play.

Our cultural heritage has provided us with a work/play dichotomy that is clearly reflected in our language, but some of our activities do not lend themselves to such categorization. Synonyms for work include such words as "drudgery," "toil," and "struggle," which are never applied to play; those for play include "revelry," "frolic," and "amusement." It is unfortunate that we are limited to labeling an activity with one word, as either work or play, because although analysis is work, it is also play. This dichotomy is not present in all cultures, and some have no comparable words with which to conceptualize such a distinction. The Protestant work ethic, firmly rooted in Judaic tradition, has had a profound influence in this country on our view of work and play, and Freud's cultural background was also "job-minded" (Riesman, 1950, p. 2), contributing to his attitudes toward work and play and the contrast he drew between the reality principle and the pleasure principle. As Riesman (1950) wrote: "The workaday world with its productive machinery, its markets, [and] its other economic processes, was [for Freud] sharply marked off from the play-world, the world of fantasy and gratification" (p. 3).

It is impossible to define "play" satisfactorily. Play requires active participation, is pleasurable, voluntary, without extrinsic goals, and is distinguished from "reality." Although these are all aspects of play, they are not always present in the activities we call play, and they are sometimes present in activities we do not regard as play. The referents of the term are protean and, although we all seem to recognize those activities we label "play," this does not necessarily mean that they are all intimately related conceptually. We play chess, we play a character in a play, we play the piano, we play with our food, with our pencils, with ourselves, we play a joke on someone, we "play around" with ideas, we play a fish, "make a play" for someone, play up to someone, we play out a rope, we play upon people's sympathies, we play a record, we play on words—and so on ad infinitum. These activities have characteristics in common, but each is also present in other states, making it impossible to abstract a set of common characteristics that would provide a comprehensive definition. This does not mean, however, that we cannot usefully discuss characteristics and classifications of play. In fact, only if we do this can we then see if there are indeed parallels between childhood play and adult psychoanalysis.

Huizinga (1955), in one of the first major "works" to take play itself seriously as an object of study (aside from the study of play as related to the treatment of children), produced a definition that we may use as a starting point to discuss the characteristics of play: "Play is a voluntary activity or occupation executed within certain fixed limits of time and place, according to rules freely accepted but asolutely binding, having its aim in itself and accompanied by a feeling of tension, joy and the consciousness that it is 'different' from 'ordinary life' " (p. 28). This difference—that play is pretend or nonliteral behavior—is the most significant aspect of play. Freud (1908) made a similar comment when he wrote that the child "takes his play very seriously. . . . The opposite of play is not what is serious but what is real. In spite of all the emotion with which he cathects his world of play, the child distinguishes it quite well from reality" (p. 144). In a similar vein, Greenacre (1959) wrote that "play may appear as a kind of paradoxical make-believe reality testing—a reality testing, however, in which the child holds the joker through the fact that much of play *is* make-believe even when expressed in overt action. It is not then 'real reality' " (p. 66). And Garvey (1977) noted, that "all play requires the players to understand that what is done is not what it appears to be. It is this nonliteral attitude that allows play to be buffered from its consequences" (p. 7). Rosen (1960) described the "implicit contract" in both play and psychoanalysis as an agreement to engage in imaginative make-believe play, which can tolerate the ambiguity of a situation being simultaneously real and fantasy. The make-believe quality of play, which disconnects it from the usual consequences of reality, was also described by Reynolds (1976), who noted that play is "behavior in the simulative mode" and studied it from the standpoint of its role in the organism's processing of information. The term "simulation" is used here in the same sense that contemporary technology uses it in referring to simulations of operations designed to produce information about performance without undertaking the "real" operation. Play is make-believe, buffered from the usual consequences of behavior, not "real reality," but a simulation only in the nonliteral mode—a special state protected from reality. The player must be simultaneously in touch with both fantasy and reality and have a "playful" tolerance of this ambiguity.

The mode of make-believe, which is characteristic of play, is also important to activities we call work. Simulation, though make-believe, is an integral part of many scientific procedures. But theoretical formulations are themselves fantasies of a sort—internal play—although their testing requires more traditional, orderly, and consciously directed thought. The play-work of artists, creative writers, and analysts depends on make-believe translated into reality-effective thought and behavior. By convention, we call some things work and others play, but no single criterion, including that of make-believe, is adequate to make the distinction.

The activity of play is pleasurable from the moment of birth, or so it seems to the observer. The mother's play with the infant almost immediately after birth results in sounds, movements, and expressions that are invariably interpreted as pleasure. Throughout life, this continues to be a dominant feature of play, and the idea that pleasure is inherent to this activity is fundamental. The concept of pleasure in play as intrinsic to the process itself rather than in external reward is widely accepted. Waelder (1933) referred to it as "functional pleasure"—"joy in the activity itself"—in contrast to "gratification-pleasure," which lies in "the *success* of an action" (p. 210), that is, the reward. Much of the study of play has been devoted to its related activities, but Csikszentmihalyi (as reported by Chance, 1979) focused on what a person *feels* in play rather than what a person *does*. Those who feel the most enjoyment in any activity, play or otherwise, describe a mental state that he calls "flow" (p. 11), a pleasurable state of great concentration. As adults, we are aware of it in a variety of activities, certainly in the pleasurable concentration of play.

Many activities important to the survival of the individual and the species are associated with pleasure, and this association ensures their exercise. Play is one of these. Pleasure motivates and strengthens behavior, and play, motivated by intrinsic pleasure, is crucial in the establishment of mother-infant attachment and in learning adaptive behavior. This pleasure could result from intimacy with the mother during play or feedback from the activity of play itself. Or, pleasure may become associated with the activity of play through learning *because* it means intimacy with mother. However we conceptualize intrinsic pleasure, it can motivate the individual to engage in play, which has survival value for individual and species. Pleasure for *both* mother and infant in play is essential to its maintenance and the developments that stem from it (for a discussion of motivational systems with affect resulting from the approximation to goal, see Rosenblatt & Thickstun, 1977). Culture is transmitted through play in childhood and in games throughout life. And although particular play may seem frivolous, the capacity for it is not, nor are its gains. Play is an essential feature of our species, not an incidental byproduct of evolution, and the intrinsic pleasure we find in play makes sense from a phylogenetic and ontogenetic standpoint.

Pleasure in play is also derived from wish-fulfillment under conditions that minimize danger. This includes the wish for mastery and for relief from anxiety, as well as the wish for the satisfaction of basic impulses. In addition, the "free zone" provided by play includes pleasurable escape from pressures of reality and superego. In 1908, Freud discussed the wish-fulfilling nature of play, fantasy, and dream and wrote: "As people grow up . . . they cease to play, and they seem to give up the yield of pleasure which they gained from playing. . . . [However, this is not so because the child actually] gives up nothing but the link with objects; instead of *playing*, he now *phantasies*" (p. 145). Later, Freud (1920) discussed the *"economic* motive [for play], the consideration of the yield of pleasure involved" (p. 14) in the "disappearance and return" game of a child of 1½ years. In like fashion, Simmel (1949) discussed the satisfaction of Oedipal impulses in the childhood game of playing doctor and patient. And Peller (1954) postulated that sexual and destructive urges are satisfied in play in increasingly sublimated form. Similarly, the psychoanalytic process provides satisfaction of sublimated forms of the analyst's infantile needs. In both patient and analyst, "regression in the service of the ego" reveals these basic needs to the analyst, whose symbolic play with the material provided leads to new understanding that is useful to both. Sublimated pleasures are a constant part of the process of psychoanalysis for the analyst, who is actively involved in the internal play of fantasy, which delivers unconsciously gained insight to his conscious thought processes. Not only is the awareness of new insight a pleasurable intermediary outcome of the analytic process, but there is pleasure gained in the wish-fulfillment of fantasies, even when these are regressions serving the purpose of analytic insight.

The distinction between work and play is blurred. When pleasure in process dominates and other gains seem incidental, we tend to regard the activity as play. When external gains dominate, the activity seems more like work and less pleasurable. Work is serious, has a purpose, and is a means to an end. Play, like work, may be very serious, but its pleasure is intrinsic, and if given external rewards, it tends to become work and lose its pleasure. On the other hand, it is possible to make the *process* of work itself rewarding, and when this can be done, work assumes the fun quality of play. (It is noteworthy that there is now a widespread industrial movement to alter the character of work in ways that would increase worker involvement and pleasure in both process and outcome.) Work appears to develop out of play, following a path from the wish-fulfillment of symbolic play to reality-adapted behavior. Piaget and Inhelder (1969) described a stage in the development of play they called "games of construction," which provides a transition from symbolic play, oriented to wish-fulfillment in symbolic form, to nonplayful activities, which "constitute genuine adaptations," such as constructions that are solutions to reality problems. Kris (1952) made a similar comment when he wrote that childhood play provided "a bridge enabling instinctual satisfaction to take a form adapted to reality" (p. 182). It appears that a turning from the pleasure principle to the reality principle, or from the pleasure of wish-fulfillment to reality and external rewards, constitutes the transition from play to work.

Anna Freud (1965) posited a developmental line from play to work and described certain "advances in ego development and drive control" (p. 82), which she saw as necessary precursors to the achievement of the capacity to work. These appear to form continua in their development and include control of aggressive impulses and their constructive use, the ability to execute goal-directed plans with a minimum need for immediate gratification and maximum regard for outcome pleasure, the capacity for sublimation of instinctual drives and, as previously mentioned, a "transition from the pleasure principle to the reality principle" (p. 82).

The idea that the pleasure of play is intrinsic in the activity itself may be applied to the psychoanalytic process. Assuming that the goal of psychoanalysis is a successful outcome (whatever that may be), then everything else in the process must be a means to that end. These means may then be regarded as goals in their own right, and pleasure may result from their attainment—pleasure intrinsic to the process, even though the ultimate pleasure is in the final outcome. But the goal of the patient-analyst system is more usefully viewed as the maintenance of the analytic process. The analytic result is the outcome of the process, not the result of striving for a particular goal of symptom relief or characterological change. In fact, the outcome may not be what was initially desired, because this may change as a result of the analytic process. This process may be conceptualized in information processing and systems theory terms (Rosenblatt & Thickstun, 1977, 1983), in which case the superordinate goal of maintenance of process includes subordinate goals in hierarchical arrangement. The relative match or mismatch through feedback from the system's activity with the established goals of the system provides information resulting in pleasurable or unpleasurable affect of varying intensity and quality. This affect would be the intrinsic pleasure (or displeasure) in the process. Play itself may be regarded as the activity of an innate "motivational system" (Rosenblatt & Thickstun, 1977), modifiable through experience, and of a level of peremptoriness below that of the safety, sexual, and feeding systems. Reynold's system view of play is compatible with our hypotheses.

Whether work or play, every analyst has experienced pleasure in the process of psychoanalysis. This is not consistently sensed, however, for there are hours that are more apt to call to mind the work-related synonyms (e.g., drudgery, toil, and struggle) than process pleasure. The state of "flow," perhaps first felt in infantile play, may also be an aspect of work, although, too often, work is drudgery. Because play is antecedent to work, it seems likely that the pleasurable, creative, high-concentration aspects of work are derivatives of what we call "play" in childhood, and without good experiences of pleasurable childhood play, the adult cannot enjoy work. The hours in which "flow" is experienced by the analyst are usually ones in which the patient also experiences this, and they occur when patient and analyst are in intimate empathic communication and seem to be associating in the same channels (i.e., when resistance is minimal and the process is functioning smoothly).

The pleasure gained in the play-work of psychoanalysis is complex, involving as it does the sublimated satisfactions of the analyst's earliest impulses, "functional pleasure" in the process itself, pleasure in the attainment of intermediary goals, pleasurable relief from anxiety, and satisfaction in understanding achieved. However this pleasure is conceptualized, the analyst must be able to take pleasure in the process itself, because his ability to do so is an important factor in his capacity to maintain it. Other rewards are often minimal in the course of an analysis and, if sought by the analyst, interfere with the process. If the analyst requires extrinsic rewards from the patient in addition to the fee (and he is apt to if intrinsic rewards are lacking), then the process will be disrupted. Of course, there are extrinsic rewards in addition to the fee, such as improvement in the patient's functioning, release of latent capacities, relief from suffering, and increasing ability to enjoy life and attain satisfactions previously forbidden, which are all gratifying to the analyst. However, these are *outcomes* of the process, and unless the analyst realizes satisfaction in the activity of the process itself, his own distress (or lack of satisfaction) when such outcomes are minimal may result in regressions leading to behavior destructive to the process, such as antianalytic modifications in technique or failures in sublimation with the resultant expression of unsublimated sexual, aggressive, or narcissistic needs.

Play has been classified in many ways, depending on the interests and theoretical orientation of the authors. The activities we call play form a heterogeneous group and serve a variety of functions. Specific play forms appear at different developmental stages, overlap in development, change in style and function, and gain or lose dominance. It is little wonder that no single classification does justice to the field. Peller (1954), in her classic paper on play, pointed out that specific anxieties and related fantasies are characteristic of different age groups, and play in these groups differs in "style, in social aspects, and in other respects" (p. 182). Earlier forms of play do not disappear but are modified in the course of ego development so that they become more complex and are sustained for longer periods of time. These statements represent the orientation and interests that psychoanalysis brings to the study of play – that play reveals, and deals with, the dynamic constellations and structural developments of the child and the adult. Peller's classification, therefore, was based on the psychoanalytic concepts of psychosexual and ego development and divided play accordingly into "play originating in the relationship to one's own body," "play rooted in the child's relationship to the preoedipal mother," "play instigated by conflicts on the Oedipal level," and "postoedipal play." The 30 years since this paper was published have seen numerous advances in psychoanalysis that augment this classification, although the basic orientation remains. Two other classifications can also be dealt with briefly: one of a descriptive orientation and the other based on the development of logicomathematical structures.

The first of Peller's stages requires revision according to our present understanding of the infant's earliest relationship with the mother. The earliest play is social play rather than solitary play with one's own body, although the latter also occurs during infancy, and the importance of the social aspect of early play cannot be exaggerated. This earliest play consists of innately determined interactions that are dependent on the partner's responsivenesss and may include finger play, jiggling, rocking, play while dressing and changing, play at the breast, cooing sounds, baby talk, and facial expressions. These innate interactions were described by Brazelton, Tronick, Adamson, Als, and Weise (1975) in discussing mother-infant communication when they wrote that this is "a reciprocally organized system in which the infant makes skillful adjustments of his actions in response to the displays of his partner" (p. 138).

The unfortunate mother who cannot enter into such play easily and joyfully fails to facilitate the delighted and engaging responsiveness of the infant. Ainsworth (1982) noted that:

> infant behaviors such as vocalizing, smiling and bouncing were associated with playful and contingent maternal behavior. On the other hand,

mothers who initiated interactions silently or who sustained a matter-of-fact expression while *en face* had babies who tended merely to look at them. (p. 38)

Such failures in empathy result in disturbances in the development of attachment, basic trust, confidence, cognitive-affective behavior, and object relations. The strength of an infant's attachment to another individual increases with the amount of empathic social interaction between them (Bowlby, 1969), and much of this stems from play. In addition, capacities for social and self-regulation begin in this early play, as well as in other social interactions, and are important in the later elaboration of more complex adaptive regularities. Social play is vital for the optimal development of such regularities, concepts of self and other, imagination, creativity, mutuality, and successful adaptation. Psychoanalysis depends on these basic characteristics arising from the early relationship with the mother; without them, the psychoanalytic relationship cannot withstand the deprivations, regressions, and transference intensities necessary to the process.

Chance (1979) subdivided the field into *physical play* (the vigorous romping of many animals, including human young), *manipulative play* (the infant's manipulation of objects), *symbolic play* (manipulation of reality, pretense, fantasy play), and *games* (play with rules). Piaget and Inhelder (1969), whose work examined the development of logicomathematical structures, divided play into four categories: *exercise play*, which occurs during the first 18–24 months of life and consists of the pleasurable repetition of activities "acquired elsewhere in the course of adaptation"; *symbolic play*, which is dominant between the ages of 2 or 3 years and 5 or 6; "*games with rules* . . . which are transmitted socially" (e.g., marbles and hopscotch) rather than games, more generally, as any "play with rules"; and *games of construction*, which provide "transition between symbolic play and non-playful activities" (p. 59, fn. 3). The former is wish-fulfilling, which is to say that the environment is modified, used symbolically, or assimilated to the needs of the self. In the latter, the interaction with the environment results in newly constructed or modified schemes, and these internal constructions represent an increase in knowledge of how the world works and therefore the capacity for adaptation. As previously stated, this category provides a transition from play to work. Games may provide another avenue for this, because "play with rules" deals with issues of authority and obligation, which have a "work" quality. In addition, team games deal not only with rules of the game itself but with rules of social relations among team members. These rules limit the freedom and spontaneity that are important aspects of play, but games are really turned from play to work when external rewards exceed the importance of intrinsic pleasure, and the rules are established and enforced by the rewarding authority.

Chance's "manipulative play" and Piaget and Inhelder's "exercise play" seem closely related, as do their categories of games. However, Piaget and Inhelder appear to be considering only the socially transmitted games, whereas Chance is referring to all play with rules. Both include a category of symbolic play, which is the dominant play of the Oedipal period and which coincides, therefore, with Peller's third phase of play development. Symbolic play deals with wishes and conflicts from various developmental levels, although such play arises during the Oedipal phase and deals mainly with the conflicts of that period.

In analysis, one sees derivatives of these levels of play, but a distinction should be made between derivatives of the activity of a play form itself and those of the dynamic constellations that were dealt with through that form of play and through other means as well. Play, dreams, neuroses, and other creative productions express such constellations of impulse, defense, and solution.

At the level of symbolic play, Piaget and Inhelder are concerned with the development of logicomathematical structures involved in symbolic thought. This is the Oedipal level of play, and although analysts are concerned with symbolic activity itself, their greatest interest lies in the way it is used to deal with Oedipal impulses and conflicts, and in understanding the inner workings of the child that observation of play gives us. Anxieties of this age are related to being small, unable to do what adults do, feeling helpless in the face of threatened dangers such as castration, and being made to feel insignificant. Compensatory fantasies include being big, powerful, and invulnerable. Fears, narcissistic injuries with their compensatory fantasies, and competitive, aggressive, and sexual impulses become organized into the central constellation of this age – the Oedipus complex. These fantasies and a wide range of emotions are expressed in play, and as Peller (1954) noted, the dramatic play of this period may be complex and present a whole story. Production of such a drama from the Oedipus complex requires creativity and the use of symbolic objects that may or may not possess objective similarity to the referent. Garvey (1977) separated such play into several components: "(1) roles or identities . . . (2) plans for action or story lines . . . and (3) objects and settings. . . . Carrying out the make-believe is largely a matter of communication" (p. 86). Certainly, the patient assigns roles to the analyst, has unconscious "plans" for his story, and needs the appropriate setting (i.e., the analysis) within which he can recreate his story and its leading characters – and the process depends on communication. This form of dramatic play is the transference neurosis. Pretend play does not really appear until about 3, although it often occurs in rudimentary form much earlier. It peaks in middle childhood and wanes thereafter, all but disappearing in puberty. As this kind of pretend play diminishes, it is replaced by fantasy – "really just a kind of internal pretend play" (Chance, 1979, p. 6) – which continues throughout life.

The foregoing play forms require imagination, creativity, and what has been called divergent thinking. The mood of such play is joyous, at times triumphant, and the activity and plots are often shared with other children. This sharing is important to the development of object relations and concepts of self. The gains of such play include pleasure in function, in the satisfaction of sublimated sexual and aggressive impulses of the Oedipal situation, in relief from injured narcissism, and in the working through, repair, and relief from the anxieties of this developmental period. Other gains resulting from this play include preparation for adult roles, development of social and communicative skills, and the cognitive-affective developments mentioned earlier. The impulses, defenses, and anxieties of the Oedipal situation continue to be important throughout life as part of our creativity and our individual and social play, and the creation of Oedipal dramas continues in our fantasies, in our overt behavior, and in psychoanalysis. The creation of such a drama in psychoanalysis by patient and analyst and its relation to childhood play have been discussed extensively (Freud, 1908; Greenacre, 1959; Greenson, 1966; Loewald, 1975; Schafer, 1977; Stone, 1961).

The post-Oedipal child, having achieved some resolution of the Oedipal situation, turns to team games, which deals with rules and authority in groups. Identification with and attachment to groups, as well as to individuals, is a prominent aspect of this age. Such latency play is more relevant to the development and consolidation of defenses, superego, and social relations than to the search for satisfaction of the Oedipal wishes. Although Oedipal play is more often an ad hoc personal creation, latency games are relatively impersonal and conventional, and thus are helpful in the formation of socially shared internal structure.

An analogy may be drawn between games and the psychoanalytic process. Analysis requires a sense of freedom, and though the analyst cannot afford to be rigidly authoritarian, neither can he afford to abandon rules necessary to the game and to the patient's ultimate advantage. The analyst establishes various rules necessary to the process and fosters freedom within those rules. An essential rule of play, as we have seen, is the mutual understanding that such behavior is in the nonliteral mode (i.e., that the game is imaginary action, free from the ordinary consequences of reality). This is also true of psychoanalysis. Rosen (1960) discussed the importance of imagination in the analytic process and disturbances of its function in patients who cannot deal adequately with the ambiguity of imaginative play, which "must keep simultaneous contact with reality and fantasy" (p. 244), and stated that in games and other forms of play "there is an implicit contract between the participants. *This contract also has its analogue in the analytic situation* [italics added]. . . . [It is an] agreement to treat the game as simultaneously illusory and real in its denouement" (p. 244).

This contract, then, is a basic rule of play and of psychoanalysis. Other rules of psychoanalysis include the "fundamental rule" of free association, the "rule of abstinence," the maintenance of confidentiality, and mutually understood arrangements regarding the fee, the schedule, and the use of the couch. Some of these rules are simply established by the needs of the psychoanalytic process, whereas others may be negotiated between patient and analyst. All are subject to an evolving understanding during the course of analysis and should not be presented arbitrarily, but should be discussed in an effort to gain mutual understanding of their necessity and role in the analytic process. Some, however, allow for little modification because of basic needs of analyst or process. Hence, analysis has rules, and although the freedom of play is vital, such freedom is not possible if the rules are not maintained, because the process, or game, simply cannot be played without them. Like marbles, hopscotch, or chess, the game cannot occur without mutual agreement and understanding of the rules by both participants.

The fundamental rule of free association is generally accepted as necessary to psychoanalysis, but it is presented and maintained in various ways. For example, the presentation may range from a requirement that the patient "pledge" to free associate to a statement such as "here you may say whatever you wish." Kanzer (1981) has pointed out that, "The fundamental rule . . . elicits a special organization of associations between patient and therapist, a special mental set yielding associations not forthcoming under other conditions" (p. 74). In his view, this pact between patient and analyst is the "standard therapeutic alliance," and a "normal superego," as well as a "normal ego," is "assumed as a prerequisite for the demonstration of unshakable loyalty to the work of analysis. The pact is two-sided and requires an analyst whose behavior is also guided by it so that he is the guardian of the fundamental rule" (p. 72). The analytic process "sets in motion the conflict between the promised loyalty to the fundamental rule and the disposition to defy it" (p. 74).

This is the basic alliance of psychoanalysis. Exception is taken to its modification, such as giving "permission" rather than requiring a "pledge." These differences, of course, affect the nature of the analytic process. It is my impression that the "pledge" aligns the analyst too strongly with the superego which, in my view, would emphasize the compulsory aspects of the relationship to the detriment of the necessary freedom and would present difficulties in the analysis of an authoritarian superego. In the case of simply giving permission, the necessity of following established procedures to attain a goal is ignored. This could place the analyst in the position of the overindulgent parent who fails to assist the child in developing adaptive regularities necessary to eventual autonomous activity. Another option, which is my preference, is to discuss with the patient the role free association occupies in psychoanalysis, explaining why this is an essential part of the analytic process on which the patient is embarking. The issue in resistance then becomes: Inasmuch as the patient understands the role of associating and the necessity of this in achieving the goal he seeks, what is it that interferes with what he wants to accomplish? This allies the analyst with the developmental goals of the patient, rather than with either the authoritarian or the overindulgent parent.

However, in all three of these instances, if the process is analytic, resistances to associating will repeatedly be interpreted, and in this way, it will become apparent to the patient that there is a "rule" or procedure being followed. There are, after all, many rules in analysis that are not necessarily stated explicitly—rules, that is, in the dictionary sense of "an accepted procedure, custom, or habit," which the patient becomes aware of over time. The rule of abstinence, for example, may be explicitly discussed with the patient but, if not, will become apparent both through interpretation and through the analyst's nongratification of expressed desires. Rules that are explicitly presented often become focal points for the expression of conflicts of various impulse-defense constellations and transference issues and may require repeated, though not necessarily explicit, restatement and interpretation. In addition, there are rules attributed to the analyst that are the patient's own products, which also become objects of the analytic process. To repeat: In analysis as in games, there *are* rules, some more necessary than others. But this process, like play, requires freedom within the necessary structure if it is to function effectively.

Learning has been widely discussed as a function of play and may well be the most important of its "secondary gains." Garvey (1977) pointed out that play, identified by certain kinds of conventions, is buffered from the usual consequences of behavior, and because it is safe to experiment in this mode, play and learning are closely related. "Although the properties of an object . . . may be known to some extent, new possibilities for its use or its potentiality for combination may be discovered in the course of playing with it" (p. 48). As previously noted, Reynolds (1976) discussed play as a "simulative mode" of behavior, uncoupled from the usual consequences of reality. In this mode, one may experiment freely and learn from this without being limited by fear of the consequences. Animals that play also show other features of what he termed the "flexibility complex," which includes ontogenetic plasticity of behavior, a relatively long period of immaturity, dependence on parental care, and a capacity for learning. Organized sequences of behavior are conceptualized as "affective-behavioral systems"; each such system is ordinarily coupled with other systems, and its activity has predictable consequences that are monitored by feedback. The play system is designed to "borrow" behavioral patterns from other systems. Under these circumstances, the behavior *resembles* that of the borrowed system but does not have its usual consequences. An "affective-behavioral system" thus borrowed is detached from other systems with which it is usually linked. This allows for "simulations" of behavior, which may be carried out without fear of danger but with feedback informing the organism of the results. Thus, information is gained about the possible consequences of action, and the organism learns which behavior is adaptive and which is maladaptive. This feedback needs to be an accurate representation of environmental response, yet the behavior must not expose the organism to actual damage. A play system is regarded by Reynolds (1976) as "specialized for the transmission of information between the environment and the non-play systems" (p. 627). Thus, a play system provides the nonplay systems with valuable information without risk. The importance of this "simulative mode" of play for learning is evident, and it makes a significant contribution to individual adaptation and the transmission of culture.

Chance (1979) reported Kirschenblatt-Gimblett as stating that learning seems to be facilitated by play in "a kind of play-competence spiral: learning leads to more sophisticated play, and play provides a kind of mastery that leads to more learning, which leads to more sophisticated play, and so forth" (pp. 23–24). It allows the child to extend his understanding by testing his beliefs about the way the world works and to attempt new behaviors when old ones fail. In early infantile games, he begins to comprehend the idea of pretending, that things need not be what they seem, and that he can create reality as he wishes it to be. Pretend play allows the child to grapple with new concepts, to gain mastery over them without the usual real-world consequences of failure, and to develop the ability to think metaphorically.

Such play is believed to aid in the development of communicative and social skills and in the ability to empathize. The opportunity for the child to take various roles and to experience thereby a variety of situations and feelings appear to enhance his capacity for understanding the feelings and thoughts of others. In addition, he learns that the meaning of behavior depends on context and that behavior can be evaluated and revised. The most creativily gifted adults tend to have been particularly imaginative and playful as children.

In psychoanalysis, "playing" with ideas in an atmosphere of freedom leads to insight and lends itself to the development of "play-competence spirals" eventuating in behavioral as well as intrapsychic changes. The psychoanalytic situation, uncoupled from external consequences, allows for the imaginative exploration and manipulation of thoughts and feelings leading to new conceptualizations of experience. Reynolds' discussion of "behavior in the simulative mode" elucidates the learning that occurs through such make-believe behavior. The earliest such simulations are made in "playful" behavior, but later ones may be more formal and consciously oriented to the solutions of realistic problems. This is, again, like the transition from play to work. Formal, conscious, secondary process simulations are derived from play behavior and are still make-believe, but they are not identical to the play from which they were derived. Such "experimental kind of acting" (Freud, 1911, p. 221) is important in both analyst and patient, and it is created *between* the two as feedback occurs from one to the other. In psychoanalysis, these actions occur initially in the form of exploratory thought processes, which are facilitated by the analyst's and patient's capacities developed in childhood play and are made possible in the analysis by the "implicit contract"—the play mode of our work. This leads to actions in the "real" world, often tentative at first, then with growing confidence and conviction.

The ambiance and space within which play can best occur interest us because the analyst provides such an ambiance and space within which the psychoanalytic process takes place. Play is facilitated by certain settings and inhibited by others. Freedom is the most important aspect of a good play environment—freedom to experiment, to explore, to fail, or to succeed. Permission to play can be an aspect of both physical and psychological environments. The absence of conventional constraints on the handling of ideas and materials is essential to play, which is inhibited by a nonplayful, authoritarian attitude. In an atmosphere that implies relaxation and acceptance, the possibility of divergent, creative, imaginative, playful thought is enhanced. Of course, the word "playful" is not used here in the humorous or jocular sense, but in the sense of free play of thoughts and feelings in the simulative mode. Nor is there any intention to suggest that the analyst adopt a "playful" attitude, in its common connotation. There can be humor in psychoanalysis, but it is generally a serious form of play unenhanced by jocularity.

As previously noted, the mother-infant system is innately provided with extremely sensitive interactive mechanisms, and play has a prominent role in establishing the earliest attachments of infant and mother.

This early play leads to the previously mentioned developments if the mother can provide a playful ambiance for the infant and if the infant is not impaired in his capacity to respond. Winnicott (1967) has discussed a somewhat later, although still early, play space–an imaginary psychological space. He argued that play becomes possible in this "space" between the infant as "fused" with mother and the infant and mother as separate entities in the infant's dawning awareness of self and other. This can only happen with a mother who is free enough herself to enjoy play with her infant, while providing loving, empathic satisfaction of her infant's needs as well. In favorable circumstances, this space is filled with the symbolism of play–a creative activity of the infant. According to Winnicott (1967), in the "transitional object, the first not-me possession, we are witnessing both the child's first use of a symbol, and also the first experience of play" (p. 369). The use of this "potential space" is determined by early experiences. It is within this space that the most intense experiences occur, and this space can only develop if the mother-figure is dependable, thus making possible the development of confidence within the infant. Similarly, "analysts need to be aware not to create a feeling of confidence and an intermediate area in which play can take place and then inject into this or to blow it up with interpretations which in effect are from their own creative imaginations. Such interpretations accumulate as persecutory elements (Winnicott, 1967, pp. 371-372).

The older child's physical play space may be populated with toys, dolls, pets, boxes, imaginary beings, and all manner of things that lend themselves to the imaginative manipulation of reality and ideas. In addition, it is of interest to note that other children appear to be a stimulus for playful behavior, whereas the presence of adults is often inhibiting. The play space provided by the analyst–physically the office, psychologically the analytic process and relationship–is soon populated with all manner of beings by the patient, with the assistance of the analyst. So the analyst provides the ambiance and the spaces, physical and psychological, for playing the game of psychoanalysis.

The space and ambiance within the analyst's office provide him with a necessary sense of security and comfort, and the meaning of this space for him is derived from a long succession of such spaces earlier in his life. Anxiety aroused elsewhere in the analyst's life is often relieved by the security of his office and by absorption in the patient. However, there is danger in this. If the analyst has lost the flexibility and freedom necessary to play with his own unconscious through fantasy and self-observation, thus mastering his anxiety rather than simply defending against it, he may use the analytic situation for the purpose of isolating or denying his disturbing affect or to act out elements of his conflicts rather than working them through. The analyst's pleasure in the "play" of his analytic work would suffer, as would the work itself. In this play-work, there is little opportunity for the abreaction of intense feelings, such as those experienced in childhood play, because these must remain muted in the analytic process. The analyst, therefore, must find different avenues for such expressions of emotion, and adult play other than in the psychoanalytic situation is one of these.

Human play shows elements in common with the play of other species, but it also shows features that are found in no other species arising from man's enhanced capacity for symbolic thought. The human child brings new elements to the play situation—some tangible, some intangible (e.g., the rules of games that are established by his culture)—but the creative products of his mind are the most significant contributions of all. The child's play space is enriched by his physical modifications of its contents and, far more significantly, by the attribution of new meaning through symbolic manipulation. Such actions reveal cognitive style early in life, and play encourages acts of creative imagination that transform reality. Garvey (1977) makes the point that play has systematic relations to activities we do not regard as play: "Play has been linked with creativity, problem solving, language learning, the development of social roles, and a number of other cognitive and social phenomena" (p. 5). The nature of these links is not clear, but all of them depend on symbolic thought.

Symbolic thought allows the child to use one object to represent another and thus to engage in play with objects quite different from the play of earlier periods. External support of realistic objects seems necessary to early play, but as the child increases his capacity for symbolic thought, less realistic objects actually seem to facilitate his make-believe, allowing him freedom from the concrete and greater use of nonliteral resources such as imagination and creativity. In addition, play appears to foster divergent thinking as opposed to convergent thinking, which depends on convention and an orderly solution to problems—a distinction similar to that between primary process and secondary process thought. The characteristics of play that promote freedom also facilitate insight into the solution of problems, and children who display nonliteral or imaginative behavior are the most effective problem solvers. In addition, they produce more imaginative ideas, use more divergent thought, and can manipulate and recombine materials and ideas more effectively. Garvey (1977) added the speculation that pretending facilitates the development of abstract thought.

The concrete props of childhood symbolic play are no longer necessary to the preadolescent because, at 11–12 years of age, he becomes capable of manipulating reality intrapsychically through symbolic transformations and is no longer bound to it in the concrete. Thus, as Freud wrote in 1908, symbolic play with external objects is replaced by fantasy creations. Such fantasies are rich sources of analytic material and of creative thought in general. Freud (1908) wrote that the creative writer and the child at play behave alike, because each "creates a world of his own, or rather, re-arranges the things of his world in a new way which pleases him" (pp. 143–144). Freud related the dynamics of fantasy formation to the work of creative writing via the concept of wish-fulfillment: "A strong experience in the present awakens in the creative writer a memory of an earlier experience . . . from which there now proceeds a wish which finds its fulfillment in the creative work" (p. 151). Fantasy follows the same path in its development: A current impression provokes the wish, which "harks back to a memory of an earlier experience (usually an infantile one) in which this wish was fulfilled; and it now creates a situation relating to the future which represents a fulfillment of the wish" (p. 147). Both are acts of creative imagination: "A piece of creative writing, like a day-dream, is a continuation of, and a substitute for, what was once the play of childhood" (p. 152).

These capacities for imaginative, creative, divergent, problem-solving thought, which developed out of, or along with, play, are crucial to the psychoanalytic process in both patient and analyst. The ability to produce "a piece of creative writing," such as the joint authorship of the drama of the transference neurosis, develops out of the "the play of childhood," as does the "day-dream" or fantasy, which is also a creative product informing us of the "wish" and difficulties in the path of its fulfillment. Adult play, like the child's, is a creative activity, whether internal symbolic play (fantasy), one of the varieties of overt play (e.g., games), or spectator participation in the symbolic play of the artist, dramatist, musician, and writer. Like the creative writer, the analyst evokes the child at play when he assists the patient in re-creating his internal world. The fantasies of both patient and analyst are related to childhood play and its wish-fulfilling character, and are important in the creation of the analytic drama.

Thus, during the analytic journey, a drama called the transference neurosis is developed out of the interaction between patient and analyst. Actually, adult analysis requires an imaginative, problem-solving relationship from which the creation, or re-creation, of the life drama of *both* participants arises. The drama of the patient is center stage, but the re-creation of the analyst's life drama is an ongoing process, with ever-changing modification over the years of his play-work. This drama is written and rewritten throughout life by those outside analysis, as well as inside, but it is during analysis that the intensity and preoccupation with it are at their height. Although much of one's childhood "playfulness" is lost to the adult, it is antecedent to the "playing with ideas" and the creation of life drama in adult analysis. Creative thought similar to the "symbolic play" of the child is active in the adult's expression and mastery of anxieties and in the future-oriented, problem-solving thought of "real" life, and one frequently creates aspects of his family drama in symbolic play. The child's—and the adult's—re-creations of his relationships do not coincide precisely with actuality, but represent his fantasies as well. These dramas more closely approximate "reality" as analysis progresses, but they are never free from the influence of fantasy in either analyst or patient. The analyst uses his life experiences—his drama—to assist in understanding the patient's. This empathic understanding, however, can become troubled and distorted when the analyst's life drama becomes too pressing and the patient's drama thus becomes misunderstood in terms of the analyst's. This danger makes an ongoing examination of the analyst's drama a necessary part of his work. But this activity is also a gratification of his need to understand and complete his drama in order to be as much at peace with himself as possible—to be master in his own house—not only for the benefit of the patient, but for himself as well. During analysis, both analyst and patient are immersed in their childhoods, and the analyst reexperiences the satisfactions, as well as the pain, of his own early life. Each analysis is part of the analyst's life journey, and each adds to his understanding of himself and enhances his life drama. Psychoanalysis is a creative activity on the part of both patient and analyst, which possesses many of the elements of infantile and childhood play grown up.

Freud related play in the child to the wish to grow up, and Greenacre (1959) wrote that pleasure in play was "not merely . . . relief of anxiety, but . . . pleasure in functioning, i.e., satisfaction of maturational potentials" (p. 69). Such a wish for progression, or development, is also a major motivation in the patient who undertakes analysis. A corresponding wish of the analyst is to assist the patient in his wish to grow up, which is the same wish that the (healthy) parent has for his child. Developmental progression, both childhood and analytic, may follow on periods of "working through," after regression. We have seen such working through as a function of play, as well as analysis.

Greenacre (1959) has discussed mastery and working through as a part of childhood play, and an analogy between such play and psychoanalysis is easily drawn. She noted that the child is in control of his play and can therefore represent and rework reality in measures that can be tolerated, whereas in the real world, he is often the passive victim of overwhelming reality. This working through is also at the heart of adult analysis. The analyst attempts to adjust the amount of distress and understanding to the capacity of the patient to make use of it and to move at optimal speed while not allowing the analysis itself to become a source of unbearable trauma. Because play is make-believe, it is possible to expose feelings of an intensity that would be too threatening in "real reality" and to experiment with otherwise dangerous or forbidden thoughts. But in the same sense, analysis is not "real reality." The intensity of transference feelings is real enough, but the recognition of the make-believe nature of the analytic reality makes it possible to experience these feelings and to see the analyst as the transference object *because* he is not. Patients who cannot tolerate, or comprehend, the ambiguity of analysis as both real and make-believe may be unable to develop the necessary intensity of transference, or—sometimes devastatingly—may be unable to accept its illusory nature and develop what has been called a transference psychosis. As Greenacre (1959) noted, "The anxiety provoking problems of today in the child's life become the subjects of the play of tomorrow" (p. 66), and of the analysis of tomorrow as well. Working through and mastery are achieved by the child in play, and by the adult in psychoanalysis.

The analyst occupies the role of participant-observer in the drama of the patient's life and identifies with many of its major characters in a manner similar to Freud's (1908) description of the writer who "split[s] up his ego, by self-observation, into many part-egos, and ... [personifies] the conflicting currents of his own mental life in several heroes" (p. 150). This is similar to the role-playing of the Oedipal-age child, which appears to enhance the capacity for empathic identification so essential for the analyst. Different elements of the analyst's personality lend themselves to the various identifications necessary to this drama, and there must be something in the analyst capable of being attuned to each character in order to do this. In particular, the analyst must have access to himself as child, because without this he cannot empathize adequately with the patient in the reconstruction of *his* childhood. Greenson (1966) also discussed the creative process in psychoanalysis, the drama-creating role, and the necessity of empathic identification with the role of the patient. The capacity for play in the sense of drama, or "play acting," is important in the analyst, who "becomes . . . a silent actor in a play the patient is creating . . . The interpretive work of the analyst as he listens to what the patient fantasies is at its best related to the creative process in literature, music, and art" (p. 22). Freud (1908) spoke of "ready-made" material with which the writer may deal, from which he may choose, and in which he can make changes in his creative writing: "In so far as the material is already at hand, however, it is derived from the popular treasure-house of myths, legends and fairy tales" (p. 152)—which, of course, are derived from the treasure-house of the unconscious and are recognizable from person to person as variations of basic themes familiar to psychoanalysts. It is part of the creative work of the psychoanalyst and patient together to recognize and construct from present material the hidden dramas of the patient's past. Thus, a conscious, newly conceptualized understanding of the nature of one's life and capabilities is developed, and a new future is constructed from this understanding.

Greenacre (1959) discussed the relation of play to creativity, both present in psychoanalysis, and wrote that a "meaning of *play* contains the notion of make-believe or even imitative action, as children who are *playing* at being grown up, or actors *playing* on the stage. . . . We speak of play . . . as recreative, i.e., renewing or reviving" (p. 62). The analyst does need to engage in internal make-believe action (although the "action" in this is not overt, but is thought as trial action), and he may feel his "work" exhausting at times, but he also experiences it repeatedly as "renewing or reviving." Greenacre (1959) also pointed out that much of play is "acted-out fantasy" and that "fantasy of special quality is the stuff of which creative productions are made" (p. 73). The analyst assists in the development of the patient's fantasy play and creates his own fantasies about the patient's dramas. These are tested for their approximation to the reality of the patient's past life, his current life, and his fantasized future. According to Greenacre (1959): "Creative imagination . . . aids in delivering the unconscious fantasy and harmonizing it with the external world," and an aspect of such functioning is the capacity to switch from "subjective creator to objective audience" (pp. 76–77). This switching occurs in both patient and analyst during the analytic process, and the analyst must possess this aspect of creative functioning in order to make use of his unconscious and his primary process thinking to inform his conscious secondary process. This is done in an imaginative form that may be connected with objectivity and the "external world" in a way that reveals, or creates, new meaning for patient and analyst from the patient's behavior and associations. Analysis requires the ability to switch from role to role, to be empathic, to be objective, to be creative, to be in touch with the present, the past, and the future, to function in both primary process and secondary process, and to be analyzing oneself and the patient simultaneously. No analyst manages to do this perfectly. It's no wonder that disturbances in the process are produced by both participants and amazing that it works as well as it does.

If "play activity in the human being serves the same function at all ages," as Adatto (1964, p. 826) suggested, then the grown-up play activity of the analyst should function for *both* participants in the mastery of traumatic experiences, in the developmental drive toward increasing maturity, and in the satisfaction of hidden instinctual impulses. Indeed, this does happen. Day after day, the analyst overcomes anxieties related to his own childhood through his play-work with his patients. This mastery of anxiety is attained not only through increased understanding of himself, but also through his role as the powerful helper and in his identification with the patient who, though distressed, is also helped and protected. Trial behavior activity of the free play of thought and feeling in analysis is not only useful for the patient, but for the analyst as well – as long as the analyst is consciously able to make use of this capacity to enhance understanding of the patient and is not caught in a regression, identification, or countertransference of which he is unaware.

Loewald (1975), Schafer (1977), and Stone (1961) have discussed the psychoanalytic process and the transference neurosis as play and created drama. Loewald (1975) wrote: "The fantasy character of the psychoanalytic situation is its character as play, in the double sense of children's and adults' playing and of drama as a play" (p. 294). As we have seen, children engage together in pretend play wherein each takes, or is appointed to take, a role in the play they develop. The Oedipus complex and its antecedents in the child's fantasy play are re-created in the analysis; this requires from both participants freedom of creative imagination and "playfulness" such as the child developed during those periods in his life. Loewald (1975) described the development of the transference neurosis in much the same way that one might describe children in pretend play when he wrote that "analyst and patient conspire in the creation of an illusion, a play" (p. 279). "Thus the transference neurosis . . . is revealed as . . . a dramatic play having its roots in the memories of original action and deriving its life as a present creation of fantasy from the actuality of the psychoanalytic situation and its interactions" (p. 281). Although the "original action" re-created in the transference neurosis was the "infantile neurosis" (arising from Oedipal conflicts), he included, in addition, adolescence and noted that pre-Oedipal issues have become for some the "original action."

Schafer (1977) also saw psychoanalysis as the stage for re-created drama with the transference neurosis as its central feature: "The analysis becomes primarily the contemplation of the fantasized or invented aspects of the relationship" (p. 347), and interpretation provides a simplified, abstract organization for the transference repetitions, which are not, in the descriptive sense, as unvarying as they may then seem. The ongoing development and interpretation of transferences create a metaphor that is "a new experience rather than a mere paraphrase of an already fully constituted experience" (p. 353). The major therapeutic impact of psychoanalysis lies in the development of this metaphor.

Stone (1961) wrote that the transference neurosis "differs from the initial transference, in the sense that it tends to reproduce . . . an infantile *dramatis personae*, a complex of transferences, with the various conflicts and anxieties attendant on the restoration of attitudes and wishes paralleling their infantile prototypes" (p. 74). Again, this is like the production of a play, with various actors who are often unaware of, and at times confused by, the roles the patient has assigned them.

These authors see the central feature of psychoanalysis, the transference neurosis, as a drama created by patient and analyst, similar to children in pretend play. Through this initially unconscious re-creation of the past, the patient comes to see his life experiences in a different light and is freed to use his capacity to create alternative dramas and to live them out, rather than simply to repeat the old. The capacities of both patient and analyst to engage in re-creating this drama together imaginatively are derivatives of childhood play essential to psychoanalysis.

To recapitulate, play and psychoanalysis have much in common: Both are make-believe, simultaneously real and illusory, uncoupled from the usual consequences of behavior, and simulations of reality. Patient and analyst enter into an implicit agreement to engage in such make-believe. In order to pursue this successfully, both must bring to his process capacities developed in their own childhood play: tolerance of ambiguity, imaginative problem solving, creativity, communication, empathy, divergent nonliteral thought, and the use of regression and primary process thought in the service of progression and the secondary process. The play mode of psychoanalysis provides the freedom to experiment with new, outlandish combinations of ideas and to risk failure without the usual fear of consequences. Psychoanalysis thus creates an optimal situation for learning. Experimentation with fantasy and reality lead to new solutions and new behaviors, at first within the safe play space of analysis and later by advances into "reality." This occurs in the learning and developmental style of childhood play. Regression, repetition, working through, mastery, and progression lead to changes in intrapsychic structure and overt behavior.

The analyst provides a play space, both physical and psychological, within which psychoanalysis can occur. This requires the establishment of rules for spatial boundaries and play appropriate to that space. These rules must be limited to those *necessary* to the "game" of psychoanalysis, allowing for the creation of an atmosphere of freedom. This is true for childhood play as well as psychoanalysis, and it makes experimental thought, feeling, and fantasy possible. Both rules and freedom are part of the play space and the ambiance necessary for the psychoanalytic process. The make-believe nature of this play makes transference possible, and the patient and analyst together re-create the patient's childhood drama. (The analyst's childhood drama is also re-created and reunderstood during the analytic process and is useful both to the analytic process and to the analyst himself.) The transference neurosis is a drama, and its development goes hand in hand with the construction of a new understanding of the patient's life. This new understanding is the foundation for the creation of a new future.

Freud used the "wish," an organizing concept of great power, to explain dream, symptom, fantasy, and other creative productions. In analysis, as in fantasy, "the wish makes use of an occasion in the present to construct, on the pattern of the past, a picture of the future" (Freud, 1908, p. 148). The analytic situation arouses these wishes, and a "pattern of the past" is developed in this process which leads to a "picture of the future"—altered by the play-work of patient and analyst together.

REFERENCES

Adatto, C. (1964). On play and the psychopathology of golf. *Journal of the American Psychoanalytic Association, 12,* 826–841.

Ainsworth, M. (1982). Early caregiving and later patterns of attachment. In M. H. Klaus & M. O. Robertson (Eds.), *Birth, interaction and attachment* (pp. 35–43). Skillman, NJ: Johnson & Johnson.

Bowlby, J. (1969). *Attachment and loss: Vol. 1. Attachment.* London: Hogarth Press.

Brazelton, T., Tronick, E., Adamson, L., Als, H., & Weise, S. (1975). Early mother-infant reciprocity. In *Parent-infant interaction* (Ciba Foundation Symposium, *33,* new series). New York: Associated Scientific Publishers.

Chance, P. (1979). *Learning through play.* New York: Gardner Press.

Freud, A. (1965). *Normality and pathology in childhood.* New York: International Universities Press.

Freud, S. (1908). Creative writers and daydreaming. *S.E.,* 9, 143–153.

Freud, S. (1911). Formulations on the two principles of mental functioning (p. 218–226). *S.E.,* 12.

Freud, S. (1920). Beyond the pleasure principle (p. 7–64). *S.E.,* 18.

Garvey, C. (1977). *Play.* Cambridge, MA: Harvard University Press.

Greenacre, P. (1959). Play in relation to creative imagination. *The Psychoanalytic Study of the Child, 14,* 61–80.

Greenson, R. (1966). That "impossible" profession. *Journal of the American Psychoanalytic Association, 14,* 9–27.

Huizinga, J. (1955). *Homo ludens: A study of the play-element in culture.* Boston: Beacon Press.

Kanzer, M. (1981). Freud's analytic pact: The standard therapeutic alliance. *Journal of the American Psychoanalytic Association, 29,* 69–87.

Kris, E. (1952). The psychology of caricature. *Psychoanalytic explorations in art* (pps. 173–203). New York: International Universities Press.

Loewald, H. (1975). Psychoanalysis as an art and the fantasy character of the psychoanalytic situation. *Journal of the American Psychoanalytic Association, 23,* 277–299.

Peller, L. (1954). Libidinal phases, ego development, and play. *The Psychoanalytic Study of the Child, 9,* 178–198.

Piaget, J., & Inhelder, B. (1969). *The psychology of the child.* New York: Basic Books.

Reynolds, P. (1972). Play, language and human evolution. In J. Bruner, A. Jolly, & K.

Sylva (Eds.), *Play: Its role in development and evolution* (pps. 621–635). New York: Basic Books.

Riesman, D. (1950). The themes of work and play in the structure of Freud's thought. *Psychiatry, 13,* 1–16.

Rosen, V. (1960). Some aspects of the role of imagination in the analytic process. *Journal of the American Psychoanalytic Association, 8*(2), 229–251.

Rosenblatt, A., & Thickstun, J. (1977). Modern psychoanalytic concepts in a general psychology. *Psychological Issues, 11*(2–3, Monograph 42-43).

Rosenblatt, A., & Thickstun, J. (in prep). The psychoanalytic process: A systems and information processing model. *Psychoanalytic Inquiry.*

Schafer, R. (1977). The interpretation of transference and the conditions for loving. *Journal of the American Psychoanalytic Association, 25,* 335–362.

Simmel, E. (1949). The "doctor game," illness, and the profession of medicine. In R. Fliess (Ed.), *The psychoanalytic reader* (Vol. 1) (pp. 291–305). New York: International Universities Press.

Stone, L. (1961). *The psychoanalytic situation.* New York: International Universities Press.

Waelder, R. (1933). The psychoanalytic theory of play. *Psychoanalytic Quarterly, 2,* 208–224.

Winnicott, D. (1967). The location of cultural experience. *The International Journal of Psycho-Analysis, 48*(Pt. 3), 368–372.

11 Becoming a Psychoanalyst

Vamık D. Volkan, M.D.

I received Dr. Reppen's invitation to contribute a chapter to *Analysts at Work* just as I was putting the finishing touches to a book entitled *What Do You Get When You Cross a Dandelion with a Rose?* (Volkan, 1984), my account of the psychoanalytic process as it had unfolded in the case of one of my patients. Some months before starting this book, I had been asked to be on a panel for discussion of psychoanalytic technique. Everyone going to this symposium had been asked to prepare for it by reading Paul Dewald's book *The Psychoanalytic Process* (1972). Now widely read in the psychoanalytic community, this book gives the transcript of the tape-recorded sessions of a young woman in analysis (who agreed to its publication) and Dewald's own views of what took place during each of her hours.

When I later met Dewald at a conference, I learned that he did not know his book had been used in our symposium, which had been attended by analysts trained in a variety of programs, some of which were approved by the American Psychoanalytic Association. I had expected all to be in general agreement with Dewald's formulations and to approve of his technique. To my surprise, however, mostly everyone disagreed with Dewald and even disagreed among themselves on the central themes that his patient's analysis exemplified.

Struck by the paucity of writing that gave any detailed account of an adult analysis from start to finish, I was moved to write on the analysis of a patient of mine who tended to classify people, including himself, as either "dandelions" or "roses," assigning undesirable qualities to the former and desirable ones to the latter.

The writing of this book required a review of my detailed notes made over a period of 4 years, with a reexamination of my analysand's communication, both verbal and nonverbal, and the recollection of my own reactions to such communications. This provided me with a sort of "private laboratory" in which I could try to evaluate myself as an analyst. Accordingly, I welcomed Dr. Reppen's proposal to have various psychoanalysts write about how they arrived at formulations of patients' problems, the therapeutic stories involved, and the day-to-day professional involvements in which they were engaged. The timeliness of this proposal was underscored by the news that the International Psychoanalytic Association had chosen the same focus for its 33rd Congress held in 1983 in Madrid. The Association's newsletter notes that the title of the program, "The Psychoanalyst at Work," was chosen with the goal of working "with enthusiasm to create an organizational frame where psychoanalysts might interchange their definite experience about their daily clinical work with their patients." "Our job," the newsletter goes on to state, "has been centered in clinical work."

My conscious reason for undertaking *What Do You Get When You Cross a Dandelion with a Rose?* was to follow Dewald's pattern of exemplifying the analytic process in detail so that my methods could be studied by others and compared with the styles of other analysts. However, I felt obligated to search for an unconscious motivation in view of the fact that I had detailed notes on many patients but somehow felt uniquely compelled to cite this one, whose mother had been adopted and remained in ignorance of the identity of her real parents, secretly believing that she was of noble birth. Although she grasped intellectually that this grandiose view of her origin was pure fiction, she had managed to convey the notion to her son (my patient), who experienced certain psychological consequences. The representation of his unknown grandfather, continued by the family "myth," exerted considerable influence on my analysand, a physician. His grandiose notion of his bloodline was supported by his mother, who, by extension, was thus able to compensate for her feelings of deficiency incident to her status as an adopted child. Before his analysis was completed, the son had to consider the possibility that he came from "dandelion" stock (i.e., gypsies) rather than "rose" stock (i.e., nobility), and he searched for the true identity of his grandfather. Although the search had been futile, he had come to "mend" the split that had led him to perceive himself and others as clearly classified as one or the other and had adopted a more integrated perception of things.

Inasmuch as he had mentioned the possibility that his unknown grandfather had been "an author," it seemed to me as I wrote my book that I was gratifying my patient by assuming this role for myself. But looking inward, I became aware that my writing was also an attempt to integrate my own identity further and to consolidate it. Like my analysand, I had an "unknown" person in my past, and it is only recently that I have come to grasp the extent to which his representation has influenced me.

My mother was the oldest child in her family, a brother named Vamık being somewhat younger than she. This uncle had left Cyprus, my family's homeland, to study engineering in Istanbul and had disappeared while a student there. Fifty-three days after he vanished, a body was found floating in the Sea of Marmara, and it was identified as his after the burial by the examination of bits of clothing found on the corpse. This event took place 6 years before my birth; I was given the dead man's name. The failure to identify the body itself as that of my uncle may have fed the illusion held by my mother and grandmother that he was still alive. As my grandmother lived in our household when I was a child, this unjustified and wistful belief of the two women influenced me; psychologically, it was true that he still lived. His representation was kept alive in me!

I had never consciously recognized my role as a kind of "replacement child" (Cain & Cain, 1964; Poznanski, 1972; Volkan, 1981a) nor realized that I inherited a past history of legendary performance and expectations pertaining to a dead uncle. However, I do recall having examined my uncle's few remaining photographs and having compared his appearance with my own. I was fascinated by the notion of a likeness, which I both longed for and feared to see. I concluded that in one picture, in which he wore a soccer uniform, the likeness was striking. I now wonder if my inability to play soccer well in high school while longing to do so might point to a need to differentiate myself from the representation of a dead man.

I do not recall my analyst's dwelling, in the course of my training analysis, on my having been a replacement child. This may very well have been due to my success in sublimating the influence of my dead uncle's representation. As might be expected, his memory was idealized in our family, and I somehow managed to uphold it by being a good student with idealized goals of my own. I recall that it occurred to me once during my analysis that my uncle may have committed suicide; I suspect that this was an attempt to lay him to rest!

To return to my choice of the dandelion-and-rose patient as the subject of my book, I was partly motivated (although I had been unconscious of this at first) to "gratify" myself by identifying with my analysand. I was "becoming" his unknown grandfather so he could locate his roots, which had so greatly influenced him. By projective identification with my patient, I, too, could find my lost "important other" (my uncle) in my effort to consolidate my own identity further.

Although clearly I had largely identified with my uncle's idealized representation, which had been impressed upon me by my mother and grandmother, his representation also had remained an unassimilated, though influential, object representation in my psyche. My attempt to "find" him was thus an effort to reduce the tension between the self that belonged to me and the representation of the man that remained "foreign" to me.

I can now see rather plainly how being a replacement child influenced me, and I can realize my lifelong efforts to deal with it. For example, while a medical student in Ankara, I wrote a play with such fury that its writing took only a few days. My sudden preoccupation with it suggests that I was trying to protect myself from anxiety. The play's theme had come to me suddenly: A young Cypriot student (obviously, one representing myself) was searching throughout Turkey for the six murderers of an uncle killed years earlier. I learned only recently from an older sister visiting America that our grandfather had sought the aid of a psychic to solve the mystery of his son's death and had been told by the psychic that his son had been murdered by six "friends." My family did indeed have a picture of the dead man with six friends, and they came to believe that these were the murderers. I am sure that I had heard this and that my turning to the story of the murder while feeling rejected and anxious about interpersonal stress in medical school was an attempt to find "solutions" for my discomfort by finding "solutions" for the mystery of the murder that provided the plot for my play. I submitted my play to the Turkish State Theater, but to my great disappointment, it was rejected.

After my sister's reference to the photograph of my uncle and his six companions, I was surprised to find it on the first page of a photograph album in which I kept pictures from my early childhood in Cyprus. In a sense, this album contained the pictorial representations of my early years, and it was a striking revelation to see how I had made room for my uncle's picture on the first page, as though my life had started with him. I had, of course, had this picture with me when I left Cyprus for Ankara 33 years ago, and had brought it to America 7 years later.

I can now better appreciate one of the "unconscious" reasons why I fell in love with and married a girl whose father had been killed in World War II when she was 8 months old. My wife's mother had idealized the dead soldier's representation, and she had conveyed this idealized representation to her daughter, who grew up without having known him in real life. Because of this experience, she was my "traveling companion" in her relationship to an idealized dead man, and through displacement, she also represented the grieving women of my early childhood whose grief I needed to repair. Also, I now believe that the death of the uncle I never saw contributed significantly to my becoming a psychoanalyst and, further, to my selection of certain topics to study psychoanalytically and to teach and write about. Although my play attracted no attention, I have been luckier in sublimating my involvement in psychoanalysis and being able to share some of my ideas in print, in lectures, and in seminars with my students, colleagues, and others.

A list of my books (disregarding my journal articles and papers in edited volumes) points to an unconscious desire to deal with the influence of my dead uncle's representation. My first book, *Primitive Internalized Object Relations* (Volkan, 1976), refers to my interest in self- and object representations, the interaction between them, and the appearance of object relation conflicts in the clinical setting. Then, after making a field study soon after the 1974 war in my homeland, Cyprus, I wrote a book on war and the adaptation following a war (Volkan, 1979). My search for roots, for my identity, and my early relationships is very evident in this; it opens with a dream I had during my analysis. Among other things, this dream reflected my perception of my developing self in an extended family caught up in complicated mourning and dealt with the process of mourning for losses sustained in the interethnic troubles. In my third book, *Linking Objects and Linking Phenomena* (Volkan, 1981a), I focus directly on mourning and offer the concept of "magical" links between the dead and those who mourn. Those caught up in complicated mourning make an inanimate object (or something such as a song) into a meeting ground for the representation of the dead individual and that of the mourner to come together. Such "linking objects" or "linking phenomena" magically keep alive the illusion of there being a choice whether or not to "kill" the dead. In my midteens, I saw my grandmother take a box from some secret hiding place. It contained belongings of my dead uncle and newspaper clippings about his disappearance. It may have been the anniversary of his disappearance. She opened the box, touched its contents, and sobbed for a while before closing the box and putting it away once more, presumably in its former hiding place. This was the only time I ever saw her go through this performance, but over 30 years later, I published a book on linking objects! One chapter in my book deals with "living linking objects"—individuals who represent to those who mourn a bridge between the present and someone cherished who was lost in the past. In my case, the "someone cherished" was my uncle. Although I do not call myself a living linking object in my book, it is an identification I have thought about privately.

I worked for more than 7 years with Norman Itzkowitz, a Princeton historian, on my next book, *The Immortal Atatürk: A Psychobiograph* (Volkan & Itzkowitz, 1984). A revolutionary and creative leader, Kemal Atatürk, the founder of modern Turkey, had been born in a house of death and was a living linking object, a number of siblings having lost their lives before his birth. His dominant wish throughout life was to "repair" a grieving Turkey and change sorrow into joy. This theme continues to be important in my writing. I have indicated some of the reasons behind my choice of one particular analysand in my most recent book. And at present, I am editing a book on *Mourning, Depression, and Depressive States* (Volkan, in press).

Considerable attention has been given in the literature to the genesis of creativity in childhood experiences of object loss and the influence upon a child of grieving adults unable to resolve their grief (Bonaparte, 1933; Hamilton, 1969, 1976, 1979a, 1979b; Neiderland, 1965; Pollock, 1961, 1977; Volkan, 1981a). Both Pollock and Hamilton indicate that Freud's childhood loss of his next younger sibling may have been a significant factor in his life. Julius, Freud's brother, died when Freud was 19 months old and most likely disturbed his relationship with his mother and his nursemaid. Milton Rosenbaum (1982), another psychoanalyst, writes of the effect the deaths of two brothers had upon him; at the age of 5, he lost a year-old brother, and at 7, he lost one aged 5. Rosenbaum recalls being "separated to a certain extent from my mother by virtue of her illness," describing her as utterly grief-stricken. He goes into some detail about his early object loss and the "loss" of his mother to her complicated mourning, describing how the death of his 5-year-old brother "and its ramifications were cardinal and crucial factors in my becoming a doctor, as well as a psychiatrist."

Children who experienced object loss and whose parents were grief-stricken differ in their response to such stress. Not all become "creative" in useful and adaptive ways; some even become psychotic (Volkan, 1981a; see the case of the "Night of the Living Dead," chap. 14). But as a child, I believe that I was caught up in the psychological process of "generational continuity" (Volkan, 1981a) and was sensitized, from childhood on, to psychological issues. My concept of generational continuity refers to the "depositing" in the next generation of the unassimilated object representations of the antecedent generation; it would appear that these can be conveyed as "psychological genes" into the representation developed by the next generation. Besides being the storeroom of the representations of the dead (usually idealized), a living linking object must face the consequences of being reared by parent(s) who suffer from complications in mourning/depression.

Olinick (1980) suggests that "a powerful motivation for the psychiatrist dedicating himself to the psychoanalytic relationship is the genetic effect of a rescue fantasy having to do with depressive mother, the latter having induced such rescue fantasy in her receptive child . . . For such relatedness of mother and child to be formative, it must be early, though the necessary duration is not clear" (pp. 12–13). Olinick adds, however, that depression (or grief) on the part of the mother is not a sufficient determinant in itself: "in addition, the maternal character must be at least in certain aspects alloplastic" (p. 13). In writing of rescue fantasies, Searles (1979) seems to take into account the other side of the coin, that is, what happens when a person cannot sublimate the influence of a sad or depressed early mother or one engaged in complicated mourning. Searles himself, however, advances the hypothesis that innate among the human being's emotional potentialities "present in the earliest months of life is an essentially psychotherapeutic striving" (p. 459). Olinick (1980) returns in a later chapter to a consideration of the depressive mother's ability to induce rescue fantasies in her child: "The child will be pressed into becoming the idealized mothering one and into additionally becoming one day the rescuing champion of the distressed woman or man, for the sexualizing and gendering of the rescue motif may cut across and interpenetrate male–female lines" (p. 160).

The matrix of my choice to become a psychoanalyst may have been my development of early rescue fantasies and my responses to an idealized representation of my uncle, although I might very well have embarked on a different career that would allow me to serve others. Additional psychological influences, coming at other times in my psychosexual development, may have been condensed with earlier ones, giving direction to my specific career choice. For example, in my late latency or early adolescence, I discovered a copy of Freud's *Three Essays on the Theory of Sexuality* (1905) in a big black box in which my father kept his valuables. I do not know what had prompted my father, a schoolmaster in an elementary school, to buy it, and I do not know how much of it he had read. The black box, with its obvious symbolism, contained something tinged with "sex," and at the time, this made an impression on me. To learn about Freud was to learn about my Oedipal father, as well as to identify with him, and when I later went to medical school in Ankara, my psychiatry professor became for me an extension of my father. Both men were islanders – one from Cyprus, the other from Crete – and the Turkish speech of each was influenced by the Greek language used on each of these islands. Professor Rasim Adasal, who died in 1983 exactly on his 81st birthday and who spoke of himself as the Turkish Freud and referred to Freud constantly, had a lively mind but a rather shallow grasp of Freudian psychoanalytic theory. In the long run, what might have been viewed as a deficiency was good for me because he awakened my curiosity about psychoanalysis—as my father had done by storing a "sex" book in his black box—but left me intellectually unsatisfied. I had to find out more about it myself.

I did not grasp the significance of the "sex" book in the black box until much later. After emigrating to the United States in early 1956, I completed a year's internship in Chicago and then entered a psychiatric residency at the University of North Carolina. As an instructor in psychiatry at the University of Virginia 5 years later, I became a candidate at the Washington Psychoanalytic Institute. My mentor during my residency had been Dr. D. Wilfred Abse, an analyst I considered "a walking library." I followed him to Charlottesville, Virginia, and heeded his recommendation that I choose as my analyst Dr. Edith Weigert, one of the great ladies of psychoanalysis in the District of Columbia. Dr. Abse told me that she had practiced in Turkey in the mid-1930s and that she would accordingly be familiar with my cultural background. At his direction, I read a lengthy paper she had written while in Ankara on "The Cult and Mythology of the Magna Mater from the Standpoint of Psychoanalysis" (Weigert, 1938). I was impressed by this paper, although I am sure I did not altogether grasp its implications at the time. She accepted me as an analysand, but we were to have only one session because she had an accident and was incapacitated for some months and would not work with new analysands.

I was required to start my analysis if I were to be eligible for my class, so I was transferred to another analyst, who conducted my training analysis. My respect and affection for him grew beyond the customary transference idealization and persists to this day. Nonetheless, I must have had some "unfinished business" with Dr. Weigert, who died a few years ago, and it was no doubt on that account that I asked her to supervise my last control case when I became an advanced candidate. She accepted gracefully, and I saw her for over 80 hours of supervision. Although she seldom spoke of Turkey then, Itzkowitz and I sought an interview with her some years later when I was no longer a psychoanalytic candidate and we were engaged in research for our book on Atatürk. The information she provided about him was highly useful; her husband, Professor Oscar Weigert, had been Atatürk's advisor on economic affairs. He was Jewish, although his wife was not, and the couple were among the many intellectuals fleeing Hitler's persecution of the Jews in Germany who received a welcome in Turkey. Edith Weigert practiced psychoanalysis in Turkey from 1934 to 1938, before emigrating to the United States, where she saw in therapy mostly "foreigners." Among her analysands was a Turk who translated Freud's work into Turkish. Thus, Freudian thought was introduced early to new Turkey, and I feel sure that the book in my father's black box was the translation made by Dr. Weigert's patient.

In an effort to summarize what I learned from Edith Weigert, the word "dignity" comes to mind, with the connotation of *professional* dignity. I feel indebted also to my two other supervisors of control cases: William Granatir taught me how to make a formulation within the framework of structural theory, and Rex Burton conveyed the importance of influences impinging on the analysand from the real world. From both I learned dedication to our profession.

I cannot list the names of all the people who influenced the development of my career in one way or another, but among them I would include my bright students in psychiatry, some of whom, as graduates and practitioners today, make up a study group that has for more than 6 years given me an arena in which I have been able to try out some of my psychoanalytic concepts. Dr. Abse was always full of encouragement. I must mention also two psychoanalysts with whom I became acquainted through my publications. While a candidate, I wrote a paper on "the little man phenomenon" (Volkan, 1965) using a term coined by William Niederland (1956) who was practicing in New York City. I sent him a copy of the paper, and he responded favorably. Thereafter, I enjoyed brief meetings with him at gatherings of the American Psychoanalytic Association. I consider him a "poet" of psychoanalysis, and I greatly appreciate his encouraging my work on the Cyprus book, and especially my writing on Atatürk.

L. Bryce Boyer of Berkeley, California, also made a special contribution to the development of my career after he responded favorably to my early papers on clinical issues (Volkan, 1964, 1968), which concerned the psychodynamics of severely regressed patients. It was not usual then to deal with such patients psychoanalytically, but Boyer was interested in what I had to say about such treatment and took my modest contributions seriously, leading me to feel that I had an ally in this man of such distinction in the field. I was not dismayed when only five or six people came to hear my first presentation at the San Francisco meeting of the American Psychoanalytic Association in 1970, because the event gave me an opportunity to meet Bryce, the discussant, for the first time.

My interest in the severely regressed patient stems from circumstances in the real world. After completing a residency at Chapel Hill, I worked for 2 years in Cherry Hospital in Goldsboro, North Carolina. It was then a hospital for blacks rejected by their family or community because their behavior had become intolerable. My psychoanalytically oriented training made me curious about the meaning of the bizarre behavior I saw there every day, and I became accustomed to the primary process thinking of my charges. For 2 years before I began my psychoanalytic training proper, I saw each day only severely disturbed patients. During this time, I went to Chapel Hill every week and received supervision from Dr. Abse. I took psychoanalytic journals back to Goldsboro from each visit, and before long, I was familiar with the major contributions to this field.

I tried stubbornly to understand from a psychoanalytic point of view the bizarre manifestations of the patients at the state hospital; this involved the additional problem of decoding black utterances that used a rural patois. I learned quite a bit about depth psychology and about language. I was no longer surprised by grotesque manifestations of the unconscious, and I came to appreciate the nuances of the English language, although my English is still imperfect and I still need editorial help in my writing. Some years later, Dr. Granatir showed me his evaluation of my handling of a neurotic control case; he had noted that my conduct of the analysis proceeded along classic lines and that I seemed to be imperturbable throughout. This comment impressed me, although I also read it as a warning, a suggestion that it might be well for me to ask myself why I never seemed "rattled." My imperturbability does not indicate any lack of feeling on my part during an analysis; I do respond to the unfolding of an analysand's story with feelings of my own, but even to this day, I usually do not get rattled, and I hold that this makes for a good analytic position. I do not get sucked into involvement in a patient's "crises," and I can wait to analyze the *meaning* of such crises. I sense in myself an ability to regress along with a patient in order to perceive and understand on a deeper level the communications I am getting from him.

I do not suggest that my experiences at Cherry Hospital account for my way of responding to a patient. I suspect that my background as a Turkish Cypriot—over and above the aspects of my family situation already cited—makes me able to regress in the service of another (Olinick, 1980, pp. 7–12). Although I was a city child, born in Nicosia, as a youngster I visited my paternal grandparents in the country where, like their neighbors, they lived in a simple house made of something like adobe and where my grandfather threshed his wheat by having a donkey or a cow drag over it a wooden plank studded with field stones. I remember striking such stones together in an effort to make fire, like primitive man. In view of the fact that one of my sons, not yet a teen-ager, is learning at school to operate a computer, I sometimes feel that my mind holds a collection of influences and symbols that span the millennia from the Stone Age to the Space Age; a trip into the depth of a patient's mind is somehow not unfamiliar!

I have written at length about my clinical practice, but I find it hard to describe a typical day. I do not think I have ever proposed a theory without describing its appearance in clinical practice. My interest in self- and object representations does not indicate a primary focus on these phenomena in everyday clinical work. I consider myself rather conservative in my technique, and I try systematically to analyze the structural conflicts of my patients, who are usually neurotic and integrated. I do this with regard for their transference neurosis. I wrote in 1981 (Volkan, 1981b):

> Structural theory is still the best instrument for understanding the psychopathology of patients with fully differentiated id, ego, and superego, and for success in handling transference–countertransference manifestations in their treatment. I argue that this theory is not very useful, however, when applied to the treatment of patients whose dominant psychopathology reflects the reactivation of internalized object relations. (p. 449)

I am one of those practitioners, perhaps still in the minority, who consider that analysis – or at least psychoanalytic psychotherapy – should not be denied to patients with severe characterological disorders or even psychosis. In dealing with such patients, I have had personal help from L. Bryce Boyer and have been encouraged by the writings of Harold Searles (1960, 1965, 1979). We may use the tripartite model of ego, id, and superego to understand neuroses and high-level character disturbances in which conflicts center predominantly around Oedipal problems, but we may need another model for the understanding of conflicts of object relationships that patients with low-level character disturbances activate during their treatment. The content (i.e., the wishes, prohibitions, and injunctions of the two opposing parts of the conflict) may not differentiate the structural from the object relations conflict. Dorpat (1976) refers to a crucial difference between the two; in the former, the person experiences the tendencies in conflict as aspects of himself or is at least capable of doing so, even if an aspect of the conflict is unconscious. He owns both the prohibitions, values, and injunctions with which he is struggling and the aggressive, sexual, or other strivings with which they have come into collision. The opponents are generated within himself. Dorpat (1976) explains: "In the object relations conflict, the subject experiences the conflict as being between his own wishes and his representations (e.g., introjects) of another person's values, prohibitions, or injunctions" (p. 870).

In accordance with these formulations, I argue that there are important differences in the transference–countertransference phenomena of patients undergoing psychoanalytic treatment for structural conflict and those whose therapy focuses (at least primarily) on conflicts of object relations. An understanding of these differences from both a clinical and a theoretical point of view reinforces the propriety of using different models for different levels of psychopathology.

In accordance with the views of Boyer (1966) and others, I have suggested (1976) that one of the most important goals of work with patients with severe characterological disorders is to help them to differentiate in piecemeal fashion the representation of the analyst from the archaic and unintegrated self- and object images. When the representation of the analyst as a "new object" (Loewald, 1960) is assimilated into the patient's self-system as analytic functions and attitudes, the patient's integrative functions are enriched.

Like Boyer, I believe that when dealing with the severely regressed patient, one should first bypass interpretation of oedipally tinged issues and focus on conflicts in object relations. After the splits have been mended and the fragmentation of identity overcome, the analysis of such a patient can run parallel with that of a neurotic patient, but "only after the dyadic material has been repeated and worked through can investigation of the oedipal transference be fruitful" (Boyer, 1982, p. 75). Such an oedipal transference has a certain novelty; the patient is going through it largely for the first time with his newly integrated self- and object world. Child analysts can be useful to us here, for they see some children pass through the oedipal period for the first time. I read eagerly the contributions of child analysts such as Mahler, and I feel that in treating adults psychoanalytically, I am profoundly aware of their antecedent developmental experiences.

In recognition of developmental experiences, I have suggested that the kind of psychoanalytic psychotherapy I conduct with patients with borderline personality organization (Kernberg, 1966) goes through six phases. Such patients come to treatment fixated at a low level of organization that is dominated by primitive splitting (of differentiated self- and object representations) and related defenses. The framework of the psychotherapeutic work is set in the initial phase, and the field delineated. In the second phase, which I call "the first split transference," such patients repeat, as it were, a split relatedness to the therapist in a chaotic way; transference manifestations inevitably include the splitting of representations of the therapist along affective lines, contaminated with the patient's archaic object and self-representations; also included is the interaction between the split representations of the therapist and the corresponding ones of the patient himself. During this phase, the therapist provides what Winnicott (1963) and, later, Modell (1976) saw as "a holding environment."

A focalized psychotic transference occurs in the third phase. The patient regresses below his fixation point. I disagree with those analysts who hold that if such patients regress, one losses the opportunity for analytic work because in deep regression such patients will become grossly disorganized. I have found that if the treatment is going well, the patient will develop psychotic "therapeutic stories" and, if the analyst is tolerant, will *move up* again, this time to the fourth phase, which I call "the second split transference." They come back to the level at which splitting exists "naturally," but they need not be fixated there now. Indeed, interpretive work can enable them to move to an even higher developmental level, at which they develop a transference neurosis (the fifth phase). I call the sixth and termination phase "the third split transference." In this, splitting and related mechanisms appear for one final working through, this time by the patient himself, inasmuch as at this point the therapist need display only "benign neglect" toward such manifestations.

In his letter, Dr. Reppen asked me to discuss how I deal with such specific problems as missed hours. To answer such questions, I must first refer to my special circumstances in practicing psychoanalysis in the setting of a medical school and hospital. Fink (1982) has written effectively about the current state of medical schools vis-à-vis psychoanalysis, but I point out that because I am salaried, my patients do not make payment to me directly, but to the hospital. I have found this to be a significant interference with my analytic work because the anal symbolism of payment is clearly influenced by the intervention of the hospital's computers and their symbolic image. I deal with this situation extensively in my book on "dandelions and roses," explaining that in order to learn a patient's reaction to making payment for his analysis, I have him bring his check to me for forwarding to the proper authority. This method does not always work well, and the situation needs analysis. Skipped hours present a problem. If the medical center denies my right to charge a patient for treatment if he fails to keep an appointment, I cannot charge him for *psychological reasons* that I consider valid. I dislike being put in the position of a judge (superego), deciding when a patient's excuse is valid and when it is not. I do not, of course, charge patients when I am absent myself or when I create an obstacle to their arrival.

During the last decade, the academic world of psychiatry has moved farther and farther away from psychoanalysis, although there are now definite signs that the direction is changing once again and that a need for analytic divisions in the medical school is becoming better recognized. However, this is not an issue I want to pursue here. I do want to deal, however, with the question of psychoanalytic organizations themselves. I was appalled to learn, when I was considered for appointment as Training and Supervising Analyst, that the Board of Professional Standards of the American Psychoanalytic Association requires those given this status to spend at least half their time in actual psychoanalytic practice. I was being judged on the quantity, rather than on the quality, of my work! Circumstances worked out well for me, as it happened, but the issue still merits attention, although a search of the literature shows only Fink raising questions about it. Fink (1982) writes of the "50% rule": "This means that under most circumstances an analyst chairman or a professor in an academic department is excluded from playing a significant role in the analytic institute and is not a person of stature in the analytic community, even though he may have the highest status in the academic environment and among those who are recruited into the analytic institute" (p. 364). More open discussion of this on the organizational level would be beneficial.

The analyst in a medical school setting may be disadvantaged in not being able to spend all his time in actual psychoanalytic practice. I have always believed, however, that he has definite advantages. He can be more readily selective in accepting patients than if he were in private practice, and this priviledge can advance his research on some special type of patient. Who is to say whether the analyst who sees eight patients a day is better than the one who sees only three or four but who has time to review his notes, to discuss aspects of his technique with colleagues, and so forth—in short, to sharpen the focus of the profession as it is practiced?

At present, I spend less than half my professional time with patients, but even when my duties as medical director of a general acute hospital were very pressing, I continued seeing some analytic cases. I had made this commitment to myself, and this is understood by the medical school authorities. I would lose my creativity if I were to stop seeing patients. Anyone serving as psychoanalyst/general hospital director (I suspect there are only a few) has certain advantages in being able to study organizations and group processes from a unique vantage point. I find it inappropriate to elaborate on this, however, for reasons of confidentiality. My academic teaching and research is psychoanalytically tinged, and I, with the help of three other analyst colleagues, founded a division of psychoanalytic studies *within* the medical school. Its emphasis is on theory, teaching, and writing rather than on clinical practice, and it is also involved with aspects of applied psychoanalysis. Maurice Apprey, a young child analyst from Ghana who was trained at Hampstead Clinic in London, joined the division a few years ago, providing an intellectual enthusiasm for studying culturally tinged issues from a psychoanalytic perspective.

The most time-consuming of my projects in applied psychoanalysis is the study of conflicts on an international level, which reflects interests stemming from my childhood on Cyprus, where I became accustomed to the bombing attacks of both Italians and Germans. Cypriots lived in fear that their homeland would be occupied. I grew up among ethnic tensions and lost a friend, who had been my roommate at medical school in Turkey, to terrorists on the island.

My connection with the American Psychiatric Association's Committee on Psychiatry and Foreign Affairs began when Dr. William Davidson invited me to speak at the Brookings Institution meeting on Cyprus in 1969. I became a member of this group, then headed by Dr. Davidson, in 1970 and became the chairman of the Committee in 1983. We have been doing fieldwork for 7 years. We have held series of meetings in the Middle East, Europe and the United States, with Israelis, Egyptians and Palestinians participating. One of our aims is to identify the psychological impediments to the peace process in that part of the world.

I have just begun writing about my psychoanalytic observations of these exchanges and am greatly pleased with this opportunity to spread the influence of psychoanalytic thought. I am in full agreement with Mitscherlich's (1971) statement that:

> If we, as analysts, persist in restricting ourselves to an exclusively medical and clinical position, the research into collective behavior, for instance research on the psychology of war, would proceed without our participation. Predictively, this would lead to a further plundering of analytic findings and theories without analysts having any effective share in the direction of the research, nor any means of protesting effectively. Moreover, one would have maneuvered oneself into an isolation of one's own making. (p. 164).

Most members of the Committee on Psychiatry and Foreign Affairs are also associated with the International Society of Political Psychology, of which I am a founding member and of which I serve as President in the 1983–1984 academic year. I am the first person with a medical background to be this organization's president. The organization's membership comes from many disciplines such as political science, psychology, sociology, psychiatry, history, and anthropology. Through my connections with the International Society of Political Psychology, I have been invited to attend Erik H. Erikson Symposiums on Soviet-American relations. The yearly symposiums gather people from different disciplines for one week at Esalen Institute to meet Joan and Erik Erikson in an informal setting and have been very inspiring for me. This analyst is busy in his work and professionally satisfied.

REFERENCES

Bonaparte, M. (1949). *The life and works of Edgar Allen Poe: A psychoanalytic interpretation.* (reprinted ed.) London: Imago.

Boyer, L. B. (1966). Office treatment of schizophrenic patients by psychoanalysis. *Psychoanalytic Forum, 1,* 337–365.

Boyer, L. B. (1982). Analytic experiences in work with regressed patients. In P. L. Giovacchini & L. B. Boyer (Eds.), *Technical factors in the treatment of the severely disturbed patient* (pp. 65–106). New York: Jason Aronson.

Cain, A. C., & Cain, B. S. (1964). On replacing a child. *Journal of the American Academy of Child Psychiatry, 3,* 443–456.

Dewald, P. (1972). *The psychoanalytic process.* New York: Basic Books.

Dorpat, T. L. (1976). Structural conflict and object relations conflict. *Journal of the American Psychoanalytic Association, 24,* 855–874.

Fink, P. J. (1982). Psychoanalysis and academia. In J. O. Cavenor & H. K. H. Brodie (Eds.), *Problems in psychiatry* (pp. 353–368). Philadelphia: Lippincott.

Freud, S. (1905). Three essays on the theory of sexuality. *S.E., 7,* 130–243.

Hamilton, J. W. (1969). Object loss, dreaming and creativity: The poetry of John Keats. *The Psychoanalytic Study of the Child, 24,* 488–531.

Hamilton, J. W. (1979a). The Doppelganger effect in the relationship between Joseph Conrad and Bertrand Russell. *International Review of Psycho-Analysis, 2,* 175–181.

Hamilton, J. W. (1979b). Joseph Conrad: His development as an artist, 1889-1910. *The Psychoanalytic Study of the Child, 8,* 277–329.

Kernberg, O. F. (1966). Structural derivatives of object relationships. *International Journal of Psycho-Analysis, 47,* 236–253.

Loewald, H. (1960). On the therapeutic action of psycho-analysis. *International Journal of Psycho-Analysis, 41,* 16–33.

Mitscherlich, A. (1971). Psychoanalysis and the aggression of large groups. *International Journal of Psycho-Analysis, 52,* 161–167.

Modell, A. H. (1976). The "holding environment" and the therapeutic action of psychoanalysis. *Journal of the American Psychoanalytic Association, 24,* 285–307.

Niederland, W. G. (1956). Clinical observations on the "little man" phenomenon. *The Psychoanalytic Study of the Child, 11,* 381–396.

Niederland, W. G. (1965). An analytic inquiry into the life and work of Heinrich Schliemann. In M. Schur (Ed.), *Drives, affects, behavior* (Vol. 2) (pp. 369–396). New York: International Universities Press.

Olinick, S. L. (1980). *The psychotherapeutic instrument.* New York: Aronson.

Pollock, G. H. (1961). The mourning process and creative organizational change. *Journal Analysis, 42,* 341–361.

Pollock, G. H. (1977). The mourning process aand creative organizational change. *Journal of the American Psychoanalytic Association, 25,* 3–34.

Poznanski, E. O. (1972). The "replacement child": A saga of unresolved parental grief. *Behavioral Pediatrics, 81,* 1190–1193.

Rosenbaum, M. (1982, May). *On becoming a doctor—A personal reminiscence.* Speech presented at doctoral investiture, Marshall University School of Medicine.

Searles, H. F. (1960). *The nonhuman environment.* New York: International Universities Press.

Searles, H. F. (1965). *Collected papers on schizophrenia and related subjects.* New York: International Universities Press.

Searles, H. F. (1979). *Countertransference and related subjects.* New York: International Universities Press.

Volkan, V. D. (1964). The observation and topographic study of the changing ego states of a schizophrenic patient. *British Journal of Medical Psychology, 37,* 239-255.

Volkan, V. D. (1965). The observation of the "little man" phenomenon in a case of anorexia nervosa. *Journal of Medical Psychology, 38,* 299-311.

Volkan, V. D. (1968). The introjection of and identification with the therapist as an ego-building aspect in the treatment of schizophrenia. *British Journal of Medical Psychology, 41,* 369-380.

Volkan, V. D. (1976). *Primitive internalized object relations: A clinical study of schizophrenic, borderline, and narcissistic patients.* New York: International Universities Press.

Volkan, V. D. (1979). *Cyprus: War and adaptation: A psychoanalytic history of two ethnic groups in conflict.* Charlottesville: University Press of Virginia.

Volkan, V. D. (1981a). *Linking objects and linking phenomena. A study of the forms, symptoms, metapsychology, and therapy of complicated mourning.* New York: International Universities Press.

Volkan, V. D. (1981b). Transference-countertransference: An examination from the point of view of internalized object relations. In S. Tuttman, C. Kaye, & M. Zimmerman (Eds.), *Object and self: A developmental approach* (pp. 429-451). New York: International Universities Press.

Volkan, V. D. (1984). *What Do You Get When You Cross a Dandelion with a Rose?* New York: Aronson.

Volkan, V. D. (Ed.) (in press). *Mourning, depression, and depressive states.* New York: Aronson.

Volkan, V. D., & Itzkowitz, N. (1984). *The immortal Atatürk: A psychobiography.* Chicago: University of Chicago Press.

Weigert, E. (1938). The cult and mythology of the magna mater from the standpoint of psychoanalysis. *Psychiatry, 1,* 347-378.

Winnicott, D. (1963). Psychiatric disorders in terms of infantile maturational process. In *The maturational process and the facilitating environment* (pp. 230-241). New York: International Universities Press.

12 Finding the Freuds: Some Personal Reflections

Clifford Yorke, FRC Psych., D.P.M.

My task, as I understand it, is to convey something of my personal attitudes, techniques, conjectures, and beliefs—my personal philosophy perhaps—about psychoanalysis. I do not believe I have anything very new to say: I belong, by training and inclination, within a broad classical tradition. Nevertheless, the opportunity to restate what seem to me certain basic attitudes is a welcome one.

I have been deeply influenced by the fact that I came to psychoanalysis through general psychiatry. In tracing the influence of the wider discipline, I may perhaps be forgiven an autobiographical note. At medical school, formal training in psychiatry was confined to three lectures and three demonstrations. The first lecture, and its corresponding demonstration, concerned "organic psychiatry." The second concerned the "biogenetic" psychoses. The third introduced us to the neuroses. Thus, we made a first acquaintance with "general paralysis of the insane" and the "delusions of grandeur" in which one patient planned to cover with silver plating every ship in the Royal Navy, and another—a dedicated exgardener—had decided to put the whole of the south of England under glass and grow tomatoes. We were shown patients who demonstrated the "waxy flexibility" of catatonic stupor and were told something about obsessional rituals.

All these disturbances were succinctly presented in a miracle of condensation. Inevitably, the presentation of these patients was somewhat dehumanizing. None of their disturbances were presented in the context of a human life; there was no history of a personal kind; the patients unwittingly but obligingly performed their unseen script to the letter.

233

Given the time available, this was perhaps in part unavoidable, but it was only later that I came to understand that the form of presentation was not entirely due to the exigencies of time.

Histories, of course, were medical histories, and to that extent, it was puzzling to realize a whole world of psychological disability was kept so separate from the physical medicine that it was our principal aim to study. In the medical schools, disturbances were either "organic" or "functional": A diagnosis of the latter was an immediate guarantee of loss of interest and the patient's return to the general practitioner.

Subsequently, junior posts in medicine, surgery, casualty, and the like brought a strong awareness of the shortcomings of a method of practice that eschewed all but the crudest and simplest psychology. Furthermore, encounters with a number of baffling psychiatric disturbances continued to stimulate curiosity, and this was not assuaged by referrals to a specialist. The patient was then lost to view. I began to read avidly—at first from psychiatric textbooks—and reached the decisive moment when I had to choose whether or not to accept a tempting offer in general practice or to apply for a junior psychiatric post that had just become available.

Once decided, I found myself in an exciting world. I found a part-time course at the Maudsley, when working for the DPM, fascinating; there was a great deal to learn and some impressive teachers to learn from. The Maudsley, at the time, was under the charismatic leadership of Professor Aubrey Lewis, and either at that institution or elsewhere, the influence of Sir Denis Hill or William Sargeant were important. Without making an attempt at the time to reconcile different approaches, I was impressed by the therapeutic advances claimed by Sargeant, Slater, and their colleagues, on the one hand, and intrigued by an introduction to the world of medical psychology, on the other. At Claybury Hospital, where I held my first appointment, the superintendent, "Jock" Harris, was a broad-minded director who encouraged his staff to pursue their interests in all relevant fields and gave them the time and opportunity for study and discussion. Time passed quickly.

In those early postwar years, the impact of physical psychiatry made us all enthusiastic therapists, but we had some of the disadvantages that come from treating patients, sometimes with apparent success, without understanding what we were treating. Thus, the interest in general psychology fostered a deep interest in trying to acquire some psychological understanding of our patients, and it was this, I believe, that furthered my interest in psychoanalysis. Of the so-called "dynamic psychologists," Freud interested me the most. His approach seemed remarkably comprehensive. I was not attracted by what I thought of as Jung's mysticism or Adler's oversimplifications. But reading at the time was extensive without being particularly discriminating, and the need to understand and to treat patients led to a wide interest in the writings on psychotherapy of a considerable number of well-known authors. In any case, my fellow trainees and I were aware of a contradiction. Although some of the most spectacular advances in psychiatric treatment appeared to lie in physical measures, the emphasis on the physical basis of mental disorder led to a neglect of psychological understanding. The attempts at "psychotherapy" to which we were first introduced seemed to involve little more than persuasion, reassurance, and advice, and we quickly began to see the limitations of these methods. Persuasion was all very well, but as often as not, one was trying to influence a patient in directions that he did not want to follow. The problem with our reassurances was that we had difficulty in believing them ourselves: And when it came to advice, we were in no better position than anyone else to tell our patients how to run their lives. Furthermore, whatever merit these methods may have had was overshadowed by an inability to give the patient any understanding of why he thought or acted in the way he did. And so it was that we laid our hands on every book about psychoanalytic psychotherapy that we could find. Our reading was widely eclectic, because we were far from certain what was psychoanalysis and what was not. Among the authors we read and discussed were Karen Horney, Frieda Fromm-Reichmann, Harry Stack-Sullivan, Edward Glover, Melitta Schmideberg, Franz Alexander, Ronald Fairbairn, Paul Schilder, and Otto Fenichel, to name only those who immediately spring to mind. (When, finally, I decided to undertake personal analysis, I read everything Melanie Klein had published before deciding she was not for me.)

We soon became aware of our own confusion. It was clear that many of the positions taken by these authors were quite incompatible with each other. But there was enormous excitement to be gained by studying them and from the resulting conviction that it was possible, at least in some small measure, to understand what went on in people under our care.

I think my career as a psychiatrist would have been very different had I not been lucky enough to have such vivid discussions and interchanges with fellow trainees. Like me, they were struggling to find a way forward in a singularly difficult discipline. After all, we had few "scientific" signposts. We were not able to work, like the natural or applied scientists, with mathematics or physics. We had to devise, for the most part, our own training procedures, and because we had no specialized supervision in psychotherapy, we had to do so in the light of the massive attention given to psychological matters by so many distinguished writers who, nevertheless, remained outside the main traditions of general psychiatry. I think it was inevitable that these excursions into psychotherapeutic literature led, in the end, back to Freud. No one else seemed to have the same authority, combined with open-mindedness, or the speculative ability allied with compelling logic, or the rigor and austerity of thought in a field that invited so much loose thinking. Ultimately, in deciding to seek a Freudian analysis, I went to see Anna Freud for advice. I have had cause to be grateful to her ever since.

This decision did not involve the abandonment of general psychiatry or a lack of belief in the importance of the various disciplines of which it was composed. Thus, an awareness of the importance of psychoanalysis as a developmental psychology, as a theory of mental functioning, as a method of psychological research, and in appropriate cases, as a form of treatment did not imply neglect of biochemistry, neurophysiology, epidemiology, sociology, and other contributants to general psychiatry. I should add that I am no expert in any of these fields, though I continue to regard myself as a psychiatrist.

I enjoyed my psychoanalytic training at the Institute of Psychoanalysis in London, but I had not supposed that I would be in for quite so many surprises and even shocks. There was an articulate Kleinian wing of the Society, a more or less classical Freudian wing, and a much larger group of analysts who were committed to neither of these approaches. This substantial body was generally known as the Middle Group. Some years later, it renamed itself, more appropriately, the Independent Group. Many famous names were numbered among this group – Michael Balint, Donald Winnicott, Paula Heiman, and others. The student could choose between two parallel courses. Course A was run jointly for students of Kleinian or independent persuasions. It is tempting to say that Course B was for the Freudians, except for the fact that the other groups also regarded themselves as Freudian. Students dedicated to either course were encouraged to attend seminars (and especially clinical seminars) offered by the other. This had the advantage of exposing the student to a variety of influential schools of thought. Its disadvantage was that the student needed to keep a very clear head if he were not to be confused by conflicting teaching.

In my later years as a teacher and training analyst, I came to feel that the different schools of thought were not always presented in ways that underlined the differences between them; students frequently had the impression that there were greater similarities than was often, perhaps, the case. It seems clear to me now that this is not a problem peculiar to the British Society. Any issue of almost any psychoanalytic journal will express a number of viewpoints that flatly contradict each other. To some extent, this may be inevitable in a discipline as inexact as psychoanalysis, but the contradictions are not mere disagreements of a kind healthy to growth and development. Rather, they hinder progress as often as they promote it. I have come to the somewhat dispiriting conclusion that far too many candidates in our training institutions qualify without an adequate knowledge of basic Freudian principles and a firsthand experience of the way in which these can underlie the conduct of a personal analysis. I further believe that this can be achieved without the sacrifice of any independence of thought and without impeding the essential diversity of individual views, without which the many uncertainties and gaps in knowledge, in which our speciality abounds, can begin to be bridged.

I have also come to believe that experience with children and, if possible, a knowledge of (or better still, a training in) child psychoanlysis is an advantage even for those who practice mainly with adults. Experience of this kind allows the analyst to complement the genetic-reconstructive point of view with the observation of the process of development as it unfolds. Indeed, some writers would distinguish between genetic-reconstructive and developmental points of view (Kennedy, 1971). However this may be, trainees in the British Society were aware that the differences between the Kleinian approach to child analysis and the approach of Anna Freud were fundamental. Perhaps those who interested themselves in children were more aware of the significance of these differences than were many others. For although those trained only in adult analysis encountered a variety of views that they sometimes felt could be complemented and integrated, in child analysis there was, for all practical purposes, no real independent group of child analysts in spite of the long career and distinction of Donald Winnicott. Essentially, there were two child trainings, and one chose between them. Anna Freud once told me that, whatever else they had differed about, she and Mrs. Klein were firmly of the opinion that in learning the techniques of child analysis, their own approaches were so radically different that any attempt to combine them could only result in confusion for the trainee. They were both convinced that the two trainings should be kept entirely separate.

I would like to maintain this autobiographical note a little longer because it may make the reasons why I hold my present views rather more intelligible. It was perhaps my training in child analysis and my contact and work with Anna Freud that were, formatively, decisive influences. It was Ilse Hellman, to whom I already owed my start in analytic life, who supervised my first child case – a girl who was not yet 3 years old at the time she began treatment. Anna Freud supervised both my second and third training cases – an adolescent girl and a latency boy, respectively. Ilse Hellman was a close associate of Anna Freud for a great many years and shared with her a great gift in knowing just how to talk to children. I found, however, that the training in child analysis did more than open up fresh perspectives on child development and a better understanding of developmental pathology. I found it enormously helpful in work with adult patients, and it gave me a better facility in reconstructive processes.

Working with Anna Freud at the Hampstead Clinic, first as Medical Director and later, together with Hansi Kennedy, as a Co-Director did more perhaps than anything else to shape and consolidate many views and practices. It would be quite wrong to think of Anna Freud as an outstanding leader and major contributor to our knowledge of normality and pathology in childhood without recognizing her great understanding of and contributions to the psychoanalysis of adults (Yorke, 1983a). Her interest in a large number of special projects involving comparative studies of disturbances in adults and children and in a project devised by her close friend and associate Dorothy Burlingham for the simultaneous analysis of mother and child (Burlingham, 1955) exemplified the spread of her interest throughout the whole spectrum of human development. I was personally aware of Anna Freud's interest in adult psychiatry through carrying medical responsibility for her adult patients for many years, but it was an interest that stretched back to the times in Vienna when she made regular and extended visits to the Psychiatric Clinic where her tutor was the great Paul Schilder. For many years at Hampstead, she took an active part, with Tom Freeman, Stanley Wiseberg, and myself, in a group for the study of psychoanalytic psychiatry. Reference to this work has been made elsewhere (Freeman, 1976, 1983), and some of the work is being prepared for publication.

It is not possible to do justice to the influence of Anna Freud on child and adult analysis and therefore on my own practice in adult work. Perhaps her single most significant contribution to the field was the importance she attached to the question of psychoanalytic diagnosis, and her influence is evident in what follows when I describe some of my current attitudes to psychoanalytic work with adults.

I believe there are many patients for whom psychoanalysis is not the treatment of choice. I do believe that any approach to treatment will be improved if it is psychoanalytically informed, but that is a different matter. It seems to me vital, therefore, that as detailed an assessment as possible should be made at the diagnostic stage as a pointer to both prognosis and the most appropriate form of treatment. I think a training in, or acquaintance with, general psychiatry is an advantage in this. There are patients who are not, after all, accessible to any form of psychotherapy without preparatory medical treatment, though I hold firmly to the view that medical responsibility and analysis should not be held and conducted by the same person, even where the analyst is psychiatrically trained.

In making an initial assessment, it seems important to take a neutral attitude to the possible outcome. Perhaps the psychoanalyst would do well not to ask from the outset: "Will this patient be suitable for psychoanalysis?" but rather: "In what way is this patient disturbed, and what would be the appropriate treatment or management to recommend?" A sophisticated woman, who was the daughter of a well-known analyst, came to me with a request that I take her on for psychoanalysis as she felt driven to distraction by her small child and couldn't cope any longer. We went into her story and history at some length. I formed the view that she didn't need analysis, and a few sessions of mother guidance turned out to be all that was required. More difficult, perhaps, are those patients in whom the nature and extent of the pathology are particularly hard to assess, even in a prolonged interview. I believe it is worth taking several interviews for further exploration and clarification rather than to make a poorly formed assessment that may well be a matter for later regret.

However, because even the most searching of interviews has severe limitations, we are bound to make wrong decisions, and the question arises: How can we minimize these? I believe that if we try to make a metapsychological assessment, we should not hesitate to make use of Anna Freud's Diagnostic Profile (Freud, 1962; Freud, Nagera, & Freud, 1965) and certainly should always use what I call "profile thinking." This is not a mere matter of an artificial listing of material, mentally or otherwise, under headings like drive development, ego attributes, superego development, and the like. It is a matter of understanding the interrelating parts of the personality as they influence each other at the time of assessment, but it is not that alone. It is necessary to try to show how these various parts of the personality interrelate within the framework of a developmental matrix. For this we need to make use of the concept of "developmental lines" (Freud, A., 1963). It is erroneous to suppose that these lines are only applicable to children or that they are merely descriptive. They are important psychoanalytic concepts that enable us to construct the vertical dimensions against which the horizontal cross-section of the profile may be judged (Yorke, 1980). As I have written elsewhere: "the profile gives an overview of what exists at one particular time: the developmental or vertical lines show what went before and may predict what lies ahead" (Yorke, 1983a, p. 393).

Understood in this way, the profile and developmental lines can be used with great flexibility. Freeman (1973) showed convincingly the importance of the profile in assessing psychosis, and in 1976, he demonstrated the significance of the lines for the understanding of certain psychotic phenomena, in particular, neglect of body care. He referred to this work on other occasions (e.g., Freeman, 1983), and the applications of these diagnostic tools in a wide range of pathological conditions are repeatedly discussed by the group at Hampstead concerned with psychoanalytic psychiatry. The group has also drawn attention to the need for careful evaluation of the large group of conditions that do not show dissolution of structures, as in the psychoses and dementias, and do not show the formation of conflicts structured around fixation points, with or without a previous instinctual regression, as in the neuroses, whether of symptoms or of character. An attempt is under way (Freeman, Wiseberg, & Yorke, in preparation) to categorize these disorders—often labeled "borderline" or "narcissistic," as the case may be—and to conceptualize them in terms of developmental disharmonies (Freud, A., 1982), arrests, reversions along developmental lines, developmental deviations, and the like. In doing so, full use is made of basic Freudian concepts, their legitimate extension and modification by workers in the main Freudian tradition on both sides of the Atlantic, and of the contributions of developmental psychology by analytically informed child observation and by child analysis. In particular, the work draws heavily on the contributions of Anna Freud. This work implies the need for a careful delineation of the differing forms of developmental pathology in children (cf. Yorke, 1983b) as well as the contributions of early vulnerabilities to later adult disturbance. It underlines the ways in which child analysis and psychoanalytic child psychiatry have broadened and deepened our understanding of adult pathology.

Above all, the diagnostic tools provided by the profile schema and the concept of developmental lines have given us the opportunity to make *personal* diagnostic formulations in any given patient—to go beyond the wider, but highly important, psychoanalytic conceptualizations of anxiety hysteria, obessional neurosis, sexual inhibition, catatonic/hebephrenic disorders, or whatever and to place them in the vertical and horizontal dimensions of an individual personality. It is in light of these endeavors that the diagnostician is better able to decide the treatment of choice and have some idea, however rough and ready, of the prognosis. There is, however, no way in which diagnostic accuracy can be guaranteed. It was always Anna Freud's idea that assessment by profile could never be more than provisional. Better approximations can only be made in light of further knowledge—when available, knowledge gained from psychoanalysis. Furthermore, the process of psychoanalytic treatment itself can also be regarded as a form of continuous diagnostic assessment, a view to which she herself always inclined. That, indeed, was one of the reasons why she favored further profiles at intervals during treatment, as well as on termination. At the very least,

these procedures allow one to check on the validity of one's earlier formulations, based on less adequate knowledge, as well as on one's earlier
(prognostic) predictions.

Adequate diagnostic assessment ought to provide some supportive
evidence for a provisional conclusion about the suitability of psychoanalysis or otherwise, give pointers to modifications that may have to be
made, suggest what initial measures may have to be taken before psychoanalysis may be a viable proposition, or indicate what approaches to
management or treatment may be appropriate where psychoanalysis is
unsuitable. Here, it is impossible to do more than touch on one or two
points where the question of analysis may be seriously entertained.

Providing that the profile does not point to personality difficulties,
tendencies, or other characteristics that may seriously interfere with
the establishment of a treatment alliance or otherwise impair capacities
that make for analyzability, I would consider analysis in cases of inhibition, sexual dysfunction, neuroses of symptom or of character, faculta-
tive bisexuality, so-called "reactive" depressions, and the like, but I
would be wary of the perversions in general, perhaps with an exception
in the case of fetishism. In itself, however, a list of this kind is not always
helpful. Some obsessional cases may be uncommonly difficult, to give an
example, and other apparently more difficult cases may yet respond to
analysis to a point that allows the patient a more comfortable adaptation
to internal and external circumstances. This is where I think the profile
may be particularly valuable in pointing to factors facilitating
analyzability, such as the capacity for self-scrutiny, verbalization, at
least *some* capacity to relate, and above all, motivation for change. Conversely, the assessment may point to factors that militate against a successful treatment alliance, such as severely narcissistic or hypochondri-
acal features, pronounced cyclothymia, and a severely impaired
capacity for self-observation, to name some of the most striking ones.
This said, it should be emphasized that no one item is in itself decisive
one way or another; it is not a matter of diagnostic categories alone or of
single aspects of the personality that may be expected to foster or
impede analysis. It is a question of the functioning personality as a
whole that must be taken into account. Furthermore, detailed assessment may point to expectable resistances or treatment difficulties,
which may alert the analyst to problems he may encounter, without otherwise suggesting that psychoanalysis is inappropriate.

It is perhaps in the field of the nonneurotic developmental disorders
that the most careful consideration needs to be made in assessing
analyzability, and here is where the findings of child analysis can be expected to throw particularly useful light. This is a field that urgently
calls for further exploration because disorders of this kind often give

rise to considerable difficulty for those analysts who approach their patients with a model of neurosis in mind. It has been pointed out elsewhere (Yorke & Burgner, 1980) that we have to distinguish between a conceptual model of the mind, a conceptual model of illness (which will, of course, derive from the general model but otherwise differ from it), and a conceptual model of treatment. The analyst whose conceptual model of illness is modeled on that of neurosis – perhaps in part because his personal reasons for seeking his own analysis were based on a neurosis of symptoms or of character – is bound to be disappointed and frustrated when he undertakes treatment of the more severe developmental disorders of the kind discussed. His model, not only of illness, but of treatment, will be inappropriate, and he may be led, in his dissatisfaction with his work, to question the Freudian conceptualization of the model of the mind itself. It may be for this reason that a number of practitioners find themselves prey to some of the newer schools of psychology which, however much they may claim to the contrary, have little in common with psychoanalysis itself.

In any case, we can accept the more challenging and difficult cases in many instances if we are prepared to modify our techniques without losing sight of analytic aims. In cases where access to free association is barred, at least in part, we would still feel justified in regarding our treatment aims as psychoanalytic ones, provided that certain general principles were maintained. Thus, the consistent attempt to reach pathogenic material, to understand it, and wherever appropriate, to interpret it would remain a cornerstone of the method. After all, we regularly do something quite similar to this in child analysis without thinking it very remarkable. This is not to say that child techniques can be transferred to the adult, but the inappropriateness of doing so does not do away with the principle. But whatever modifications we felt called upon to introduce, we would have to be prepared to recognize that there are cases in which our techniques could not be expected to reach beyond the limitations imposed by intrinsic difficulties and the nature of the available material.

It is difficult to select aspects of clinical work for discussion in a brief presentation without an element of caprice. Such a charge can certainly be leveled against what follows, in which I select one or two points that I find of interest and hope they are also of interest to the reader.

The first session of a psychoanalysis is almost invariably a pointer to some of the key problems that will require exploration in depth at an appropriate stage. It has often been said that the first words spoken in an analysis are indicators of a major underlying conflict. In my experience, this is often, though not invariably, true. Thus, one young woman announced at the very outset of her treatment that her father was a vile and despicable man of whom she was deeply ashamed and about whom it was difficult even to speak! Her admiration and intense Oedipal tie soon became a central focus of the early phase of the analysis. Another patient's first thought in analysis was of a "gas course" undergone during army training. He was amused by the pun, but had some way to go before the anal components in his personality began to make themselves felt or a hitherto repressed fantasy of anesthesia and surgery in early childhood came into consciousness. But of course, one should not try to make too much of an isolated statement. It only becomes a pointer when taken in context, when its possible significance may be suggested by what follows. There is no need for guesswork, but one can still pause and wonder. I do not remember who first told the well-known story about the patient who began his analysis with the statement, "My mother and father never had intercourse," but no one could fail to be impressed by it.

It is a common experience that analysis may open with a major resistance. This may have been anticipated from the anamnesis and assessment, but it may come out of the blue. One patient of mine was splendidly articulate in the diagnostic interviews, while at the same time showing a capacity for self-reflection, which augured well for the future. But as soon as she lay on the couch, she displayed a terror-stricken silence. To become horizontal was, for her, a frightening sexualization of the analytic situation. She had to be allowed to sit up before consequent fears could be dealt with sufficiently for her to allow herself to proceed in the usual way. It later turned out that the initial situation prompted the reexperience of childhood anesthesia when she felt she was sexually overpowered.

A more difficult situation arose when a patient had been very cooperative during the initial assessment though perhaps just a little too compliant. She had understood well enough the basic rule to lie down and follow her thoughts, but in her very first session, she did neither. She stood at the opposite side of the room with her back to the analyst and refused to utter a word. Here, defiance of the parents, and its immediate emergence in the transference, clearly had to be dealt with first, but it taxed all the analyst's resources. Gradually, we were able to learn how the patient was always expected to mold herself on the model child held up to her by her mother to a point at which she had no identity of her own. Only in later life had she been able to regard herself as anything like a person in her own right. Now she was expected to forego that identity once more, to comply with the analyst's expectations. Only with the recognition of her fear of virtual annihilation as a person was she able to begin to form a true working alliance.

It is my impression that in dealing with some of these difficulties, whether or not they occur at the beginning or later in analysis, we do not always make use of appeals to the ego when such an appeal might well be helpful. My experience as a training analyst indicates that many students think that anything other than a transference interpretation is unanalytic. Assuming that the patient would not be there unless he had indicated a strong motivation for treatment, it is that very motivation which may have to be mobilized during certain periods of resistance. A patient, for example, may feel unable to say what is in her mind. She has a thought, a series of thoughts, an experience, an affective state—something that she cannot put into words. The analyst accepts her difficulty. She is not obliged to divulge an embarrassing content (if that is the immediate problem), but she might be willing to consider, if invited, what it may be that makes her afraid of so doing. Even the verbalization of embarrassment, for example, without naming the embarrassing content, may be a useful step forward. It may be objected that this is all very well for a minor holdup but of little use in the case of silence as prolonged or massive resistance. It is true that the latter can be a major problem for the analyst and test his resources to the limit, but the principle still holds. Appeals to the ego, made without any suggestion of nagging or intrusiveness, and seeking to enlist the support of the observing part of the ego, inviting it to join forces with the analyst in the patient's self-scrutiny, as Sterba (1934) pointed out over 50 years ago, strike me as useful techniques in the analysis of clinical resistance. Certainly, patience and flexibility are indispensable. But I do not believe that there is much point in sitting in prolonged silence in the hope that something will turn up or in making arbitrary interpretations in the absence of any evidence to support them. Nor is the patient's response to an appeal necessarily a simple reflection of a desire to please the analyst. No doubt she could do that much better by following her thoughts in the first place.

Dealing with resistances in these and similar ways are but particular examples of winning a treatment alliance. Such an alliance may be jeopardized from time to time, but it can generally be restored once it has been won initially, and it will normally withstand the vicissitudes of transference, positive and negative, however intense these may be. Where such an alliance cannot be won or where it is too tenuous to withstand the emotional upheavals inseparable from analytic work, then, I believe, analysis will cease to be viable and end in failure.

Matters such as these have to be examined in light of certain special conditions provided by the analytic setting. That setting is designed to foster some degree of primary process intrusion through the use of the supine position in fostering regression and instinctual recruitment, through the inability of the patient to see the analyst or to look at anything more stimulating than the ceiling in a bid to diminish reality distractions and to stimulate fantasy, through the use of free association, and through the relative immobility of the patient so that excitation is discharged through recollection, fantasy, and affect rather than motor activity (McAlpine, 1950; Yorke, 1965). All these are technical tools in the struggle to make the unconscious conscious. It would, however, be a mistake to conclude that the patient is involved in a measure of primary process thinking throughout the analytic session. Even a brief consideration is enough to indicate that this cannot be so. When the analysis is going well, the patient may be involved in his inner world and follow his thoughts and feelings as these willfully pursue their way. But the patient must be able to return, at a moment's notice, to secondary process functioning. The moment the analyst begins to speak, to give an interpretation, the patient must abandon his regression and become the functioning adult who tries to make sense of whatever the analyst has to say. What is called for, in short, is flexibility, a capacity to move with a certain facility between two types of mental process, and the degree of primary process functioning fostered by the analytic situation must always, for the patient, be within manageable limits.

The absence of such flexibility in the patient is a serious barrier to treatment. I have occasionally encountered this difficulty in fairly severe forms. In these instances, instinctual regression was matched by a degree of ego-regression that made any rapid return to adult ego-functioning almost impossible. The patient would be immersed in a toddler-like state, and when the analyst tried to communicate his thoughts about it, the patient would be unable to make any sense of his words. In such an instance, what is effectively lost is the capacity for the ego to maintain a self-observing function. It may be impossible to conduct analysis with the patient lying down, at least to begin with. And even in those cases where some measure of analysis can be conducted with the patient supine, the regressive experience may be so intense that, unless the patient is encouraged to sit up for the last few minutes of the session, he may not find it easy to abandon his regression at the end of the session and resume an adult role.

I have elsewhere (Yorke, 1965) attempted to describe both the conditions that make interpretation possible and the metapsychology of the interpretive process itself. That account was written at a time when, at least in England, transference interpretation was widely held to be almost the only legitimate form of analytic intervention, whether in formal psychoanalysis or in so-called "psychoanalytic psychotherapy." Accordingly, it was necessary to examine the metapsychology of the transference in order to consider the nature and modus operandi of the transference interpretation and to distinguish it from other interventions such as "confrontation" (Devereux, 1951) and "clarification" (Bibring, 1954; Rogers, 1942). In subsequent years, I became aware of the inaccuracy, as well as the incompleteness, of certain statements in the paper, which certainly needs revision, but by and large, a good deal of what I wrote still seems to me to hold true. Nevertheless, we are still sadly short of a metapsychology of the analytic treatment process, and it surprises me, in view of a considerable amount of literature on technique, that the gap remains unfilled.[1] For present purposes, I want only to touch on a few matters relevant to this brief personal statement, and the problem of transference must necessarily be one of them.

Nowadays, there are at least two major kinds of problems in relation to the concept of transference, which tend to complicate its discussion. The first is particularly widespread in Great Britain but is by no means confined to its shores. I refer to the fact that the original concept has suffered a fate similar to that of "acting out" and the "negative therapeutic reaction," in that its meaning has been gradually broadened until it includes a much wider range of phenomena than originally envisaged. According to some adherents of this widening concept, the term "transference" encompasses the sum total of all the reactions of the patient to the analyst, whether conscious or unconscious, whether experienced exclusively in the present or revived from the past, whether massively distorted or modified through projection, displacement, or any other mechanism, whether based on reasonably accurate perceptions subject to minimal interference from such maneuvres, or whether displaying such phenomena as transitivism as in psychosis. This broadened concept is sometimes extended to a point at which everything that is done or said by the patient within the analytic hour is, or includes, a transference manifestation.

On this occasion, I confine myself to the first of these two groups of problems and one or two technical points that seem to arise from them. Personally, I do not find a blanket definition of transference very helpful, but it is not difficult to see how such a definition comes to be taken seriously. Every object relationship is patterned on, or influenced by, an earlier one, and certainly, the influence of the past is bound to leave its stamp on subsequent stages of development. But caution demands that we accept the complexities of human development. We have to consider the changing interrelationships of environment, maturational factors, and the vicissitudes of conflict in the internal world. We need to know how far object relations, even intimate ones, change and develop and how far they remain at the mercy of a timeless and unchanging unconscious. We need to remind ourselves, in any case, that the repression barrier proper is not fully established before the res-

---

[1]Such a metapsychology should indicate an attempt to conceptualize the analyst's use of intuition, empathy, and reflective thinking.

olution of the Oedipus complex and that the "timelessness" will cover at least the first 5 years of developmental history and correspond to the period of infantile amnesia. Nor does this take into account the transformations of object relations in adolescence. But the study of the development of object relations is not, I suggest, coterminus with the study of transference, and I think we may be led into difficulties if we confuse the two.

Many people would agree that the relationship between patient and analyst contains a number of different elements that can usefully be distinguished from each other, some of which either do not occur, at least in accessible form, in all other close relationships, and others which have a much more generalized character.

A useful distinction has long been drawn between the spontaneous transferences of everyday life and a transference neurosis (cf. Glover, 1955). These spontaneous reactions are generalized and nonspecific, for example, a childhood attitude to a father may be transferred unconsciously to a bank manager or a policeman. The transference lacks specificity in the sense that *any* figure of authority may carry the displacement, projection, or externalization, as the case may be. The transference neurosis, on the other hand, is specific. Archaic infantile attitudes are not only unconsciously transferred to the analyst *to a degree accorded to no one else*, but in its more highly developed forms, the neurosis itself becomes structured around his person.

Some confusion may have been aroused by Freud's original distinction between the transference neuroses (symptom neuroses) and the narcissistic neuroses (psychoses), drawn on the basis of the capacity or incapacity to form a transference. But, strictly speaking, a fully blown transference neurosis can only occur in conversion hysteria, anxiety hysteria, and the true obsessional neurosis. The transference in these conditions develops to a point at which it has all the structure of a symptom. A transference regression to the relevant fixation points is followed by a restructuring of infantile conflict and a compromise crystallizes around the person of the analyst. The greater the intensity of the transference formation, and the more successful its formation, the less the symptoms intrude into everyday life, and the greater the improvement in adaptation to the outside world seems to be. No doubt this state of affairs would be brought about more often if "pure" symptom neuroses were more widespread than they are. But although they are met infrequently today, with the exception perhaps of the "true" phobias (i.e., the anxiety hysterias), the problems of this intense kind of transference neurosis need to be recognized and dealt with. There are two important dangers, at the very least. The first is that with the comparative disappearance of neurotic disturbance from everyday life the patient comes to feel that all would be well were it not for the analysis. The analysis is the source of all difficulty; it is there that the problems lie, and the only logical step is to break it off. The second danger is, perhaps, only a special instance of the first. It occurs in severe phobias. Once the transference neurosis develops, the analysis becomes the phobic situation, to be dealt with by avoidancee. Early and thorough transference interpretation is absolutely vital if premature termination is to be avoided.

None of this is meant to suggest that transference cannot be intense in patients exhibiting other than symptom neuroses. Apart from the question that elements of symptom neurosis and character neurosis frequently share the presenting picture, the plain fact is that regressive pulls of all kinds are inseparable from the analytic situation and are, indeed, fostered by it through the operation of factors already selectively listed. But there are also dangers in deciding that all transference phenomena are ubiquitous and accessible, irrespective of the nature of the clinical disorder or the stage of the treatment. This attitude can be as defeating to the patient as it is to the analyst. It was, indeed, just such an attitude that originally led me to consider the metapsychology of interpretation (Yorke, 1965). Behind it lies an assumption that everything is translatable into infantile terms in relation to the analyst as parent or as some significant figure from the infantile past.

No doubt this position brings comforts as well as frustrations, but it seems to me more of a device for conducting analysis by rote rather than by understanding. Applied unthinkingly and when the relevant material is inaccessible or cannot yet be made accessible, transference interpretations are a device that stultifies the analytic relationship and impedes any real progress. To be sure, there are patients who play into such conduct and give it a ready assent. From accounts of such analyses, one cannot avoid the impression that in many instances both patient and analyst are discussing a third person. No doubt that this spares a few anxieties on both sides.

There is another aspect of this technique to which Willi Hoffer used to draw attention some years ago. Namely that the repetition of transference interpretations, from the start of analysis onwards, may obscure the development of a true transference situation. The transference artifact remains in the foreground, and even if the formation of a transference is not thereby obstructed, the subtleties of the true situation may go undetected. It seems to me that these difficulties can only be minimized if analysts have more confidence in the analytic method. The enormous advantage of psychoanalysis carried out on a five-times-a-week basis (and I agree with the late Edward Glover that anything less should be looked on with some suspicion) is that one has time to follow developments, to free the patient's associations from undue obstruction, to listen with "free-floating attention" and to pick up the main underlying trends, to anticipate difficulties and to make timely intervention, to follow Fenichel's admirable instruction to "tell the patient what he already knows and just a little bit more" (personal communication via. W. Hoffer), to make such interventions in the context of the transference if that is where they belong, and to be ready at all times to reassess the situation in case of unexpected hitches and holdups. Under these circumstances, the delight of analytic work with an accessible patient who has formed a treatment alliance is that the patient never fails not only to teach the analyst, but to surprise him. In the absence of these experiences, one should seriously question the validity of the technique one has adopted.

Inasmuch as this account deals only with selected aspects of technique, a great deal has been omitted in a summarized statement of the kind just presented. No account has been attempted of the analyst as superego, as ego-ideal, as id-tempter, or as vehicle for externalization, to name but a few familiar situations. The entire question of transference resistance has been neglected. Nothing has been said of the important question of countertransference, the different ways in which the term is used, and its differentiation from what some of us would regard as a counterresponse, or affective response, to the patient. Inadequate attention is given to the technique of character analysis – still, in my view, to be modeled on that of Reich – and some of the auxiliary devices that sometimes further the transformation of the ego-syntonic into the ego-dystonic. Nor has anything been said of the treatment problems posed by certain severe developmental disorders. As for the so-called "transference psychoses," held to occur sufficiently often to render Freud's concept of the "narcissistic neuroses" thoroughly out of date, I would only say that I believe transference psychosis sometimes occurs, but that claims to use the phenomenon in an *analytically* therapeutic way should be treated with reserve. However, the entire matter needs more extensive discussion.

Finally, I want to emphasize the importance of understanding transference manifestations within their affective context. Without this important dimension, the analytic experience would be an arid and intellectual exercise.

This highly selective presentation contains nothing particularly novel. But it has provided an opportunity to restate my conviction that basic Freudian principles, augmented and expanded by the findings of child analysis and by psychoanalytically informed child observation, provide a sound conceptual framework that allows our discipline a continuing, healthy growth and development. Further knowledge will not be confined to those conditions *treated* by psychoanalysis. Psychoanalytic diagnostic techniques and understanding will cast further light on the more obscure psychiatric conditions, as well as the more common disturbances that still remain less than tractable. And there is no reason why we should not join hands with those related disciplines that have a bearing on the science of human development. Both for the practicing psychoanalyst and the psychoanalytic psychiatrist, we have a legacy beyond price.

REFERENCES

Bibring, E. (1954). Psychoanalysis and the dynamic psychotherapies. *Journal of the American Psychoanalytic Association, 2,* 745–770.

Burlingham, D. (1955). Simultaneous analysis of mother and child. *The Psychoanalytic Study of the Child, 10,* 165–186.

Devereux, G. (1951). Some criteria for the timing of confrontations and interpretations. *International Journal of Psychoanalysis, 32,* 19–24.

Freeman, T. (1973). *A psychoanalytic study of the psychoses.* New York: International Universities Press.

Freeman, T. (1976). *Childhood psychopathology and adult psychoses.* New York: International Universities Press.

Freeman, T. (1983). Anna Freud–Psychiatrist. *International Journal of Psycho-Analysis, 64,* 441–444.

Freeman, T., Wiseberg, S., & Yorke, C. *Studies in psychoanalytic psychiatry, a developmental approach* (in preparation).

Freud, A. (1962). Assessment of childhood disturbances. *The Psychoanalytic Study of the Child, 17,* 149–158.

Freud, A. (1963). The concept of developmental lines. *The Psychoanalytic Study of the Child, 18,* 245–265.

Freud, A. (1982). Mental health and illness in terms of harmony and disharmony. In: *Collected Writings, 8.* New York: International Universities Press.

Freud, A., & Nagera, H., & Freud, W. E. (1965). Metapsychological assessment of the adult personality. *The Psychoanalytic Study of the Child, 20,* 9–41.

Glover, E. (1955). *The technique of psycho-analysis.* London: Baillière, Tindall & Cox.

Kennedy, H. (1971). Problems of reconstruction in child analysis. *The Psychoanalytic Study of the Child, 26,* 386–402.

MacAlpine, I. (1950). The development of the transference. *Psychoanalytic Quarterly, 19,* 501–539.

Rogers, C. R. (1942). *Counseling and psychotherapy.* Boston: Houghton Mifflin.

Sterba, P. (1934). The fate of the ego in analytic therapy. *International Journal of Psycho-Analysis, 15,* 117–126.

Yorke, C. (1965). Some metapsychological aspects of interpretation. *British Journal of Medical Psychology, 38,* 27–42.

Yorke, C. (1980). The contributions of the Diagnostic Profile and the Assessment of Developmental Lines to Child Psychiatry. *Psychiatric Clinics of North America, 3,* 593–603.

Yorke, C. (1983a). Anna Freud and the psychoanalytic study and treatment of adults. *International Journal of Psycho-Analysis, 64,* 391–400.

Yorke, C. (1983b). Clinical notes on developmental pathology. *The Psychoanalytic Study of the Child, 38,* 389–402.

Yorke, C., & Burgner, M. (1980). A developmental approach to the assessment of obsessional phenomena in children. *Dialogue: A Journal of Psychoanalytic Perspectives, 4,* 35–47.

Author Index

253

Subject Index